A CULTURAL *HERMENEUSIS*
On Caste Culture, its Discontents
and Politics of Culture

A Model of Contextual Theologising

A CULTURAL *HERMENEUSIS*

On Caste Culture, its Discontents
and Politics of Culture

A Model of Contextual Theologising

JOSEPH CHITTOOPARAMPIL CMI

ISPCK
2005

A Cultural Hermeneusis – On Caste Culture, its Discontents and Politics of Culture —Published by the Rev. Ashish Amos of the Indian Society for Promoting Christian Knowledge (ISPCK), Post Box 1585, Kashmere Gate, Delhi-110006 under Contextual Theological Education Series - 29.

© Author 2005

All rights reserved. No part of this book may be reproduced or transmitted in any form or by any means, electronic, mechanical, photocopying, recording, or by any information storage and retrieval system, without the prior permission in writing from the publisher.

ISBN: 81-7214-865-8

Cover design: VIRENDRA SINGH

Laser typeset at **ISPCK,** Post Box 1585,
1654 Madarsa Road, Kashmere Gate, Delhi-110006,
Tel: 23866323, Fax: 91-11-23865490.
e-mail–ispck@nde.vsnl.net.in • publishing@ispck.org.in
Website-www.ispck.org.in
Printed at Repro India Ltd, Mumbai.

CONTENTS

Foreword	xi
Preface	xv
INTRODUCTION	xvii
Scope and Relevance of the Study	xvii
Presuppositions	xix
Limitations	xxi
Method	xxiii
Sources	xxiii
Structure of the Study	xxiii

PART ONE
A BRIEF SURVEY OF CASTE CULTURAL REALITY OF INDIA

Chapter I
CASTE SYSTEM IN A HISTORICAL PERSPECTIVE   2

1. A General Understanding of Caste   3
2. Caste system in History   6
   Interaction between Castes   7
   The Caste system and the socio-cultural encounter in Myth and History   10
3. Challenge of Religions to the Caste system   14
4. Mobility in Caste system   19

Chapter II
CONTEMPORARY EXPERIENCE OF CASTE   **24**
1. Experience of Caste Oppression   24
2. Dalit Writings and Caste Oppressions   28
3. Dalits and Christianity   33
4. The Impact of Modernity   36
5. Modern Transformation of Caste   40
6. Caste and Class   43

Chapter III
CULTURAL DYNAMICS   **48**
1. What is Culture?   48
2. Dominant and Subaltern Cultures   52
3. Caste Culture and Counter-culture   54
    Dissent and Counter-culture   56
    Politics of Culture   58

Notes : *Part One*   62

PART TWO
CASTE CULTURE AN ANALYSIS

Chapter IV
GOD-CHARIOTS IN THE GARDEN OF CASTES   **73**
1. The Chariot and the Positions and roles of Different Caste Actors   74
2. Men are Unequal   75
3. Journey of the Chariot   80
4. Festival and Socio-cultural Meanings   81
5. After the Festival   83
6. Some Caste Actors   83
    Kancha – an Untouchable   84
    Shiva Bhakta – a high-caste   85
    Kesar – a Jugi   86

Chapter V : CASTE CULTURE IN DIFFERENT DIMENSIONS — 88

1. Caste Culture and Economics — 89
   - Globalisation and Brahminism — 92
2. Caste Culture and Politics — 94
   - Who is Ruling India? — 96
   - Democracy of Dalits — 97
   - Patriarchal Authoritarianism and Brahminism — 99
   - Hindu Political Institutions and Dalitbahujans — 100
3. Caste Culture and Society — 103
   - Equality in Newar Moral Discourse — 107
   - Equality of Moral Worth vesus Social Equality — 108
4. Caste Culture and Person — 110
   - The Distorted Dalit Psyche — 110
   - I am a Person and You are also a Person — 113
5. Cultural Dimension of Caste — 116
   - Interplay of Hierarchy and Equality — 117
   - Confrontations — 120
6. Caste Culture and Religion — 121
   - Deity of Caste Hindus and Dalits — 122
   - Ascetic and Householder — 125
   - *Karma* and Hierarchy — 127

Notes : *Part Two* — 131

PART THREE
TOWARDS A COUNTER-CULTURAL INTERPRETATION

Chapter VI : COUNTER-CULTURAL VOICES AND MOVEMENTS — 138

1. Counter-culture and Buddha's Dissent — 138
2. Bhakti Movement and Counter-culture — 141
   - Sufism — 141

3. Mahatma Phule and Counter-culture 145
4. The Challenge of Periyar E. V. Ramaswamy 147
5. Ambedkar and Interpretation of Caste Culture 148
6. Gandhi and Interpretation of Caste Culture 153
7. BSP Movement in North-West India 156
    The Emergence of BSP Movement 157
    Evolving a Political Base 158
    Politics of Alliance 160
    Achievements of BSP Movement 163

Chapter VII :
THE INDIAN UNTOUCHABLES' CRITIQUE OF CASTE CULTURE 166

1. The Untouchables' Critique – Indigenous and Integral 167
2. The Articulation of the Untouchables in Counter-cultural Discourses 170
    The Critique and its Language 172
3. Counter-ideologies through Dissimulation 175
4. Practical Ethos of Living: The Idiom of Necessity 178
5. Ascetics and the Dalit Critique 180
    Politics of Asceticism and the Countercultural Discourses 181
    Counter-culture and Ascetics 183
6. The Untouchable's Symbolic World 187

Chapter VIII :
COUNTER-CULTURAL PERSPECTIVES 191

1. Option for the Poor – Liberation 192
2. Option for the Culture – Inculturation 200
    Centrality of Culture 202
    Culture, Faith and Theology 203
3. Option for Dialogue – Interpretation 207
    Culture, Language and Interpretation 208

Chapter IX :
JESUS AND COUNTER-CULTURE — 213

1. Jesus: the Prophet of a Counter-culture — 214
   - The Role of the Prophet of Hope — 217
   - Nature of the Counter-culture – Kingdom of God — 220
   - Counter-culture and the Option for the Poor — 221
2. Jesus versus Power and Prestige — 226
3. Counter-culture Demands Active Faith — 230
   - Jesus' Love and Freedom — 234
4. Jesus' Vision of a Society of Equals — 236
   - Jesus a Friend of Outcastes and Sinners — 236
   - Table Fellowship: Symbol of Cultural Revolution — 237
5. Towards a Counter-cultural Interpretation — 239
   - The Pure Versus the Impure — 241
6. A Prophetic Countercultural Movement — 244

Notes : *Part Three* — 247

CONCLUSION — 258
The Cultural *Hermeneusis* — 269
Invitation to a New Spirituality — 275

Notes — 278

BIBLIOGRAPHY — 279

INDEX — 307

FOREWORD

I feel honoured to be asked to write the foreword to the research work of Dr Chittooparampil CMI. Hailing from Kerala, the author has spent many years in north and central India involved in social, religious and theological services, and in this capacity has been able to keep a close watch on the evolving cultural scenario of this area. His serious research and reflection on what he has discovered throws light on the social and religious situation not only of north India but of the whole of south Asia, where the central theme of his study, the caste configuration, is an important influence on social life although working in many different ways.

From his observer participation in the life of the poor in these regions and an indepth dialogue with many scholars who have studied the area, he offers us a new interpretation of the dynamics of caste in India today, which corrects the somewhat static views of Dumont and other classical authors. Caste is not merely a social structure. It is a living reality constantly affected by the dreams and the dreads of its members and by the play of economic, cultural and political forces. This thesis, however much it is grounded in sociological and historical study, is not merely descriptive. The author writes as a theologian. He calls his work a cultural hermeneusis. He offers a fresh interpretation of culture by a sort of X-ray analysis of the caste phenomenon along its six principal axes singled out by Dr M. Amaladoss – economic and politics, society and person, culture and religion. Through his analysis Fr Chittooparampil shows how in practice the caste culture includes a ferment of change churning from below. In this ferment he discerns a sign of a bud of the Rule of God about which Jesus spoke. He reflects on how and along what lines the social reality calls on people committed to the service of the poor to join in their struggle for liberation. Not the least significant feature of this analysis is that it includes the recent political movements in north India represented by the BSP and similar formations.

This work belongs to the tradition of contextual theology in which the first step is a study of the social reality, its structural frames and its faultlines, so as to then confront the reality with the biblical teachings and the faith articulations of the Church and finally arrive at a new understanding of the working of god's Spirit in our history. Such understanding calls for an active commitment to help our situation come closer to the ideals of the Rule of God as visualised by Jesus. Liberation theology evolved following this method, as have many other forms of contemporary theology, and not only in he Third World countries. In India Dalit theology generally follows the same path. But although the Dalits are central in the present volume, its scope extends to the whole social reality of the caste, with special concern for the larger group of the OBC (Other Backward Castes). The central proposal of the author is the need to create a counterculture along the lines of the protests movements of India, from the Buddha down to Ambedkar and the BSP movement. He shows that this perennial movement in our culture can be enriched with the assimilation of the values found in the Gospel of Jesus. The final call of the thesis is for a new spirituality which is holistic and prophetic at the same time.

One of the valuable traits of this work is that, without being chauvinistic, it finds its roots and inspiration in many insights of Indian sociologists, historians and theologians in the last fifty years, even when the author is free enough to make use of the work of western analysts of the Indian situation. Dr Chittooparampil continues and extends the lines of reflection of George Soares-Prabhu, Sebastian Kappen and Michael Amaldoss. Every reader of this book will get a fair picture of the main trends of Indian theology in the last half a century and become familiar with the names of Indian theologians. This is a swadeshi thesis in the best sense of the term!

But this is not a book just to be read. It is rather an outline of a manual of action to be discussed by concerned groups and individuals who want to go beyond cultural hermeneusis and accept the hard demands of liberative activity in an option for the poor. The Church in India and the country in general will be grateful to Dr Chittooparampil for the guidelines he offers in this fruit of many years of commitment, study and reflection.

G. Gispert-Sauch, S.J.

May 1, 2005
Vidyajyoti, Delhi-110054

xiv

PREFACE

In the situation of many cultures and religions and many poor in India, liberation, inculturation and interpretation seem to be important theological and countercultural perspectives to work for transformation and change from the existing oppressive, death- dealing and dehumanising aspects of different cultures. In this study while entering into the problems of meaning and structures associated with life in the caste system, I try to explore the critiques of caste culture in view of clarifying the theological and countercultural perspectives capable of taking the path to liberation, freedom and justice. Here my intent is to explore a model of Contextual theologising in the Indian context.

This work is, originally, my doctoral thesis that was (submitted and) defended on 30th November, 2004, at the faculty of theology, Delhi, in Vidyajyoti. This research was undertaken while I had assignments in the teaching and pastoral fields. The Vidyajyoti administration generously permitted me to undertake in this study in this manner only because they have a clear focus in theological training and the projects they undertake — promotion of relevant and contextual theologising. I am very fortunate and happy to be a part of this mission, and express my sincere gratitude to the staff and administration. I also participated in the methodological training programme conducted by United Theological College, Bangalore, under the guidance of Dr. K. C. Abraham for doctoral students for about a month as a preliminary requirement for the doctoral programme. I am very grateful to all the staff members of U. T. C. for the support and guidance they gave me in the early stages of this study.

I am greatly indebted to many others, with whose help, support and encouragement I have been able to undertake and complete this study. I am particularly grateful to my guide Rev. (Dr.) G. Gispert-Sauch SJ who was a source of inspiration and encouragement and often challenged and took me to task. More than a guide, he has been a guru and friend supporting and encouraging me in the course of this study. I sincerely thank Dr. M. Amaladoss who contributed generously in the early stages of the research, sharing his scholarship in the field of culture and theology. Some other professors from whom I have enriched myself with valuable theological insights that they generously shared are: Dr. Samuel Rayan, Dr. Kuncheria Pathil, Dr. Thomas Kadankavil, Dr. Thomas Kochumuttom and Dr. A. R. Thumma. I gratefully remember my superiors and friends for their support and understanding by providing all the necessary arrangements for the completion of the study. Especially Rev. Dr. Antony Kariyil CMI whose generous support and keen interest has benefited me to complete the study. I remember with appreciation the Dharmaram College community for all the support and assistance they gave me when I frequented the college to study. I am grateful to Mr. Mathew Pulickan who did the proof reading.

Fr. Joseph Chittooparambil CMI

INTRODUCTION

Scope and Relevance of the Study

Those who watch the Indian scenario will observe a socio-cultural crisis which is expressed explicitly in the discontent of the people. Its root is found in the caste cultural system that affects the self and society in general. The development in science and technology has not alleviated the rampant poverty, hunger and disease. The electronic era characterised by fast communication and action has produced an increase of unemployment and cultural imperialism. The ecological imbalances caused by rapid militarisation and industrialization is a danger signal to the quality of life and a threat to nature. The growing intolerance and the cult of violence surfacing in the militant sections of different religious traditions and the resultant attacks and atrocities on 'others' are of great concern to subaltern groups and minorities.

The caste system and the life associated with it is an important feature of the Indian cultural and religious ethos. The alarming socio-cultural realities mentioned seem to be closely related with the caste system. Though laws and democracy abolish untouchability, it is still practiced in India. The traditional hierarchical ideology has a decisive role in our cultural systems. In the United States, the black people bought from Africa were subjugated in a way similar to the Dalit subjugation in India, but a legal and political end to this situation took place through the liberator Abraham Lincoln, who gave his life for the sake of equality and justice to all men and women. In South Africa, an equally cruel system called apartheid was recently brought down legally and politically, after a heavy price paid by the victims. The South African apartheid had all aspects of cultural domination – social, political, economic and religious – as we find in the Indian caste system.

Culture really is for the people, for their well-being. The people on the one hand create and recreate it, to preserve and enhance life in the world, and to make it more human; and on the other hand challenge and destroy all the elements that are dehumanising and death-dealing. This is an ongoing process in which the day-to-day experiences of people interact with culture, creating, modifying, preserving and changing it because they become more sensitive to the justice done to other lives and cultures when they are considered equal partners. Vatican II says that people are conscious of their being "the artisans and authors of the culture of their community".[1] Culture demands introspection, discernment and an interpretation that promotes and liberates the self and society. There is always the tendency or the risk that discourses and interpretations detach culture from their lived worlds and turn the self, life and action into an arid and one-dimensional cosmos. Culture then becomes dominant and oppressive, erasing the "others". In such cases movements supported and guided by theological and hermeneutic discourses motivate and create countercultures capable of taking the path to liberation, freedom and justice.

By their experience of pathos the subalterns are better placed to meet the challenge of injustice and subvert all elements in the cultural life that are oppressive and hegemonic. A. Thumma states:

> The marginalised subaltern people have come to discover their glorious heritage, ancient roots and identity, dignity and nobility, history and culture, and wisdom and theology. They have also realised that their present struggles and radical movements for life, justice and liberty, contain many insights

---

[1] Gaudium et Spes, 55.

and continue in line with their traditional wisdom. These insights and wisdom of people, that arise out of their past heritage, present struggles, and their hopes and aspirations of the future, form the content of People's Theology.[2]

My attempt in this research into the Indian cultural caste situation is to make a contribution to the struggles of the oppressed by isolating and challenging all elements of domination and subjugation and to pinpoint and clarify some of the countercultural and theological perspectives for an alternative counterculture that can hold together all men and women in freedom, equality and justice. By this I participate in the process of liberating the marginalised and oppressed subaltern groups, especially the Dalits, seen as the main victims of the Indian culture. Jesus Christ, a prophet and a mystic, through his teaching and pastoral action, inaugurated a countercultural movement challenging all dehumanising cultural forces and invited all to join the movement by responding to the divine call to create this world anew and make it better place to live in. This movement has been advanced by other great visionaries and leaders like Buddha, Dr. Ambedkar, Mahatma Gandhi, Jotibha Phule, Sri Narayana Guru etc. The focus and concern expressed in this work is not restricted to the promotion of one or other group, caste or religion. But the marginalised and the victims of oppression deserve primary attention. The socio-cultural transformation we want can take place only if we identify the causes of the cultural crisis that has plagued the Indian society for centuries, and seek adequate remedial measures through a counterculture that has a relevant theological and hermeneutical basis and keeps a holistic perspective.

Presuppositions

The relevance and importance of the area taken for the research, "The Caste Cultural Conflict: Towards a Countercultural

---

[2] A. Thumma, *Wisdom of the Weak*, Delhi: ISPCK, 2000, 1.

Interpretation," is clear from the remarks given above. The concerns I had in the selection of this research shall be clarified a little more. It is part of my search for a relevant contextual theology and interpretation. Today most theologians have reached a consensus that theology and interpretation have to be contextual, and that the methodology for the same should undergo a change from the traditional, dogmatic approach. The National Seminar on People's Theology affirmed this contextual need in theologising, emphasising the theologians' involvement and commitment to people's struggles, and a lived experience in the theologising activity:

> The starting point of this theology is the life of the people especially of the marginalised groups with their struggle and quest for justice and dignity. A necessary condition for developing a valid theology of the people is a deep commitment to the people through a life of involvement. Our traditional approach, which begins with scripture and tradition and speculative, abstract, doctrinal formulations, has as its main preoccupation an other-worldly concern and safeguarding of orthodoxy. It cannot provide us with an adequate tool for people-centered theologising.[3]

The slogan for this change of approach says, "theology has to be reborn at the 'grassroots', i.e. in the midst of life and lived experience of the people."[4] Contextual theology is "an intentional and thought-out effort to do theology in and for a given context, an effort, that, furthermore, is undertaken by people who belong to that context and make use of its own intellectual, religious and spiritual resources".[5] Contextual theologising is more than inculturation. While contextualisation

---

[3] National Seminar on People's Theology, Statement and Papers, *Jeevadhara*, 22 (1992), 237-238.

[4] J. M. De Mesa & Lode L.. Wostyn, *Doing Theology*,Quezon City: Claretian Pub., 1990, 3.

[5] R. Latourelle and R. Fisichella (eds.), *Dictionary of Fundamental Theology*, New York: Crossroad, 1994, 1098.

includes the whole context, indigenisation and inculturation may be narrowly understood. "Inculturation and indigenisation are apologetic methods focussed on the translation/interpretation of a received text for a given culture, whereas contexualisation sees this translation/interpretation as a dialectical process in which text and context are interdependent."[6]

Caste cultural conflict is a contextual question, and is the most significant issue in the socio-cultural reality of India, with its rampant poverty and pluriform religiosity that affect the lives of the people individually and in society. The change in the approach to theology and interpretation is urgent for any kind of relevant theology that seeks the total liberation of people in society in their different dimensions: economic, political, psychological, social, cultural and religious. So this research seeks a kind of cultural hermeneutics. It approaches it with a cultural framework of having the different dimensions mentioned above, and shows that it is important to approach any reality (here the Indian reality of the caste) holistically and integrally, avoiding attempts to one-dimensional approaches. There is also a conscious bent towards the subaltern view, i. e. the caste cultural reality is seen from the victim's perspective, from the stand point of the dominated and marginalised, which involves a call for conversion to the dominant groups. At all the stages of the work the researcher is comfortable with his Indian and Christian roots that have grown in him in a dialogic and ecumenical way.

Limitations

The caste system is a vast area where there is much history and literature, especially in the sociological and anthropological fields. The focus of the study is the caste conflict and its different dimensions, economic, political, personal, social, cultural,

---

[6] R. O. Costa (ed), *One Faith, Many Cultures*, New York: Orbis Books, 1988, xii.

religious etc.; that is, caste is approached in a holistic perspective. For the analysis, the sources explored are especially the authors and writings of such perspective. The objective of the study and research is not to describe a counterculture in all detail, but to point out and clarify theological and countercultural perspectives integral to a continued dialogue in hermeneutics, without any claim to be exhaustive. The treatment is subject to further development. Though content and method are inseparable, the approach of the project leans more towards the latter. The process involves three stages: experience, analysis and interpretation.

Method

The conceptual framework and the approach used in this research are basically hermeneutical, holistic, and contextual. The starting point is dissatisfaction with and the resultant suspicion over the prevailing caste cultural situation. Though the Marxian tool of analysis is useful for the socio-economic situation, it falls short of the holistic and integral approach we pursue in this project. The cultural and the religious dimension, which is generally overlooked in Marxian analysis, needs to be taken into consideration when we approach the caste system in India. The pluri-dimensional aspect of the caste reality and the mutuality between its different dimensions are accepted and the study is envisaged as a dialogic dynamics, which follows an ongoing hermeneutical movement. At the same time the interpretation process is not done from a neutral stand: there is a conscious bias in favour of the subalterns, the victims of the oppression.

The method used is largely the explorative cultural analyses and interpretation done from a countercultural perspective. Both analysis and interpretation cannot be understood as two separate activities or functions distinguished in time and place, but as two aspects of a process of theologising and hermeneutics. For the sake of understanding, the two aspects are distinguished and their different aspects and parts are explored. Some kind of overlapping is possible when different sections and sub-sections

Introduction

are treated. We seek an interdisciplinary approach and the understanding of their interconnections and functions is achieved through the medium of dialogue, in a critical and creative way.

Sources

The primary source is experience: one's own and others in the caste cultural life. The researcher's own experience in the caste cultural conflict and the participation, dialogue and interviews with people who are struggling with the discontent and the quandaries of caste life as different caste actors. The researcher also explores the experiences of others as reflected in the literary works they have produced, which stand as powerful witnesses of the reality of caste. The resources that are used in this study mainly belong to two areas, that is, in the caste cultural analysis and in the theological, countercultural and hermeneutical explorations. I mention here a few authors from whom I have benefited much in the above mentioned areas, although I am listing them in the detailed bibliography: They are S. M. Parish, M. Amaladoss, Kancha Ilaiah, R. S. Khare, Andre Beteille, C. J. Fuller, S. Kappen, George Soares-Prabhu and Felix Wilfred.

Structure of the Study

The entire work is divided into three parts. The first part surveys the caste cultural reality and consists of three chapters. The first chapter unfolds the experience of caste in history. And in the second chapter the stress is given on the contemporary experience of caste. These two chapters (of the first part) are intended to give a general picture of the vast reality of caste system in the long history of India in view of converging our focus on the analysis of the caste cultural conflict that is to come in the second part. In the whole study the approach is holistic and so the framework and the dynamics is consciously set in the milieu of experience and culture. In a general look the caste system seems to be a sociological category. But, as mentioned, a holistic perspective takes us suddenly to the subtle realities of culture, life and experience, which elicit theological and hermeneutical responses. That is why the cultural dynamics is worked out in the third chapter of the first part.

The hermeneutical suspicion emerging from the experience of the ground realities of caste takes us into the second phase of the study, i.e., the part two, with an analysis of the caste culture in two chapters. To facilitate a deeper understanding of the caste cultural conflict in the different dimensions given in the second chapter, we first make use of an important study by S. M. Parish who enters into the consciousness of different caste actors in the celebration of a Hindu festival, with its major event of the chariot pulling. The second chapter of this part is an analysis of the caste cultural conflict in six dimensions. The analysis in six dimensions is aimed at entering to the subject in a detailed manner, but this does not mean that the six dimensions are to be understood in exclusive terms: rather they are mutually interdependent.

As the study is targeted to a countercultural, theological and hermeneutical exploration at the level of perspectives, the third part can be considered as the most important. It has four chapters. All the chapters are interpretations based on the analysis done on the caste cultural conflict in different levels. In the first chapter, caste is approached in a historical perspective; the second from the perspective of the subalterns, the third studies it in a theological perspective and the fourth offers a Christian response focussed on the countercultural message of Jesus for the establishment of the kingdom of God, in tune with his values like freedom, fellowship and justice.

PART ONE

A BRIEF SURVEY OF THE CASTE CULTURAL REALITY IN INDIA

I study caste and culture not as a researcher in anthropology or sociology, but as a theologian with the aim of arriving at a theological discourse about it seeking the pastoral and theological relevance for the Gospel ideals in India today. In part one I attempt to discuss generally about caste in history and in contemporary times, and the dynamics of culture from within the world of caste. This is in view of analysing and critiquing it so as to discover the perspectives and trends that contribute to a transformation and change of the society away from the death-dealing aspects of caste culture.

CHAPTER I
CASTE SYSTEM IN A HISTORICAL PERSPECTIVE

The caste system is a complex social phenomenon, which is a festering wound in the body of Indian society[1]. It involves glaring inequalities in wealth, prestige and power; and naturally the tendency of the rich and powerful is to exploit and oppress the weak. Inequalities and the resultant oppression of the dominant over the weak, are very much a part of Indian cultural and religious ethos. As the chief feature of the Indian cultural and religious ethos the caste system will not disappear, if past experience is any indication. Max Muller observes, "Caste cannot be abolished in India. As a religious institution caste will die; as a social institution it will live and improve"[2] The study of the caste-culture, especially the encounter between the dominant caste culture and the Dalit culture, and the resultant conflict arising out of it takes today the centre stage in the researches of anthropologists and social scientists on Indian society.

In such a large and diverse country with a billion population, caste cannot possibly have the same meaning or the same legitimacy for all Indians. With the advent of modernisation and democracy, changes are taking place in the caste system. The educated Indians know that the law has abolished untouchability, and that its public manifestations are slowly disappearing. However, they are unclear about what the caste and its socio-cultural expressions mean to them as members of a society that is part of the modern world. Beteille says: "No one can say that it is easy to give a clear and constant account of the meaning and significance of caste in India today".[3] From the recognition that there is no one standpoint from which the scholar must investigate the 'objective', the stable reality of caste, it is necessary to insist what caste is and what it means are now very much in a state of flux, but that scholarly discussion of the topic cannot ignore the discourse on caste found in contemporary Indians.[4]

Amaladoss finds two sorts of approaches in the study of caste system.[5] One is phenomenological, studying in depth a particular caste or a group of castes in a particular village.[6] The other is theoretical, exploring the characteristics of the caste system, using, besides field data, literary songs (and other literary forms) that express the self-understanding of the people who belong to the system.[7] There are also general surveys and discussions of issues and problems[8]. I do not plan to research into the caste system. I want to profit from these studies to enrich my own personal experiences in view of understanding the problems and perspectives of those who are deprived and oppressed, specially the Dalits.[9] I want to analyse the caste culture from the contemporary experience. This, I submit, is the first step in a theological response from a Christian perspective to the challenges that the dominant caste-culture poses. In this chapter I try to explain caste-culture in a historical perspective.

1. A General Understanding of Caste

The word caste is of Portuguese origin, '*casta*' being a feminine adjective meaning "pure" and used in old *Iberian* languages with reference to "lineage" or "breed". The Portuguese used it to refer to the *jatis* they found in India, meaning race or breed.[10] Caste is an endogamous kinship group of people, usually living in a particular locality or area, formerly characterised by some occupational specialisation, linked to other such groups co-operatively, but in a hierarchical order, graded in terms of status and ritual purity.[11] The caste of a person in the caste system depends not on wealth as in the classes of modern Europe but on the traditional importance of the caste in which one has the luck to be born.[12] The caste had a separate arrangement for meeting out justice to its members different from that of the community as a whole, within which the caste was included as one of the groups.[13] The governing body of a caste is called the *Panchayat*.

A characteristic principle by which a caste is intelligible in relation to the system is its underlying hierarchy. As society now stands, said the Mysore Census in 1901, "the place due to each community is not only distinguishable, nor is any common principle of precedence recognised by the people themselves by which to grade the castes. The *Brahmin* at one end and the admittedly degraded castes like the *Holeyas* at the other, the members of a large proportion of the intermediate castes think or profess to think that their caste is better than their neighbors' and should be ranked accordingly".[14] One concrete expression of ranking of different castes in the hierarchy is found in the rules that govern the giving and receiving of food and of women in marriage.

The caste includes two distinct realities: *varna* and *jati*. The two are different.[15] Caste first corresponds to *varna* in the Brahmanic literature of the post-Vedic period although the mention of mixed castes (*sankara-jati*) and also of outcaste classes (*antyavasayin*) are found in such literature. The term *varna* comes first in Rig Veda to distinguish between Aryans and the 'Dasyus'.[16] The Division of people into four varnas: brahmana (priest scholar), kshatriya (ruler-warrior), vaishya (merchant), and shudra (peasant), is generally attributed to the Brahmanical tradition. The mythological tradition gives the origin of these four groups of people: from the mouth, the arms, the thighs and the feet of the primordial person (*Prajapati*) respectively, from whose sacrifice the whole universe emerges.[17]

Away from this *varna* complex the *Chandalas, Pipilikas, Nishadas* and others were called *'Panchamas'*, the 'fifth group', later called 'Untouchables'. There is no fifth caste. To explain this, *Manusmrti* put forward the concept of "mixed castes", which means those who were born of intercaste marriages. The main divisions of such marriages were *anuloma* and *pratiloma*. In the case of *anuloma* the male partner belonged to the higher caste and the female to the lower caste, and in the case of *pratiloma* it is *vice versa*. According to the Manusmrti, the most hated groups were *Chandalas* and *Sapakas*, who were the offspring of a *Sudra* male from Brahmin women, and *Chandala* male and a *Pukkasa* female respectively.[18] We find many expressions and directives showing the inhuman and degraded treatment of the outcastes in different parts of *Manusmriti*.

Though *varnas* provide an overall framework in the classification and hierarchical ordering of people, the living sociological reality is *jati*. Amaladoss observes:

> There are many *jatis* as endogamous units within a *varna*, and these also may be hierarchically ordered. For example, among the Brahmins, those who are specialists in ritual are considered inferior in rank to those who specialise in the sacred sciences.... In any case the untouchables stand outside the *varna* scheme, more as slaves than as servants[19].

Most Indians recognise both the meanings of caste, but now they think of it more as *jati* than as *varna*. In ethnographic literature the term *jati*, more colloquially, *jat*, has other associations as it is commonly used to cover a series of identities of increasing degrees of inclusiveness from sub-subcaste through caste to religion and language. In Indian languages caste generally refers to *jati* and I understand caste in this sense. Amaladoss explains:

> A caste is different from a tribe, which is a social unit in itself, which is not linked to other units in a system. Ideally a tribe is a socially and culturally closed group in a particular

geographical area. It is normally self-governing, though it may have commercial relations with others outside the tribe. The tribe is not an element of a wider social system. Tribes, however, have sometimes been integrated into the wider society as castes. [20]

Caste is based on birth and ascribed status of ritual purity. Caste as a system is peculiar to India and those countries that came under the influence of Hindu culture. "A caste becomes simply a kinship group, if economic, political and religious developments lead to the breakdown of status or ritual differentiation".[21] Kolenda sees the tribe, the caste and the kin-community as transformations of a single underlying descent-group structure. Today the kin-community is adapted to the institutions of the modern occupational, political and educational environment. It operates for the welfare of its members, on whose behalf it functions as a family, a resource network, a pressure group, a voluntary organisation, or an ethnic group.[22]

2. Caste System in History

The caste system seems to have developed in the early kingdoms of northern India as a system of division of labour and land control. Harold Gould in the module, *Caste and Class: A Comparative View*, shows the parallel in the development of the Indian division of labour, embodied in the caste system, with developments of division of labour in other ancient states[23]. Amaladoss suggests two ways of reaching a historical view:

> One can analyse the available literature; the *Vedas*, the *Puranas* and the *Dharmasastras* (Mukherjee, 1988). But these documents present the view of the Brahmins, the people on the top. It is not unbiased. It may be a more legitimisation of existing order or even an ideological claim than a factual report. Another way is to focus on the known historical facts like the invasions, the social conflicts and movements. One approaches these facts for an explanation of a system that is already in place. The explanation depends on the key that

one uses to interpret these facts. The key varies according to what one's view of the caste system is: for instance whether the phenomenon is seen as economical: class (Kosambi 1987); socio-cultural: race or tribe (Bose 1975); political: conquest-subjugation (Wilkinson and Thomas,1972: 1-32, Mukherjee 1988:103-104); or religious: purity-pollution (Dumont 1970).[24]

I do not intend to explore in detail the caste system in history in one of above mentioned perspectives, but to look at it from an integral cultural perspective that searches for and identifies what will contribute to the better understanding of it and its oppressive structures, in view of change and transformation. The authors whom I refer to more frequently are: M. Amaladoss (1994), Parish (1997), Ilaiah (1996), Khare (1984,1998), Freeman (1979), Maliekal (1980), Fuller (1996). These authors approach the caste reality in a cultural framework and in an integral way.

Interaction between Castes

Amaladoss speaks about the interaction between the different castes and the way the dominant castes establish their identities and give themselves mutual support after the entry of Aryans into India:

> When Aryans entered into India around 1500 BC (Thapar 1966:24) and progressively established their hegemony in the north, there must have been the division between the dominant Aryans and the subjugated local peoples. Among the Aryans there must have been an ongoing rivalry between the spiritual and temporal powers: the priests and rulers-warriors. The reform of the Buddha is often seen as Kshatriya reaction to the domination of the Brahmins and their rituals. The subject peoples may not have been simply a mass, but a social group diversified into tribes and classes, especially since there had been earlier migrations and conflicts. As these multifarious groups got organised into a social order, the Brahmins as the

intellectuals legitimise their dominance by elaborating their *varna* scheme and by building up a boundary wall around themselves in terms of their ritual purity. The Kshatriyas also protect their identity as the ruling group. The Brahmins and the Kshatriyas support themselves mutually to uphold the social order. The Brahmins provide intellectual services and religious legitimation to the rulers. The rulers in turn protect the rights of the Brahmins.[25]

Amaladoss guesses how the interrelationships between groups especially between the dominant castes and the masses of people, possibly developed into social, economic and political strata which ultimately gave to each one their position in the hierarchy:

By the side of this two-fold dominant group, there are the masses of people. Since the *varna* boundaries were supple in the beginning, the dominant groups among the local peoples may have been integrated with the Aryans. We know this to be true of the Kshatriyas. Any group that attained political power created a mythological ancestry helped by a willing Brahmin scholar, obtained legitimisation from the Brahmin priesthood, since it was convenient to the latter to be on the side of the actual rulers, and become Kshatriyas. Similarly the Kings had a certain freedom to set up a group as Brahmins. While this process of adaptation and integration was going on among the dominant groups, the dominated groups might have sought to adapt themselves to the situation. Among them there must have been a group of the poorest who were the slaves and servants and who eventually become the Untouchables. In between is a middle group divided between the Aryans (Vaisyas) and others (Sudras). The middle groups must have sought to model themselves on the dominant ones, whether Brahmin or Kshatriya, and protected their own social space with the refusal to inter-dine and inter-marry. The political or economic power, or the favour of the ruler and/ or priest, enjoyed by a group in a particular place must have determined its place in the local hierarchy.[26]

There are also other factors that helped the emergence of caste system with its socio-cultural specificities:

> Two further factors may have helped the emergence of the caste system. When the first big empires emerged from a set of warring units - say with the Guptas - there must have been a variety of 'tribal' groups, with their own cultural and religious specificities, even political leadership, geographically distributed, but united under one ruler. The empire provided an overall political organisation and also possibilities of geographical mobility. But the rulers wisely decided on not imposing cultural or religious uniformity, as we see, for instance, in the edicts of Ashoka. This means that the groups preserved their 'ethnic' identity while they interacted at political and commercial levels. The occupational specificity and diversification must have developed slowly. In the context of such commercial and political unity, the cultural and religious unity emerges, not through imposition, but through slow permeation and integration of different elements, thanks to the desire of the middle groups, even minor kings, to imitate, in a search for social legitimisation and status, the habits of the dominant Brahman-Kshatriya combination. As M.N. Srinivas remarks: 'Every caste tended to imitate the customs and rituals of the topmost caste, and this was responsible for the spread of Sanskritisation... Caste enabled Hinduism to proselytise without the aid of a church'.[27]

In the powerful presence of the dominant groups, those who are below in the overall social framework will have to either follow the way of the dominant groups or suffer exclusion. We see this dynamic operative in protest groups like Buddhism and, much later, Sikhism or groups like Islam and Christianity being obliged to conform to the existing social order at the risk of total marginalisation or extinction[28]. In India the identity of different groups from the powerful high castes to the powerless low castes, even to the present times, is defined by the high castes. The outcastes, who do not even come to this category of castes, dubbed as impure, untouchables and polluted, carried on with the occupations and way of life as dictated by their masters.[29]

The Caste System and the socio-cultural encounter in Myth and History

There are some examples of cultural encounters where mutual influence and enrichment between different groups take place, "The gods and goddesses of the various groups are equalised, identified or related in matrimonial and family relationships. The Tamil God Murugan is identified with Kartikeya, a son of Shiva and Parvati. The various local goddesses become manifestations of Shakti, the divine mother, and are married off to Shiva in his various manifestations, as, for instance, Minakshi to Sundareswara in Madurai. These new identities and relationships are sanctioned by appropriate mythical histories. All this happens under the control and inspiration of the intellectual classes. Thus we have a cultural unity in diversity."[30] This is the context where cultural integration and mutual enrichment takes place between cultural groups, each one keeping its identity, but as integral parts of the whole. Referring to this cultural dynamics Amaladoss writes:

> Such a social order may have been fluid in the beginning. But then the lawgivers give it an elaborate legal framework and the religious ideologues elaborate myths and doctrines to legitimate the existing order. This ideology in its turn shapes the minds of succeeding generations and is interiorised. Many have noted the role of the Epics, the *Ramayana* and *Mahabharata*, in helping such interiorisation. Thus the dialectic between ideology and social order rigidifies what must have been a fluid system. Once it becomes a commonly accepted ideological system it continues its way uncontested through history. The ideology spreads with the religion and the culture[31].

There were many different races in India, the Aryans, the Dravidians and other local races, which can be considered as

Caste System in a Historical Perspective

the dominant ones who were instrumental to the present Indian culture and religion. Another observation is that the domination of one group over the other can take place socially, economically and politically, but imposing one's culture on others does not take place without a process of interiorisation in the receiving culture.

Until now, in general, authors of Indian history have treated the Dalits as those who were always at the margins.[32] The *Vedas* speak about the conquered local population as *dasas* or servants. References to the *Chandalas*, who lived on the margins of society and looked after corpses and funerals, can be found in Buddhist Pali texts. The texts of *Upanishads*, which started being composed around 800 B.C and completed towards and of the third century B.C, addressed the outcastes as Chandala. The law books, dating from 3rd century A.D speak about the *varna* scheme and elaborate rules to preserve it. That the *varna* boundaries were not rigid and a certain mobility across them was possible in its early stages is acknowledged by most historians.[33] Suniti Kumar Chatterji in his work *Indo-Aryan and Hindi*, mentions about the existence of the pre-Aryan people of India. *Dasa*, *Dasya*, and *Nisadas*, whom he has also addressed as the 'Original Indian Austric People' or 'aborigins' or 'Dravidian'.[34] The general term he used for them is 'non-Aryan', which itself shows that 'Aryans' are subjects, and others mere objects. 'Non-Aryan' of course are conquered *dasas*, who, according to Suniti Kumar Chatterji, later on were divided either into Sudras (the serving caste) and slaves, (present Dalits). The Aryan according to him are Vaishyas, Kshatriyas and Brahmans.[35]

Massey refers to Romila Thapar's historical writings where Dalits are shown to be treated as objects dealing with the subject of 'society and historical consciousness', she says:

> "The *Ithihasa Purana* Tradition, has given a number of examples from the *Rig Veda*, *Mahabharata* and *Purana* by which it is proved that a number of historical myths were

created to legitimise some of the prevailing aspects of that time's social or religious life".[36]

She speaks about the myth of *Prithu* created "to legitimise the expulsion of such groups when land was cleaned and settled by agriculturalists". According to the story King Vena who became wicked for not performing the sacrificial ritual and had to be killed by the *Risis*, who alone had the right to depose the rulers. *Risis* churned Vena's left thigh to get a successor, and a *Nisada* came out, who was inadequate, dark short and ugly: therefore he was sent to the forest as a hunter and from him started all the communities of forest dwelling people. Then from the right arm of Vena the *Risis* churned king *Prithu*, who was a cattle-keeper and an agriculturist.[37]

In the *Ramayana* there is reference to a *Shudra* boy losing his life by the hand of Lord Rama because he undertook *tapasya* in order to attain divinity, which was only allowed to the first three upper castes.[38] In another story of the *Mahabharata*, *Ekalavya*, an indigenous boy, who had to lose his 'right hand thumb' because he learnt the art of archery unaided and unguided by anybody and had acquired a proficiency surpassing Arjuna, a Kshatriya.[39] The *Manusmrti* completely took away the human identity of Dalits. The following *slokas* narrate the degraded non-human state of the Dalits:

> The dwelling of Chandalas and Svapakas (should be) outside the village; they should be deprived of dishes (*apapatra*), their property (consists of) dogs and asses, their clothes (should be) the garments of the dead, and their ornaments (should be) of iron, and their food (should be) in broken dishes and they must constantly wander about. (*Manu* X:51,52)

Dr. Ambedkar reports that the *Balais* did not heed to the demands of the high caste. As a result they had to abandon their homes and had to migrate somewhere else and normal life was not possible for them.

The normative prescriptions by the *Manusmrti* have an aspect of fixation that makes social mobility unacceptable in the divine order of Hinduism. As the Brahman sprang from Prajapati's mouth, as he was the first of born, and as the possessor of the Vedas, he is by right the Lord of this whole creation. [*Manu*.1: 93]. A Brahman may seize without hesitation, if he is in distress for his subsistence, the goods of the *Shudra*. [*Manu*. VIII: 417] A Brahman may compel a *Shudra*, whether bought or unbought, to do servile work, for he is created to be the slave of the Brahmans [*Manu* VIII:413]

Gandhi also graphically describes the plight of the Dalits. The situation, particularly for 80% of the rural Dalits has not changed:

> Socially they are lepers. Economically they are worse than slaves. Religiously they are denied entrance to places we miscall houses of God. They are denied the use of the same terms as the caste Hindus, of public roads, public schools, public hospitals, public wells, public taps, public parks and the like. In some cases their approach within the measured distance is a social crime, and in some other rare enough cases their very sight is an offence. They are relegated for their residence to the worst quarters of the cities and villages where they particularly get no social service. Caste Hindu lawyers and doctors will not serve them as they do to other members of the society. Brahmans will not officiate at their religious functions[40].

Al-Beruni, a visitor to India, wrote in his book about the ill treatment suffered by the Dalits during the Muslim period:

> The people called Hadi, Doma (Domba), Chandala, and Badhatau (*sic*) are not reckoned amongst any caste or guild. They are occupied with dirty work, like the cleaning of their villages and other services. They are considered as one sole class, and distinguished only by their occupations. In fact, they are considered like illegitimate children, for according to general opinion they descended from a Shudra father and

a Brahmani mother as children of fornication; therefore they are degraded outcastes.[41]

Massey refers to Ambedkar's impression on India's Constitution and its flexible character as it affected the life of Dalits:

> Dr. Ambedkar did say on Nov. 4, 1948, it (the Constitution) is 'workable' and 'flexible', but even this character of our Constitution has been used only to maintain the status quo of our set rule of life in our Indian society. Because it has only gone in favour of a few powerful, not the masses of powerless people (Dalits). The Constitution itself, as Dr.Ambedkar said, is not bad, it is the use of it being 'flexible' which proved 'bad'.[42]

As a result of this, the history of Dalits even after independence has not improved. Massey concludes by pointing out the role of religion in the plight of the Dalits even in the post-independent times:

> Here the main point is not the rights of the Dalits. The rights of the Dalits have been taken away with force and oppression for centuries, and religion has been used as an instrument to oppress them. But now in the post Independent period, by offering them the same tool of oppression, that is 'religion', their very human freedom (identity or dignity) has been taken away.[43]

Historical studies show clearly that the caste system in India has provided a stable, though oppressive social order.

3. Challenge of Religions to the Caste System

In the history of India, the domination of Brahminical values and caste rigidities has not gone unchallenged. There have been many protests and reform movements. A rapid overview of the fundamental struggle that determined our cultural history will be informative.

The popular discontent against the ritualistic religion of the Brahmins found expression in dissident sects like Jainism and Buddhism. The Buddha brushed aside all metaphysical questions as irrelevant. His concern was with the alienated existence of human beings. He saw the sum of human alienation as sorrow [*dukha*], which has its source in craving – the craving for pleasure, for life, for power. Only the elimination of all craving can ensure complete emancipation.[44] The Buddha affirmed the centrality of friendliness [*maitri*] and compassion [*karuna*], which, along with joy and equanimity, go to form the four cardinal virtues of his teaching. He extended the horizon of love to cosmic proportions to include all living creatures. The universal love he advocated is not only a help to attain *nirvana* but *nirvana* itself.

The Buddha also initiated a radical critique of contemporary religions, especially the ritualistic religion of Brahmins. His spiritual path [*marga*] and effort [*sadhana*] were open to people of all castes. In the *sangha* [monastic community] too, there were no caste barriers and no special privileges. On the contrary, Outcastes and women were welcome to join the community. He said:

> "A man becomes not a Brahmin by long hair or family or birth. The man, in whom there is truth and holiness, he is in joy and he is a Brahmin".[45]

Repudiating caste system and the notion of the ritual purity he also says:

> No Brahmin is such by birth,
> No outcaste is such by birth.
> An outcaste is such by his deeds,
> A Brahmin is such by his deeds[46].

He suggested to his monks that just as the great rivers lose their names once their water merge in the ocean, monks too give up their original family and personal names, when they enter the fellowship of the Sangha[47].

Much later the *Bhakti* tradition repudiated Vedic sacrifices and the practice of ritual purity as they contained oppressive elements. *Bhaktas* saw no meaning in the devotion to the Lord divorced from neighbourly love and the practice of justice. Kabir (1440-1518) and Nanak [1469-1539] were great prophets in the *Bhakti* movement. Kabir says:

> The Lord Maker hath moulded one mass of clay into
> vessels of diverse shapes.
> Free from taint are all vessels of clay
> Since free from taint is the divine potter[48].

One of the Tamil poets, *Siddha,* declares how he is decided to make use of his free will and act against the set dominant ways:

> We will set fire to divisions of caste
> We will debate philosophical questions in the market place,
> We will have dealings with despised households,
> We will go around in different paths.[49]

The *bhakta* debases himself before that God as though he had no will, no option, no joy of his own. This doesn't mean he lives in fear and trembling, but rather the opposite. For God is conceived as the divine lover. The devotee is transported into another world of joy and rapture where he loses himself completely.[50]

We often hear the protests of the untouchable *Bhaktas* against their inability to enter the temple to have a *darsha*n of the Lord. According to tradition, when the south Indian Shivite Nandanar, standing outside the temple protested at his inability to 'see' the Lord, the image of the bull, which, as his vehicle and as his devotee, is normally found facing the Lord at the entrance to Shivite temples and so hides the view from one who is outside, moved aside to let him have *darshan* (contemplation).[51]

Chokhamela, from Maharashtra, protests in the following words:

> Run, run Vithu, don't come slowly.
> I am beaten by the Badve for some transgression.
> They ask: "How can you wear the garland of Vithoba?"
> They abuse me and curse me: "Why have you polluted God?"

I am your dog by your door; don't let me go without mercy.
O Lord of the wheel, you are the creator of our lives.
I, Chokha, hands clasped, beg you, O God,
Don't be angry at my importuning.[52]

It is a historical fact that the different religious traditions that did not accept the caste system as an ideology and even opposed it were isolated. The legitimisation of the existing social order was there done very easily as the resistance was weak. Many Dalit groups became converted to Islam and eventually to Christianity to escape the system and improve their social status.[53] However, they share the many disabilities the caste system imposes on their cultural and material life.

Muslims were not interested in appeasing the spirit of casteism and Hinduism. They differentiate between those who can claim to belong to the group that originally came from Arabia and the local converts, who carry with them their former social rank within the community of Muslims.[54] There were many occupational groups among Muslims, which do indicate differential status and rank. While inter-dining may be in vogue, inter-marriage among different sub-groups is not frequent. The conflict between the Sunni and Shia sects and the fierce battles which were fought between them for status are common knowledge. Islam has many positive elements when it is contrasted with the Hindu caste system. It does not have discrimination based on ritual purity and pollution. We do not see much food restrictions in Islam and they do have a strong sense of brotherhood.[55]

Sikhism, which is concentrated in Punjab, is a movement, which was inspired in fact by the best of Hinduism and Islam, based on devotion, salvation, deliverance from the chain of death and rebirth to all humankind irrespective of caste and creed[56]. It repudiates social differentiation based on caste and stands for the ideal of equality. The symbols of Sikhism mentioned above are said to represent the rejection of the medieval division of society into rulers and the ruled.[57] However, the Sikhs are divided into castes and a constitutional amendment gave the recognition to their untouchables for the purposes of reservation[58].

Basavanna, the founder of Lingayats condemned the caste system. But today the caste system is very much alive among them.[59] The *Arya samaj* in Punjab and *Brahmo samaj* movement in Bengal were spearheaded by men like Dayananda Saraswati, Raja Ram Mohan Roy and Ravindranath Tagore. Both movements attempted reform of Hinduism by recruiting people from among different castes and tried to bring about changes. These reform movements still linger on but never became a counter–force to mainline Hinduism. They did not directly deal with the problems of the Untouchables. Generally the Untouchables remained in the periphery even in the new scheme of things.[60]

The S.N.D.P. [Sri.Narayana Dharma Paripalana] movements in Kerala were also based on social and religious reforms within the broad framework of Hinduism. The unity of mankind, the oneness of God and equality were the oft-repeated precepts of their leader Sri Narayana Guru. This movement was confined mainly among the *Ezhava* caste. The *Ezhavas* managed a considerable degree of social mobility, especially through the socio-economic programmes and the political movement initiated by it.[61]

Christians found a very fertile ground in India. The disunity among the Hindus coupled with social discontent, accumulated over centuries provided a favourable atmosphere for the spread of Christianity. If individual Brahmins and upper castes embraced Christianity because of its religious ethics or as an escape from the structural constraints within which they were caught, the low castes and the tribals embraced Christianity in-groups mainly for improving their social status.[62] After a detailed historical study Forrester concludes:

Whatever the differences among them, missionaries of all persuasions were united in feeling uneasy about caste. They differed in their analysis of what was wrong with caste and what to do about it. For some, the caste was acceptable if disjoined from Hinduism. For others the problem was the 'caste spirit' rather than caste itself. Some wished, somewhat naively, to destroy caste, while others favoured a more gradualist policy. Hardly any gave any kind of general approval to caste. The Roman curia showed itself consistently opposed to untouchability and the idea of hereditary pollution, while willing to encourage a policy of accommodation to many caste practices. It is hard not to see in this distinctive and well-nigh unanimous unease concerning caste the recognition of some fundamental incompatibility between Christianity and the theory and practise of caste.[63]

The new Christians while viewing their affiliation to Christianity as a higher caste identity were not prepared to accept a separation of castes within the Church as a social reality. The Church, though it has been tolerant of the caste system, has contributed to the uplift of the Dalits through education and in other ways.[64]

4. Mobility in the Caste System

Though caste is a rigid stratification of different social groups it includes elements of mobility[65]. Amaladoss hints at a paradox when he says that the caste system is getting firmer in spite of the challenges of prophetic people, the enactment of Constitutional laws and the practice of reservation:

As a social system it has not been really challenged, though prophetic individuals have not been lacking. Even the Constitution abolishes untouchability, but says nothing about the caste system as such. On the contrary the continuance and extension of the practice of reservation assures not only the continuance of the system, but even its strengthening, with even the higher castes asking to be considered economically backward.[66]

He continues:

> The rigidity of caste boundaries seem particularly strong at the extremes. The Brahmans affirm and defend their ritual purity. Their connection with religion has protected them well. They were also quick to profit by the educational opportunities in modern times and this has assured, on the whole, a dominant position for them in society. At the other extreme the Untouchables have been kept almost as slaves marked by impurity, not only by the Brahmins, but also by all the other castes. Recent changes of economic and political mobility have affected only a small group. Reform movements may have changed their own consciousness and that of some in the other castes but not so much their position in the social hierarchy. [67]

The middle castes that are between the two extremes mentioned endeavour with some success to improve the position in the scale of ranking in the system. The most effective way to rise was formerly by the acquisition of territory either through conquest, or, if the land had previously been sparsely populated or empty, by peaceful occupancy. [68] Another way today is Sanskritisation, by which process the lower castes manage to come closer to the brahminic ideals. Amaladoss comments:

> At a lower level, a particular caste group may become economically dominant, the economic power often translated into possession of lands. Thus they acquire certain dominance in a region. Such dominance gives rise to a desire to improve their caste status. The usual way seems to be to imitate the social customs of one of the higher castes, usually the Brahmins, but sometimes also the Kshatriyas. This means becoming vegetarians in food habits, refusing to inter-dine with castes that they wish to consider inferior to themselves, promoting child marriage and forbidding widow remarriage, enforcing seclusion of women through *purdah*, etc. Giving the daughters in marriage to grooms of a higher caste is also a slow way of improving ones comparative status. One also

Caste System in a Historical Perspective

attempts to change religious habits by adhering to brahmanic Hinduism in terms of the gods one worships and of the life cycle rituals performed for them by Brahmins. They also have to create a past for themselves that traces their origins to mythical high-caste ancestors, leading eventually to a change of caste name. This process is called Sanskritisation, taking Sanskrit as a code for a higher caste culture seen as the norm. [69]

M.N. Srinivas introduced the concept of Sanskritisation, standing for the claim to "twice born" *varna* status. In secular India there is no official arbiter for claims to higher rank. However, *jatis* continue to try to improve their rank in the local caste hierarchies by changing the general public's view of their jati's rank, a kind of arbitration by public opinion.[70] Supplementing such elite emulation, an upwardly mobile *jati* may try to improve its status by "pulling" rank – refusing to take food or water from the *jati* of the next high rank.[71] Sanskritisation is a very slow method for a *jati* to raise its status. It is successful only if reinforced by economic or political power. Sanskritisation results in a proliferation of the number of existing *jatis*. A division of a *jati* occurs in two segments by the very process of Sanskritisation – the segment that has successfully Sanskritised, and the segment that had not. The former segment would refuse to give daughters in marriage to the members of the other segment and the more Sanskritised group might or might not receive brides from the less Sanskritised.[72]

Commenting on the effect of mobility among different *jatis*, and the division and disunity caused by such tendency, Kolenda says:

> The proliferation of *jati* units due to the division resulting from Sanskritisation and elite emulation may be a feature of stability in the Indian caste system. Thus, Hindu society is not composed of a small aristocracy and a large mass. If the twice-born is equivalent to an "aristocracy", within that aristocracy there are many rankings. Likewise, among the

Shudras and Untouchables, there are rankings, based largely on customs relating to the purity–pollution values. Such distinctions in purity rankings prevent the development of unity among the Indian "masses". [73]

To understand caste mobility one has to recognise the role of modern education, especially the increase in educational facilities extended for the *Shudras* and *Dalits* by the Christian Mission. Studying the *Jatavs* Lynch says that some educated members of the *Jatav* community developed by sending their children to the Christian mission, Arya Samaj and government schools. [74] Kolenda observes:

> Attainment of wealth, especially the form of land, may enable a *jati* to sustain a luxurious style of life with much leisure time for its members, and servants to carry on the menial work on the land. Such a process seems to account for the gradual and undramatic transformation of the identities of some lower peasant *jatis* into those of higher rank. [75]

Among the South Indians the vast majority of whom belong to the middle castes, there seems to exist a fluid phenomenon where a particular caste becomes more dominant in particular area due to their fast development in economy, education, etc. Mobility has also been relatively easy within a broad hierarchical order. [76] The *Nadars* present an example of successful mobility in recent times. [77] Unless there is economic or political improvement in terms of power or influence, it seems difficult to attain upward social mobility with mere change of social habits. But even economic and political betterment and an improvement in awareness of personal dignity have not helped the Untouchables to change their place in the ranking system.[78]

India is a large and diverse country and with the advent of modernisation and democracy it is difficult to give a clear and constant account of the meaning and significance of caste today. A personal and experiential approach to the caste system using the advantages of scientific studies of cultural dynamics will be beneficial to the understanding of the significance and power of the caste. The brief discussion on the caste system in history in this chapter and the contemporary understanding of it in the following is in view of exploring the contemporary caste culture, the conflicts and the resultant discontents and the conditions of the Untouchables in India.

CHAPTER II
CONTEMPORARY EXPERIENCE OF CASTE

Indians know that caste exists, but they are unclear and troubled about what is its significance for them as member of a society in the modern world. [79] In an address of 1957, entitled "Caste in Modern India," M N Srinivas drew attention to the continuing if not increasing importance of caste in public life. [80] *The Times of India* commenting in the editorial on 21 January 1957 said that the role of caste was greatly exaggerated. It was pointed out that the caste barriers were falling, both in ordinary interchanges among peoples and in ceremonial life. Yet the same newspaper reported shortly afterwards that caste loyalties were being greatly utilised for mobilising political support in the general election that followed in a few weeks. [81] The view that caste is not only a pre-eminent institution but permeates every area of life is accepted by many.

1. Experience of Caste-Oppression

The evil and the oppression of the caste system are to be understood primarily from the point of view of those who suffer most, the Dalits. Violence against the Dalits is growing, says *The Human Rights Watch Report*, New York, released on April 14, 1999. The report, "Broken people: Caste Violence Against India's Untouchables" indicts the Indian Government for its failure to prevent massacres, rapes and exploitation and calls on it to disband private armies and implement national legislation to prevent and prosecute caste-based attacks. [82] Though legally untouchability is abolished through the Constitution, the Dalits still suffer discrimination, harassment and victimisation both in villages and in urban areas. A Dalit as professor in a university, a bureaucrat in India's several administrative services, a public servant, an official in a private firm or a clerk, a coolie, a scavenger, a sweeper, all are victims of a "hidden apartheid".[83]

V. T. Rajashekar describes in strong words the victimisation and discrimination of the subaltern Dalits in India: "The monstrous caste-system, that let leashed the world's longest and the worst form of apartheid and slavery on millions, a subaltern people of India for millennia, is still at large, assuming new forms and subtle ways of discrimination and exploitation".[84]

The Dalits are for the service of the high castes, and are not supposed to dress well so that they may not be mistaken as equal to their masters. One needs to travel to the rural parts of our country to see the social discriminations met by the Dalits. If they rebel, they will have to face atrocities and social boycott. Some recent information came in a Karnataka daily: "Wherever the Dalits are asserting their rights to a greater share in political-economic cake, social violence is also on the higher side according to Prof. Ram."[85]

Mark Juergensmeyer reports the results of a survey he conducted in Punjab in 1978: "I found that old practices, although frequently less common, die hard: eating, smoking and sitting with upper castes were denied; separate wells were maintained for the lower castes; free labour was common; and the wives and daughters of the lower castes were subject to sexual abuse". [86] Occasional efforts by Dalits to demand that the law abolishing untouchability be taken seriously attract severe reprisals from the higher caste people. The names of places like Marathwada, Belchi, Khanjawala, Villupuram, Tsunuru, Ponnur etc. have become symbols of anti-untouchable violence. Gail Omvedt reports:Those who dared to assert themselves are boycotted and assaulted, their fields ploughed over and their crops stolen, their women raped, their leaders murdered, their houses burned and innocent women and children thrown screaming into the fire. [87]

A.R. Thumma writes about the plight of the pauperised:

> Poverty, pollution and powerlessness go hand in hand in India. The poor are not only economically exploited but they are politically dominated and socio-culturally degraded by the rich upper castes. The coincidence of class and caste makes economic, social, political power and status accumulate in the upper castes, pushing down others to cumulative inequality. The caste system, entwined with patriarchy, has created a stratified male-dominated society based on inequality and hierarchy. The "two Indias", that of 20% powerful minority and the 80% powerless majority (*Dalit bahujana samaj*) are getting alienated more and more from each other, as the powerful care less and less about the majority, on whose labour they prosper. [88]

Amaladoss gives some statistics showing the discrimination in the field of land and agriculture by the powerful landlords towards the labouring class:

> The Dalits are nearly 15% of the population in India, which means over 140 million people. Over 80% of these live in rural areas and are agricultural labourers. Due to land reform enactment they may have lost even the precarious tenancy rights they have had and become landless labourers- 52% in 1971. Owing to the increase in population and the scarcity of resources many of them may be unemployed or not have full employment. A considerable number may be bonded labourers, at least in practice, because of the loans they took from their landlords. 71% of all Dalit agricultural labourers were in debt in 1974–75. A 1976 survey found 2.6 million bonded labourers in agriculture alone of whom 62% were Dalits. [89]

Scholars speak of slave labourers in agriculture in the past. [90] The vast majority of the poor belongs to low caste people, mostly Dalits and Adivasis, who serve as bonded labourers or as underemployed, underpaid landless workers. More than 60 million of their children toil as child labourers while the number of unemployed adults is mounting. [91] Thumma continues:

> Oft repeated promises, slogans and policies of "socialistic pattern of government", "*garibi hatao* (banish poverty)", "development with social justice", "mixed economy", etc have not prevented the leadership in India to follow the western model of development and capitalistic pattern of economy. State capitalism is the hallmark of the "socialist state" of India. [92]

The voices of the victims grow louder in the Narmada valley when the height of the Sardar Sarovar dam increases:

> When the valley lives, we are alive
> when it dies, we die with it. [93]

This is the voice of Loharia of Jalsindhi village whose farms and houses are getting submerged along with their village, and 50 other villages, displacing about 2500 Dalit and Adivasi families among others. The Dalits, Adivasis, peasants, all victims damned by the dams, and their movement, the Narmada Bachao Andolan(NBA) cry:

> Pani Chahiye, Pepsi Nahi
> (We want water, not Pepsi)
> *Iangal jammen koniniche?*
> Amriche, amri che
> (Whom do the forests and land belong to?
> To us, to all of us). [94]

Almost hundred and forty million people of our country are considered polluted, impure and untouchables. They live a miserable existence working from dawn to dust as scavengers, chained by the landlords as bonded labourers or doing any other jobs. They do not have an identity or dignity of a human person.

2. Dalit Writings and Caste Oppressions

Caste oppression has a great impact upon the lives of the Dalits. It affects their consciousness. They develop a self-image, which has a stamp of all the heavy burdens they are forced to carry in their lives with a feeling of shame. [95] They have attitudes of dependence and fear.[96] They have a sense of helplessness that paralyses initiative.[97] The poems and songs of the Dalits picture for us graphically the indignity and oppression they suffer. [98] They are very impressive and expressive as they come from experiences of real life situations, full of human emotion and pathos.

Pariah is a poem by Amrita Pritam. The term *pariah* can either mean a stray dog or a community of Dalits. There is a conjoining of these two references for the term in south India and the Dalits and dogs could be spoken of as being part of the same reference.

> Years ago
> you and I went our separate ways
> without regret.
> Only one thing I never quite understood—
> when you and I said good bye
> and the house was sold
> some empty vessels lay outside
> in the courtyard
> staring at us.
> Others lay overturned,
> hiding their faces.
> A wilted creeper
> climbed down the door
> perhaps complaining to us
> or to the water tap
> about the lack of water
> All these are now memories.
>
> I only remember
> that pariah

> who entered our empty room
> for some unknown reason
> And the door was locked outside
>
> Three days later
> when the deal was clinched
> our house was sold
> we exchanged the keys for money.
> The new owner
> was shown each room
> And in one of the rooms we found
> the corpse of that dog.
>
> I have never heard that dog bark
> I only remember the smell of its corpse
> That still haunts me:
> it returns from everything I touch. [99]

The poem has its roots in the notion that Dalits are less than human and ought to be kept outside the contours of the societal household, just as dogs are to be kept outside the living space of the human house. The following is an old slave song heard in the Pulaya congregation in Nagercoil:

Chorus(repeated after every verse):

> Our slave work is done
> our slave bonds are gone
> For this we shall never
> henceforth forsake Thee, O Jesus!

Verses:

1. To purchase cattle, fields, houses
   and many luxuries (we were sold);
   (Now) Messiah himself has settled on the land
   a people who once fled in terror.

2. The father was sold to one place,
   the mother to another;
   The children also separated.
   But now...

3. The owners who enslaved as
   often caused as much suffering:
   But will it comfort us
   to relate all the oppression in full?

4. After exhaustion with labour in burning heat
   in rain and cold and dew,
   They beat us cruelly
   with thousands of strokes.

5. Dogs might enter streets,
   markets, courts and lands;
   (But) if we went near
   they beat and chased us to a distance.

6. As the unclean lepers must run and hide in the jungles,
   so we outcastes must leave the road
   after warning those who approach.
   But now...

7. As the Lord freed from slavery
   the much suffering Israelites in Egypt,
   so He has freed us
   From our distresses.

8. The scripture teachings came
   sent by the triune God:
   Through this, slavery was ended
   and liberty was gained. [100]

Waman Nimbalkar writes from his life experiences, the very process of interiorisation of shame and consciousness of lowliness, weakness, etc.

> When I know nothing, I knew
> My caste was despised (low, despicable)
> The Patil had kicked my father,
> cursed my mother.
> They did not even raise their heads.
> But I felt this 'caste' in my heart.

When I climbed the step to my school
Then I knew my caste was low.
I used to sit outside, the others inside
My skin would suddenly shiver with little thorns,
My eyes could not hold back the tears,
Our lips must smile when they cursed.

I don't understand anything-
I heard this, I learned that,
I became a man like a man

Even now I don't know-
How is caste? Where is it?
It isn't seen so does it live inside the body?
All the questions float like smoke,
And the wick of thought in sputtering.
But when I knew nothing then I knew
My caste was low. [101]

Another Dalit poet, Arun Kamble pictures the contrasts that are existing between the Mahar and the Brahman

If you were to live the life we live
(Then out of you would a poem arise)?
We: kicked and spat at for
    Our piece of bread

You: fetch fulfilment and
    Name of the Lord

We: down-gutter degraders
    Of our heritage

You: its sole repository
    Descendants of the sage.

We: never has a paisa to scratch our arse

You: the golden cup of offerings in your bank
Your bodies flame in sandalwood.
Ours you shovel under half-turned sand

> Wouldn't the world change, and fast,
> If you were forced to live at last
> This life that is all we've ever had? [102]

A poetess from Andhra Pradesh expresses her deep-seated feelings of helplessness and anger that arose from the exploitation of women at the hands of the perpetrators of caste and male domination.

> The lives of Dalit women
> Are tales of woe and agony
> The darkness of unjust fate
> Clothes their shame and misery.
>
> We rise up long before dawn
> And run to our master's houses,
> To clean and scrub and hurry over
> To their fields and our daily labour,
>
> Our bodies are bony cages
> Our lives untidy as our unkempt hair
> Are we earthen vessels with flickering breath?
> Broken bangles mock our shattered lives.
>
> We go to work for we are poor,
> But the same silken beds mock us
> While we are ravished in broad day light;
> Ill-starred our horoscopes are
>
> Did God ordain our fate?
> Will men decide our lives?
> Are we faggots for burning in the funeral fire?
> No, we will rise and free ourselves. [103]

James Freeman points out the struggles and problems of life portraying one of the untouchables from Orisa:

> Muli's life history portrayed conflicts between ideals of his caste, his own expectations and led him to idealise his youth. His attempted adaptations were in the long run unsuccessful. He failed to solve both his internal problem of negative self-image and the external problem faced by almost all

untouchables of his village: poverty, discrimination, and failure to benefit from the growth of the new city... Muli and other Bauris have failed, not because they embody expectations of failure or accept their lot, but rather because the Bauris face social and economic disabilities that they are presently powerless to change.[104]

In Dalit literature we see the outpouring of the self of the victims of caste oppression. Their voices, their wisdom, though coming out in the wounded self, are really powerful and prophetic. The heart-rending expressions of poem and prose by the contemporary Dalit writers are the expressions of passionate protests of the rejected. The consciousness of the marginalised long suppressed by the dominant caste ideology, has been aroused out of its inferiority-complex. The search for the psychic and cultural liberation emerging from the subjugated and marginalised ones: their aspirations for a just society and a life with dignity: their yearning for higher learning and a prosperous life, etc. are the resources for a cultural revolution. The challenges the subalterns pose for themselves to meet the onslaught of cultural imperialism and the feudal and patriarchal dominant culture will show the way to a project of counterculture seeking a new value system, an egalitarian pattern and a reinterpretation of traditional cultural system.

3. Dalits and Christianity

Generally Christianity is considered as an egalitarian religion, and a number of Dalits thought that they would escape the burden of untouchability if they left Hinduism and joined it. Seventy five percent of the Christians of India were drawn from Dalit and tribal socio-religious background.[105] A desire for an improvement in their social status, rather than economic benefits has been at the root of many mass conversion movements in India.[106] But soon they have discovered that the difference in status, both within their religious community and in the wider society was marginal. According to a study in South India, they seem to have made less progress both economically and politically than the Hindu Dalits in the area[107] They suffer a two-fold oppression: as they are on the margins both in the society and in the Church.

After a survey studying the conditions of the Dalit Catholics in Tamil Nadu, Anthoniraj points to the many discriminations that still continue in many places:

> Separate chapels, separate places in the church and cemeteries, discrimination with regard to the roles that the Dalits can play in the celebration of the liturgy, exclusion of the Dalit streets from the processional routes during festivals, refusal to accept their financial contributions during festivals so that they may not claim equal participation, etc[108]

In some churches the voting system and candidates proposed for election to some posts are skilfully manoeuvred by the wealthy and clever high caste Christians. Marriages between the high caste and Dalit Christians are rare. On January 15, 1925, the Dalit Christians of Thiruchirappilly sent a memorandum to Bishop Alexius Maria Henry Lepierier, the Visitor Apostolic for India, enumerating the discrimination that they suffer from the high caste Christians:

> The absurdity of their pretensions to enforce their distinctions of caste against us in the house of God is only matched by the arrogance with which they put them forward. They demand in writing, signed and sealed by his lordship the Bishop of Trichinopoly, (1) that we should for ever be segregated as untouchables in the house of God, (2) that Holy Communion should be distributed to them first, and that after they have all been served, then and there only the officiating priest should carry the sacrament to us, (3) that our children, under no circumstances, be admitted in St.Joseph's College, in the Catholic Boarding Houses, the Convents, the Holy Redeemer's School, the Seminaries and other institutions. We have waited long and patiently. As Catholics we demand

our Catholic privilege for equal treatment in the house of God and for equal educational facilities. [109]

In the recent CBCI Meeting at Varanasi, the Bishops declared: "The prevalence of caste-based practices, not only on society but also in some parts of the Church in India even at the close of the 20th century, is a matter of shame and disgrace to all of us... Discrimination against anybody on the basis of caste is a sin against God and humanity. This needs to be proclaimed from the housetops so that caste-based practices will be removed from the Christian community totally as part of our preparation for *Yesu Krist Jayanti* 2000".[110]

Theologising on the subalternity of the Dalits, the Dalit liberation theologians speak of "Dalit awareness" or "Dalit consciousness" that provides a new sense of self to Dalits at the margins.[111] Though some Dalit liberation theologians make the criticism that the missionaries and their work among the Dalits in the 19th century did not contribute to awaken them, there are many who argue that the Christian mission did bring about a change of consciousness among the Dalits. J. Samuel argues:

> The missionaries believed that it was conversion to Christ and the new life in Christ that provided the depressed class believers a new identity and a transformed view of the self and this in turn, brought social change and very often upward mobility. The missionaries provided education and health care and these facilities contributed positively to the well being of the depressed class Christians and to their sense of personal worth. [112]

The Church, though tolerant of the caste system, has contributed partly to the sociocultural uplift of the Dalits. Even if the motive behind the conversion of the Dalits to Christianity was their uplift by a change of place, occupation and style of life so as to improve their living conditions, yet the Church could not make any dent in the hierarchical system that gave the Dalits a low rank in the society.

4. The Impact of Modernity

It is an undeniable fact that the caste system proved to be the stable social structure of India for about three millennia. Even Buddhism or the *Bhakti* tradition could not bring about significant change in the system. In this stagnant situation the impulse to change can only come from outside.[113] But Islam, though it came from outside, did not make an impact for change, as it was a traditional society and its impact on India was rather tradition reinforcing than otherwise.[114] The real challenge to change came from the British. Yogendra Singh enumerates the prominent aspects, which caused the change:

> Its components were: a universalistic legal system, the expansion of western form of education, urbanisation and industrialisation, speed of new means of communication and transport and social reforms. Along with these modernisation norms structural modernisation also took place. For instance, rational bureaucratic systems of administration and judiciary, army, and industrial bureaucracy, new classes of business elite and entrepreneurs came into being. These were accompanied by the emergence of a political elite and a nationalist leadership by the middle of the nineteenth century.[115]

The consequences of this impact in the area of caste were a number of reform movements as noted by many:

> There was a new awareness among the Dalits, some of whom were able to profit by new educational and job opportunities. Their demand for equality as well as the egalitarian ideologies of the West also provoked movements among the higher castes. Kesab Chandra Sen and his *Brahma Samaj*, Dayananda Saraswati and his *Arya Samaj*, Jyotirao Phule and his *Satyasodhak Samaj*, M.G.Ranade and his *Prarthana Samaj* were some of the more organised movements.[116]

However, these movements were unable to make a substantial change in the structure of caste. Amaladoss observes four elements that contribute to change in the modern times:

The availability of caste-free jobs in production and service industries and in the government bureaucracy, breaking the caste occupational link; developing urbanisation that loosens the rigid village organisation, promotes a money economy as opposed to the *Jajmani* system of exchange of services and facilitates; a certain anonymity of the individual in the public sphere; the possibility for all caste groups of getting educated; and the advent of a democratic order that stresses fundamental rights and liberties, abolishes untouchability, promotes affirmative action and provides opportunities for political initiative and action for individual and caste groups.[117]

A kind of new freedom has come for the Dalits by the occupational mobility. Writings on the Mahar movement in Maharashtra point out the impact of many finding work in the Railways, in the Army or with European households.[118] Many possibilities and new awareness have come to the Dalits, but any attempt to go from this awareness and freedom to a movement for upward mobility is opposed by high caste groups as it is becoming a threat to their present status and the privileges. Conflict and violence in such a situation are inevitable.[119] Changes are also affecting the high castes. Increasing secularisation surely affects the purity-pollution complex. Democracy in politics and the abolition of untouchability by law promote at least the public practice of equality.[120]

In spite of some changes the caste exists and it seems to be very vibrant with a lot of influence in the question of marriage and has an increasing presence in the politics of contemporary India. It is dying only under certain aspects, as Beteille observes:

The first and most decisive casualty has been the legal basis of caste. No two texts can be more divergent in this orientation to caste than the *Manusmrti*, which we may take as the charter of traditional Hindu law, and the Constitution of India, which may be regarded as the charter of contemporary Indian law... Many of the modern proponents of Hinduism such as Vivekananda, have attacked caste instead of defending it.

There are very few contemporary proponents of Hinduism who would be prepared to argue that caste has to be saved in order to strengthen the Hindu religion.[121]

It is often said that no matter how loudly Hindus proclaim their indifference or even hostility to caste, when it comes to the question of marriage all of them - educated and uneducated, urban and rural, professional and peasant - turn to caste.[122] Still, according to Barnett, a kind of relativity is introduced to the system. A person who keeps caste rules at home and breaks them in the office has introduced a basic relativity into the system. Sooner or later the caste rules will have to be loosened. The caste group may continue as a kin group, but it tolerates individuals who do not keep all the rules. Thus a principle of individualism subverts the group principle from inside.[123]

The caste distinctions and the sense of obligations arising from such distinctions and their articulations and practice are not seen in the same way in different places, especially when we consider the rural and urban situations. Beteille observes:

> One of its principal components was the sense of obligation that the individual carried towards the caste into which he was born, to abide by its customs, to adhere to its style of life and to pursue the occupation allotted to it. Perhaps that sense of obligation, though not easily articulated is still strong among cultivators, artisans and others in the rural areas. But it has weakened considerably in the urban areas...Nothing could be more mistaken than to believe that caste was something that for two thousand years Indians merely lived by, without giving thought to its meaning or its rightness, that it existed merely as practice and not as theory. We must not lose sight of the intellectual tradition of India in which theoretical reflection and dialectical skill were used for describing, explaining and justifying the distinctions of caste by generations of individuals.[124]

Later Beteille observes:

> In 1950s, most Indian intellectuals believed that caste was on the way out, while only a few said that it was there to stay. Even those who said that it was gaining a new lease of life, could point to evidence from only a single domain, that of politics, to support their argument. No one could seriously maintain that the structures and sanctions of caste were becoming stronger, or that the many ritual injunctions and interdictions relating to food and physical contact were gaining strength, or that the association between caste and occupation was growing closer, or even that the rules of endogamy were being more strictly defined and observed. In all these domains caste was growing weaker, very slowly, almost imperceptibly in some cases, more clearly and noticeably in other cases. It is only when we turn to politics we get a very different picture.[125]

In politics, the caste is emerging as a powerful force. Rajni Kothari has remarked: "It is not politics that gets caste-ridden; it is caste that gets politicised".[126] Caste did not enter into politics all at once with independence, but it made its presence strongly felt in the first general election, and increasingly with each successive election.[127] In democracy number matters. A caste group can exert political pressure if it organises its votes as a block. Even the economic dominance of a caste can be used as political pressure. Different sub-groups who organise themselves to a larger group can enter into a coalition against a locally dominant caste. Loyalties of caste are used for the mobilisation of political support in a number of ways: by generalised appeal to caste sentiments, by activating networks of kinship and marriage and by organised activities of caste associations.[128]

The question is not simply one of the extents of the use of caste in electoral politics but also of its meaning and legitimacy for different sections of Indian society. Beteille observes a change in the orientation and ideological tone of the political leaders:

A change in the orientation of political leaders, and with them of the *intelligentia*, appears to have started in the 1970s when the politics of backwardness took a new turn with the installation of the first non-Congress government in New Delhi in 1977. It began to be argued that caste needed to be given a place in the public life not so much on grounds of Realpolitik as on grounds of social justice. The lower castes had been stigmatised and exploited in the past and they should be given special protection through extensive quotas in every domain of public life... The ideological tone was given a new articulation from 1990 when the left parties decided to join hands with Mr V.P. Singh's Janata Dal in pressing for the extension of the caste quotas in the course of social justice. This made it in effect impossible for any party openly to oppose caste quotas, so that caste has, at least for the time being strengthened its grip over politics. But it still is an unsteady grip, for, neither supporter nor opponents of caste quotas say that caste itself should be revitalised. In fact the strongest supporters of caste quotas are, paradoxically, also the strongest opponents of caste as a hierarchical system.[129]

Though the caste system remained stable for centuries, there were always changes in it through the centuries. Internal changes are seen from the traditional set up to modern times.

5. Modern Transformation of Caste

Throughout modern India, the public and political discourse about caste is dominated by perceived illegitimacy of 'traditional' caste hierarchy and by the need to overcome the effects of the persisting caste inequality.[130] Virendra Singh puts it this way: "Power is held by a traditionally privileged class but it is no longer institutionalised by tradition."[131] Whereas in the past a small section of a caste may have broken away from the bigger group aiming at upward mobility through Sanskritisation, today caste groups are coming together for political mobility.[132] Thus 'fusion' is replacing 'fission' as a factor in mobility.[133]

The political delegitimation of caste has penetrated all levels of society as the characteristic note of modernity. As Rudolph says: "Modernity has entered into the Indian character and society but it has done so through assimilation, not replacement".[134]

Fuller explains this modern transformation of caste thus:

> The contemporary understanding of caste — what it is and what it means – is above all a denial, most explicitly in the public domain, of the existence or continuing significance of caste in its traditional form.... Furthermore, when the existence and importance of caste are still acknowledged, this often takes the form of a substantialist assertion about cultural distinctiveness ostensibly belying inequality both between and within castes, although substantialisation is itself accompanied at the empirical level by increasing intra-caste differentiation. Moreover, because cultural distinctiveness retains evaluative implications, it can also provide a coded language to refer to caste inequalities. These inequalities are widely recognised and even approved in private, but normally they cannot be legitimately endorsed in public.[135]

Barnett also sees this development as substantialisation of the caste, where it moves from a transactional to a substantial mode.[136] Whereas earlier a caste found its identity and rank in relationship to other castes with which it was reacting in a given locality, now it defines its identity in belonging to an ethnic like caste bloc spread over a whole region or state.[137] To make sense of the data on caste today, it is useful to reconsider the relationship between caste and ethnicity, for Barnett's description of substantialisation as a form of ethnicisation[138] has some analytical advantages, which have not been sufficiently explored. Fuller explains:

> In Weber's original model status group stratification develops from perceived differences between styles of life, and if these differences are thought to be based on common descent and

are further reinforced by restrictions on intermarriage in particular, status groups become ethnic groups. Ethnic groups in turn can develop into castes.[139]

The 'vertical social system' defined by hierarchical relationships is decaying and castes are becoming 'horizontally' disconnected ethnic groups, putatively differentiated by their own styles of life.[140] The development of ethnicity in the west, specifically in the United States and the ethnicisation of caste in India are entirely separate processes, but the difference between them, as Beteille (1991: ch.9) insists, should not be exaggerated by asserting that West is egalitarian and individualist, whereas India is hierarchical and holistic. All the same, caste equality – unlike ethnic or racial equality – is a virtual contradiction in terms.[141] Gandhi's famous assertion that in truth all castes are equal because 'A Scavenger has the same status as a Brahmin'[142] has never been credible to any contemporary Indian.

In the political arena the electoral majorities are built upon coalitions of caste, which are considered as a political strategy for the survival or strengthening of caste system in the post-independence India. Fuller considers that treating susbstantialisation as ethnicisation helps to draw attention to connections between the politics of caste and religious nationalising. He explains:

> At first sight, it looks as if the re-enforcement of caste-group's solidarity in the political field ought to inhibit the development of a broader Hindu identity, but this is not in fact inevitable. Indian politicians are constantly trying to forge inter-caste alliances in order to build much larger blocs, and in theory this process of alliance formation could continue until all Hindu castes joined together in a single Hindu 'community' opposed to Muslims, Sikhs or other religious minorities. Such unification is indeed a major objective of the Hindu nationalist movement, the Vishva Hindu Parishad, whose rhetoric consistently stresses the need to incorporate Harijans and tribal groups within the 'Hindu nation'.[143]

In principle Bharatiya Janata Party in union with VHP, has this objective, to unite all castes, although the BJP is well aware of the problems in every attempt to create such a vast alliance. At the same time, this strengthening of Hindu communal identity is, at least in part, an extension, rather than a negation, of the ethnicisation of caste. Moreover, the substantialised, ethnic identity of a caste may be reciprocally expressed by emphasising its Hindu identity – by asserting that its distinctive caste culture is itself a manifestation of *Hindutva*, Hindu-ness.[144] Under these contemporary circumstances although the overall direction of change is fairly clear, the social fact of caste appears increasingly ambiguous, inconsistent and variable.[145]

Mobility and change have not made any substantial difference in the position of Dalits, they continue to be segregated and isolated in society even now. Economically and politically a few individuals or small groups may have improved in their status. Generally speaking as a group their social position in the caste system has not really changed.[146] Barnett emphatically says, "Now all castes keep up asymmetric transactions with Untouchables, even where they abandon them with other castes. Given this qualitative distinction, Untouchables are coming to be seen as separate "race".[147]

6. Caste and Class

Caste and class are considered as two significant dimensions of social stratification, which are closely interrelated, almost inseparable, in all the basic aspects of social life in the specific Indian situation today. Debate on caste and class has covered wide ranging issues related to the indicators of status, levels of equality and inequality, cultural and structural interaction, occupation and mobility, etc.[148] Among these two dimensions of social differentiation caste is a legacy of the past carried over to the present, whereas class is based on the development of productive forces and the production relations. D'Souza explains that though these two dimensions are different, qualitatively they are basically determined by the same variable, occupational prestige:

> The basic reasons for making a qualitative distinction between caste and class were the assumption that the caste hierarchy is qualitatively different from the class hierarchy. Whereas the former is attributed to variables such as status, honour, purity and impurity and intrinsic worth of groups, the latter is derived from the variables of economic and political power... Both caste hierarchy and class hierarchy are basically determined by the same variable, occupational prestige. What are considered to be essential features turn out, on a closer examination, to be the modes of expression of status differences among castes in their interaction. Since they depend upon the particular cultural milieu, they vary from culture to culture.[149]

Other observers think that castes are yielding their place to class formations, especially in industrial situations.[150] Amaladoss pointing out the complexity in the understanding of caste and class together writes:

> The class association may function in the public sphere, leaving caste formations to continue in the private sphere, though the very fact of such differentiation weakens the traditional caste ideology based on occupational differentiation. Sometimes the class formation, as for instance the Peasants' movement in Tanjore, may effectively be the political face of a single caste group: the Dalit agricultural labourers. Besides, the qualitative distinction between the Dalits and other castes would prevent a common class formation. A class formation irrespective of caste may be possible in a particular industrial setting. But it may be difficult for a group to retain its Dalit identity and at the same time become part of a class.[151]

Caste as status groups are defined mainly in terms of styles of life. Although a given style of life is compatible with more than one occupation, it is possible when an unlimited or too much diversity of occupation or economic status may disrupt the unity of the status group. Styles of life generally have a close association with a large number of ritual restrictions with the social honour as the caste structure brings about a social subordination and an acknowledgement of 'more honour' in favour of the privileged caste and status groups. Generally classes are not defined in terms of social honour, though class positions do tend to be associated graded honour. Classes are normally defined in terms of property, of ownership or nonownership of the means of production. The Caste system in traditional society enjoyed legal and religious sanctions, whereas classes do not enjoy such sanctions as they are *de facto* categories.

Many changes have taken place in the caste system having implications for changes in the class structure and power relations, as Sharma observes:

> The emergence of a new middle class disproportionate to the forces of production and the size of the upper and the lower classes has forged a new nexus between caste, class and power. The embourgeoisement of the families of the principal agricultural castes has given a new direction to the connection between caste, class and politics. The divide between the upper and the backward castes also adds a new dimension to the caste/class.[152]

Besides caste, the quality of the agricultural land, infrastructure for cultivation trade and commerce, invasions and migrations and power have determined social status and mobility.[153] Sharma sees a shift from the emphasis on the 'cultural' to economic-political pointing to a new power structure that approves caste-class nexus:

> A shift from the emphasis on 'cultural' criteria has made the distinctions based on economic and political power the focal theme in the study of caste system. Surfacing of incongruities between caste and other domains shows domination of caste as an all-encompassing system and the emergence of a new

nexus of economy, politics, migration, and religion as interlocking sub-systems. Since agrarian relations, economic transactions and service relations have changed; the caste system too has changed a lot setting in motion the process of 'role-reversal'... Agrarian reforms and the green revolution have affected caste, class and land relations by creating divides comprising various kinds of gainers and losers, which also has implications for the emergence of a new power structure.[154]

Neither caste nor class can serve as a tool for analysing the emerging reality of pauperisation, proletarianisation and downward social mobility among the middle and lower castes, because caste is not a precise equivalent of class. Castes are discrete, segmentary and flexible. Class relations can be analysed by juxtaposing them with caste, kinship, marriage and family. The study of the nexus between caste and class has highlighted the multifaceted nature of social stratification.

Discussing the modernisation of the Indian tradition Yogendra Singh distinguishes between categorical and instrumental values and explains that the change in the value system take place when there are changes in the mind-set and world-views of the people as it is seen in the case of NRIs:

> Categorical values refer to the worldview, value systems and social relationships that characterise culture. Instrumental values refer to elements like the means of production and communication. The impact of science and modernity can change instrumental values; it cannot by itself change categorical values based on religion or culture. Traditional categorical values could very well co-exist with modern instrumental values. People everywhere may use cars and radios without changing their worldviews and ways of relating to other.... This does not mean that categorical values are absolute or that they cannot be changed. It only means that science, economic development and political change cannot by themselves change categorical values.... the caste system

does not belong to the sphere of instrumental values. If it has to be changed it must be approached at its own level, with appropriate strategies and methods. We must change people's minds and attitudes and the world-views and motivations on which they are based.[155]

Castes and class are not polar opposites. Both are found in rural and urban areas. The nature and significance of caste is progressively becoming complex and ambiguous. Both caste and class are corporate as well as individual entities; and both have fixity and flexibility. Class is not replacing caste and the latter is still changing fast in the cultural domains of individual, social, political, economic and religious life.

By the end of the 20th century there was a feeling among many Indian intellectuals that caste was on the way out, but it did stay. Even those who said that it was there to stay could point to a single domain, politics, for evidence. We come across caste conflicts in all realms of life, a holistic cultural analysis is called for, for a better understanding of all discontents surrounding the caste cultural life.

CHAPTER III
CULTURAL DYNAMICS

This research concerns caste and the problems associated with the caste life in the Indian society, focusing on the conflicts in the encounter between the dominant caste culture and the Dalit culture. The caste system in India is analysed and understood in the framework of culture with its different dimensions. The analysis of the caste-culture and the interpretation that follows are in view of a counter-culture. But before entering into this analysis of the caste-culture with its different dimensions and going on to a theological response by pointing to a counter-culture, it will be useful to have an adequate understanding of the concept of culture, its different dimensions and dynamics.

1. What is Culture?

Etymologically "culture", like the word "cult", comes from the Latin word *colere*, which means to worship, to cultivate, or the state of being cultivated. In Latin the nouns from *colere* are *cultura* and *cultus*. '*Cultus*' means religious worship and ritual when it is applied to the gods. When the word culture refer to soil, plants and animals, it meants agriculture. When it is referred to human beings it meants education and refinement. There is a close affinity between the different kinds of work we do in relation to nature: agriculture and cult, religious rituals and culture, the various artistic expressions of the people.[156] We could distinguish between primitive and developed, and refer to the rich cultural heritage of a country consisting of art, music or literature and sometimes religion. Since it is limited to a few people in the country known for their skills, refinement, erudition etc., this understanding of the word culture is very inadequate. All experience belong to culture. It is never an affair of an individual at a particular moment of time, as it involves a complex interplay of perception, thought, interpretation and language. A recognised culture covers everything in human life. The Willowbank report (1978) makes this sufficiently clear in the concise definition given by it:

> Culture is an integrated system of beliefs (about God or reality or ultimate meaning), of values (about what is true, good, beautiful and normative), of customs (how to behave, relate to others, talk, pray, dress, work, play trade, farm etc.), and of institutions which express these beliefs, values and customs (government, law, courts, temples or churches, family, schools, hospitals, factories, shops, unions, clubs etc.), which binds a society together and gives it a sense of identity, dignity, security and continuity. [157]

M. Amaladoss takes culture as "the way in which people humanise nature and themselves".[158] The process of humanising nature depends upon the relationship between man and God, humans and nature, derived from the meaning and value system that guide one's choices in life. "Culture with its political implications is the crucial issue today in the process of humanisation."[159] The eruption of the cultural and the ethnic beckons us, therefore, towards a long-term project of humanisation. The political implications of culture are manifested when the equality-hierarchy interplay is seen as acting in society. Amaladoss explains how this process takes place: "There is a certain sense of equality among the people. As the community gets more organised and cities and trade develop, we have a more feudal set up.... Social organisation becomes hierarchical."[160]

There is a rather explanatory definition of culture by Kroeber and Kluckholn, which was reached after surveying and analysing hundreds of definitions. It stresses the very dynamics of culture affecting human behaviour, forming and changing it, as a product of action and as conditioning action:

> Culture consists of patterns, explicit and implicit, of and for behaviour, acquired and transmitted by symbols, constituting the distinctive achievement of human groups, including their embodiments in artefacts; the essential core of culture consists of traditional (i.e. historically derived and selected) ideas and especially their attached values; culture systems may, on the one hand, be considered as products of action, on the other as conditioning action.[161]

Recognising the constitutive and interpretative aspects of culture S. Kappen puts forward another definition explaining how the culture enters into the different realms of human life, in the social, economic, political, cultural, religious, etc., and establishes an authorship in the human and communitarian aspects of life:

> Culture is the organic whole of ideas, beliefs, values and goals, which condition the thinking, and acting of a community of people. Culture finds conceptual expression in ethics, philosophy and law; symbolic expression in art, literature, myth and cult. It is also embodied in economic, social, political and cultural institutions and structures. It is equally enfleshed in the psycho-structure of individuals – in their reflexes, reactions, sensuousness, expectations and hopes. Even ordinary artifacts and products are bearers of culture. The beliefs and values of a people can be read from the kind of houses built, dress worn, food eaten, and implements used.[162]

M. Amaladoss is of the view that the basic elements of culture include a world-view and a system of values based on that world-view. Concerning the manifestation in life he says:

> These elements find expression in symbol systems of various kinds: myths, particularly of origins and ends, but also historical narratives; artistic creations in word, sound, colour, stone, body or space; and rituals that help the affirmation,

interiorisation and celebration of the basic world-views and values at human and social levels in terms of community relationships.[163]

Much of the interiorisation of the culture remains at the subconscious level, unless it is brought to the level of consciousness by interpretation.

Religion is the deepest element in culture because it refers to the ultimate meanings and values, specified normally in terms of a revelation at the "beginnings", transmitted in narrative (myth) and symbolic action (ritual).[164] The symbolic structures specific to a particular religion or tradition (which is inclusive of culture, as in 'Buddhist culture', 'Islamic culture', 'Hindu culture', 'Christian culture' etc.) must be understood as existing side by side with social (economic, political, etc.) structures.

While symbolic and social structures are to be distinguished, there is also a dialectical relationship between them. In the very dynamics of culture there is a dialectic taking place between the twofold dimensions of ideological structures and meaning structures. M. Amaladoss distinguishes this twofold dimensions as social and cultural[165], S.M. Parish understands them as ideology and critique[166] and J.L. Segundo in a similar way distinguishes them as ideology and faith.[167] Amaladoss explains the dialectic interaction between the meaning structures and the concrete social structures having a new vision, which is capable of bringing transformation and change:

> Both are interrelated and in an ongoing dialectic: moments of change, which are also moments of tension, are inevitable. A new vision may lead to a change in structures and a revolutionary change of structures may evoke a new vision. This mutual relationship is not a casual one but a creative one. This is why culture escapes total conditioning from the social system. Saying that culture is at once a 'model of' and 'model for' social behaviour sometime specifies the dialectical relationship between culture and the social system. It is a

'model of' in so far as patterns of social behaviours are the ground from which cultural symbols emerge and which they reflect. It is a 'model for' in so far as a given pattern of social behaviour is one concrete realisation of a cultural symbol.[168]

This is a dynamic interaction and a creative process effecting change and transformation in the society.

2. Dominant and Subaltern Cultures

In complex societies where a multi-cultural situation prevails one distinguishes between dominant and subaltern cultures. Between the two poles, great and little, dominant and subaltern, elite and popular, macro and micro, etc., there is continuity with different middle positions or starting points. Amaladoss discusses also their interaction while distinguishing between the two:

> The elite pole refers to a more articulate, conscious, written, reflexive and technologically developed level of culture in a society. The popular pole represents the ordinary people whose culture is taken for granted, if not unconscious, oral, spontaneous. Even the elite is rooted in the popular and keeps absorbing the elements from the popular level. On the other hand, over time elite elements may filter down to the people at a popular level.[169]

The emergence of the great and little traditions that the anthropologists speak about can also be understood from the history of China and India where exists different groups of people with different languages and cultures. In India the emergence of Hindu sanskritic tradition as the great religious tradition was the result of the infiltrations of the Aryans around 9th century BCE on the one hand, while many indigenous smaller traditions and cultures of the native population existed side by side. Later there emerged different traditions and movements by the mixture and interaction of people caused by the successive wars and invasions. The great tradition is also often the more elite tradition. A great tradition may have evolved under the aegis of a ruler who brought about political unity among the various peoples and had provided the political basis for the emergence of a common great tradition.[170]

All over the world we observe the conflict between macro and micro, the big dominating the small and the small dissenting from the big. Different races, castes and classes try to interpret the world and reality in their particular way creating particular cultures. However, not all of them are in a position to impose their culture on others as universally valid. The Indian scene is dominated by the Aryan race and the Brahmin caste (Sanskritic culture).

In multicultural situations we can speak of dominant and subaltern cultures. The Italian Marxist writer Antonio Gramsci in order to counter Fascism in 1920s and 1930s made the term subaltern into a socio-political category. In India it is popularised mainly by the publication *Subaltern Studies* in nine volumes on South Asian history by a group of thinkers. Ranjit Guha in the first volume of *Subaltern Studies* gives the following description:

> The word 'subaltern' stands for the meaning as given in the *Concise Oxford Dictionary*, that is, of inferior rank. It will be used as a name for general attitude of subordination in South Asian society whether it expressed in terms of class, caste, age, gender and office or in any other way.[171]

In this research caste culture takes up the central place. And in the analysis of the caste culture and its cultural dynamics we come across the two poles: the dominant caste culture and the subaltern caste culture or the dalit culture. Amaladoss points out some of the characteristic features of the subaltern cultures:

> The subaltern cultures belong to people who are oppressed and downtrodden in a society with unequal economic, political and social structures. They can simply be the poor, who can be found in any society. But more characteristically, they are structurally marginalised and oppressed in a systematic way because of ethnicity, caste, gender, economic status etc. Their

culture integrates their oppression. The dominant culture justifies the oppressive social structure through 'myths' of origins or through racial and other prejudices. Oppressed groups as well as their oppressors, living at a spontaneous level, may accept the oppressive social structure as normal, inevitable, inherited.[172]

When some reject and challenge the premises and practices of certain culture they undergo not just a struggle with others who pursue different commitments and interests, but also they undergo an inner struggle of self against self. This self-examination, scrutinising the way the self is involved in the dynamics of social world, is very difficult and most painful part of questioning and reinterpreting the culture.

3. Caste-culture and Counter-culture

Different people deal with the unhappiness people feel from the encounter they have with the social and historical realities, differently. Each group has its own sense of reality emerging from the moral imagination, which often is entangled with its sense of what might be and what should be. S. M. Parish (1997) describes the dynamics of the process in which the human mind creatively encounters the socio-cultural world characterised by the caste culture with its different ideologies and comes out with a critique capable of bringing change and transformation in society in the form of a counter-culture.

Among the many anthropological accounts that focus on the ideology of caste, in contrast with the official moral ideologies of the West, Louis Dumont (1980) has come out with an ideology that gives an image of the Hindu as *Homo Hierarchicus*. Apart from the hierarchical inter-dependence, the individuals here have no value. Responding to Dumont, Parish says:

> This account offers an important insight; it captures a central ideological note. Yet it yields a profoundly incomplete image of the Hindu person a "totalising" interpretation that accounts

for everything, this view dangerously obscures the actual diversity of human experience in Hindu cultures. It precludes a discussion of a culture's discontents, of agency and resistance within a culture, of the tensions and quandaries of cultural life.[173]

Perusing the studies and literature concerning caste one finds that there is a one-dimensional approach in the caste ideology, which forgets the cultural and religious aspects. The ideology of caste hierarchy dominates many of the scholarly studies with a total collapse of cultural and personal dimensions of caste life in the Indian society. Parish observes:

> If ideology transforms human beings making them uni-dimensional, mere reference points for cultural practices or polemics, rendering them stick-figures suitable for rhetorical purposes for justifying some vision of society, then too often this process of over-simplification has been echoed in and implicitly ratified by academic studies... Ideological glosses on humanity, and academic glosses on ideology, leave out too much of what men and women themselves find most meaningful: their aspirations and discontents, much of their suffering, the texture of their life and flow of their experience. We need to explore such experience and not the ideology of caste.[174]

Many societies with racial, gender, caste and class hierarchies have as the central core of their socio-cultural existence a kind of hierarchy of power and privilege and value. In the theological and moral imagination our sense of reality becomes entangled with a sense of what ought to be. Parish describes:

> Discontents inspire moral fantasy, a reimagining of the world. This reimagining can take many forms which yet have kind of underlying unity: there are dreams of justice, reveries of revenge and reversal, the musings that define aspirations, the poetics of utopia, the value-statements of social critique. In all these ways and many more, people imagine themselves whole, or contemplate a world where they could be whole,

where they might not suffer, might have justice. They dream of possible worlds. The fantasy stands in counterpoint to an actual world, where some might fear even to whisper their discontents.[175]

No one can close their eyes to the terror of history and injustices we see in human societies. Those who have had first hand experiences of such injustices, terror and suffering may quite often be led to despair. Pointing out the harsh realities of life and the way in which the people face them and the resultant changes in their lives, Parish states, "Wounded in the imagination and robbed of a future and brutalised by society, violence, ethnic cleansing, the depredations of those more powerful, people may step from history as nightmare into cultural hallucination in their desperation to get the world to turn out right."[176]

Dissent and counter-culture

The victims occasionally come out positively with prophetic voices and movements, which hold a promise of creating a better world, restoring homes and lives. Parish points out the dynamics of this cultural process:

> They, the victims, may bring history violently home to others in the process. As fantastic as such cultures of justice may seem they are not to be mocked or dismissed lightly. Nor are the psycho-cultural responses of those with more power to understand the events we call history or even make such events happen. Isolating themselves in a separate, but parallel reality the more powerful may live in a state of denial and develop a culture of denial. The historical sociology and psychology of the moral imagination must pay attention to these "cultures" within culture.[177]

Discontents and displeasures force people to construct reality differently and reinvent the existing social world. Parish points out the inner dynamics of how people enter their own selves, consciousness and society to redefine and restructure them by way of critique:

> People struggle to interpret history and society in the light of a sense of moral possibility and necessity, framed in terms of their cultural ethos and experience. Such discourse rejects what is, the way society is; it aspires to define what might be and what should be, putting culturally imagined possibilities into conceptual play, pitting actuality against ideals, defining aspirations and hopes that may be felt with a certain intensity, however unreal they are in practical terms. What people imagine might be and should be, are key aspects of human consciousness.[178]

People are disappointed and discontented when they see the gap between what they desire and what actually they receive. Culture, here, is not cults and customs, but the structures of meaning through which men give shape to their experience.[179] It is the perennial desire of every human person to reconstruct the world free from all pain as to realise the dreams of justice, equality and liberty. People fall short of achieving the desired changes and transformation of society. Such disappointment and discontents propel people to come up with moral discourses that reveal their structures of feeling and power that animate the cultural life.

The disappointment due to the gap between the desire and reality is a fact of life for many. We embody it: it is a self-contradiction that signals our humanity. We confront our multiple consciousnesses with varying degrees of awareness, irony, pain or wistfulness, and we attempt to cope in terms of our own values and experience.[180] There is a world of our imagination that embodies our hopes and values, and we feel that in a certain way the real world should conform to our values, even if it does not. Parish points out that the gap between desire and reality is not easily reconciled to the fact that human history is the story of millions of lives crushed at the bottom of human societies, that thousands march to meaningless deaths even now, and that those who have claimed to solve the problems of history and inequality have probably condemned more to death and suffering than they have saved.[181]

The suggestion is not just to look at the face of the nightmares of history in bewilderment or wonder at the way our history and societies overlook our humanity, our consciousness. We have to deal with the situation as people of courage and hope even in the struggles and pains. Those who grope for emancipation will find it. They are the real makers of history, the agents and subjects of culture. Parish affirms:

> We can imagine and live our sufferings, our pains, our frustrations, and our struggles to survive and lead lives that mean something. This is surely one thread in history: a story woven in life and thought, by men and women capable of responding to what they experience, who, if unable to grasp fully all of the circumstances that create their life situations, are nonetheless both agents and subjects of cultural lives. They have no choice. They have to live. This means they must grapple with the cultural world in which they live.[182]

Once awakening take place within them subalterns come out from their "culture of silence". They come up with suitable discourses challenging the dominant ones.

Politics of Culture

In cultural practices, when some are questioned, challenged and reinterpreted, there is the struggle, not just with others who pursue different commitments and interests, but also of self against self. The hegemonical struggle would then mean a conflictual situation: 'Intellectuals' clinging on to the established ideology and the inegalitarian social order try to nullify the efforts of those intellectuals who try to mobilise and organise masses to build up a new world order with a liberating world outlook and a corresponding value system, ethics and everyday practices.[183] It is a struggle to come to the fore, a painful process of self-examination, scrutinising the involvement of the self in the dynamics of the social world. This process is called "politics of consciousness" where the symbolic forms and values of caste hierarchy are created, contested and recreated in minds and lives.

Parish explains:

> The politics of culture is more than the cultural production of critique and ideology by contending groups, whether dominant cultural elite against critical minority, those with great power against those with little, or Brahman ideologues versus low caste critics of Brahminical ideology. It is a politics of self, identity and consciousness, mind and experience, reflect conflicting visions of reality, self, life. Who I am, what I am, is grounded in culture: the process of contesting culture encompasses an inner politics of consciousness.[184]

In cultural constructions people try to define others showing them as inferior or superior, or giving them a social value that stigmatises them. Though such constructions of personhood of others, that make others objects, are powerful, they do not necessarily determine what people think of themselves. However, people contest the way that they are objectified and struggle to define themselves by way of recreating culture to make meaning for themselves.

Those who defend the dominant order, endeavour to make it seem natural, necessary and even sacred. At times even the oppressed ones experience the order that oppresses them as fair and just. They find it difficult to deny the hegemony of the other group or challenge the cultural creation that stigmatises them. In some sense they share the culture of, and conspire with, the politically and economically dominant elite to make the social order that stigmatises and oppresses them appear objective, natural, moral and just. This, however, requires a lot of self-deception. Often the dominant ones succeed, if they act with political skill. However, as Parish argues:

> People have moments of insight into the social order, moments in which they see through the cultural presentation of a 'moral' order to the arbitrary foundations of social practices. In these moments of insight they may see that the established order of their lives is a human construction and may even catch

themselves in the act of "naturalising" the arbitrary. When they do so they face a choice. They can either explore the insight, or make themselves forget what they know. Often enough, actors work to make the dominant order's often capricious foundations seem moral and necessary, and natural (Bourdieu 1977:164). Frequently, this requires that people produce in themselves a degree of cultural amnesia or blindness.[185]

Insights and blindness live together. People shift between these two. Race, caste and gender are considered as the most powerful vectors of the multiple consciousness of self and society, and in the context, not only do people sometimes have the political equivalent of religious conversion experience, they shift and adjust perspectives as they confront the realities of everyday life, and attempt to fine-tune their social existence.[186] We could conclude that in any complex society, the characteristic note would be the multiple (un)consciousness.

The integral understanding of the social order, and the encounter and the conflict between the dominant caste culture and the subaltern culture could be done in a cultural framework. It could be done either through a grid made up of six elements, [187] which are grouped, in three related pairs: economics-politics, society-person and culture-religion, or taking the different cultural components individually. I have followed the latter method in this thesis in view of a comprehensive look. This method will of course entail some kind of overlapping of these different elements. There is the need of the framework of theory and ethnography that looks at, and beyond, and approaches integrally, the ideology that constructs and justifies a social order even if one approaches the different constitutive elements of culture individually.[188] To be sure, critical and integral ethnography must present materials on the construction of the social order. The construction of hierarchy in pageants and rituals, in moral and political discourse, in the practice of everyday life and in the context of the sacred must be explored in any study of caste society.[189] Such a critical approach will help to explore the different ways the mental spaces and conflicting models existing in a culture, and even make people rethink and challenge dominant concepts of reality.

Such explorations of the mental spaces in critical moments of insight and blindness push people to the cultural process of change and transformation, capable of giving shape to alternate culture or counter-culture, counter-ideology,[190] anti-hegemonic thought[191] etc. In the face of dominating and dehumanising forces it is important to have a clear vision and leadership with prophetic voices, which pave the way for a counter-culture. Such counter-ideologies, anti-hegemonic thoughts spun out of moral imaginations and critique affect the historical development and change of culture leading to social transformation.

NOTES

PART ONE

1. M. Amaladoss, *A Call to Community,* Anand: GSP, 1994, xi.
2. P. Kolenda, 1978, 1. Quoted by M. Amaladoss, *A Call ....,* xi.
3. A. Beteille, "Caste in Contemporary India', in C.J.Fuller (ed.), *Caste Today,* Delhi: Oxford University Press, 1996, 153.
4. C.J. Fuller (ed.), *Caste Today....*1996, 3.
5. M. Amaladoss, *A Call...,* 11.
6. M. Marriott, *Village India: Studies in the Little Community,* Chicago: University of Chicago Press, 1955; R. Deliege, *Les Paraiyars du Tamilnadu, Studia Instituti Anthropos* 42, *Nettetal, SteylerVerlag,* 1988; E.R. Leach, *Aspects of Caste in South India, Cylon and North-West Pakistan,* 1960; D.B. McGilvray, (ed.), *Caste Ideology and Interaction,* Cambridge:Cambridge University Press, 1982: 34-97.
7. Mckim Marriott, *India Through Hindu Categories,* New Delhi: Sage, 1990; S.M. Parish, *Hierarchy and its Discontents,* New Delhi: Oxford University Press, 1997.
8. A. Beteille, (ed.), *Social Inequality,* Hammondsworth: Penguin,1969; J. Silverberg, (ed.), *Social Mobility in the Caste System in India,* The Hague: Mouton Publishers,1968.
9. The term 'Dalit', first used in the nineteenth century by Mahatma Jyotirao Phule and in the journalistic writings as far back as 1931 to connote the Untouchables and outcastes as the oppressed and broken victims of our caste-ridden society. But it did not gain currency until the early 1970s with the Dalit Panther Movement in Maharashtra. Dalits have been called by various names, such as 'Untouchables', 'Harijans'(a glorified term coined by Narasinha Mehta and adopted and popularised by Mahatma Gandhi); 'Exterior Castes'(used by J. Hutton), 'Outcastes','Depressed Classes'(by British Officials), 'Pariahs'(commonly, but undoubtedly derived from the Tamil word *para* or *parai,* the drum [see Deliege,1997]). In more

ancient times the tems 'Mlecha', 'Chandala'(used by Manu), also Panchama (the fifth class), Avarna (i.e., outside the four varnas), Nishada, Paulkasa, Antyaja, Atishudra, etc. are used The term Scheduled castes appeared for the first time in April 1935, when the British Government issued the Government of India (Scheduled Caste) order, 1936, specifying certain castes, races and tribes as scheduled. Prior to that these population groups were generally known as 'Depressed Classes'. They make about sixteen percent of the Indian population and number about 138 million. Dalits, Dalitbahujans etc. are the terms preferred by the Dalits themselves. Cf. S.M. Michael, *Dalits in Modern India,* New Delhi: Visthar,1999; James Massey, *Dalits in India,* New Delhi: ISPCK, 1995, Eleanor Zelliot, *From Untouchable to Dalit,* New Delhi: 1992, 271.

[10] S. Devi, *Caste in India,* 1999.
[11] P. Kolenda, *Caste in Contemporary India,* 1978, 40-41
[12] G.S. Ghurye, *Caste and Race..,*1986, 2.
[13] *ibid,* 4.
[14] Mysore Census, 1901, 400. Cf. Ghurye, 1986, 6.
[15] D. Gupta, *Social Stratification,* 1992, 28-37.
[16] K.P. Rao, *Caste and Alternative Culture,* 1995, 2.
[17] Rig Veda, 10,90:11-12.
[18] Burnell, Arthur Coke (tr.), *The Ordinances of Manu,* New Delhi:1971, p. 306,310 (Manussmrti 10.12,10.38).
[19] *ibid.*
[20] M. Amaladoss, *A Call...* 1994,12-13.
[21] *ibid.*
[22] P. Kolenda, *The Caste..* 1978, 9. Cf. by M. Amaladoss, *A Call...* 1994, 13.
[23] P. Kolenda, *The Caste....,* op. cit.,1997, 24.
[24] M. Amaladoss, *A Call to...,* op. cit., 14-15.
[25] *ibid.* 15-16.
[26] *ibid.*
[27] *ibid.*
[28] M. Amaladoss, *A Call to.... op. cit.,* 17.

29. A. Pinto, Dalits: *Assertion for Identity.N. Delhi: ISPCK*, 1999, 2.
30. M. Amaladoss, *A Call...*op. cit.,17-18
31. *ibid.*
32. J. Massey, "History and Dalit Identity", in *Dalit Solidarity*, Massey and Das (eds.), New Delhi: ISPCK, 1995, 17.
33. M. Amaladoss, *A Call to..., op. Cit.,* 15.
34. S.K. Chatterji, *Indo-Arian and Hindi,* 18, 36, 47.
35. *ibid.* 500.The original inhabitants of India as perceived by the earliest written traditions are named as *dasas, vanaras, rakshasas, nishadas, nagas, yakshas, sabaras and kirata.* Whether we can substitute the term *tribe/adivasi* with dalit is a disputed question. The argument generally given was that the word 'tribe' is an administrative, linguistic, ethnic and sociological invention used by the outsiders. 'Dalit' is a more generic term depicting the deplorable conditions of a people who are at the bottom of the Indian society. Cfr. J. Vadakumchery, "The Original Inhabitants of India: Victims of Written Traditions", J. Massey ed., *Indigenous People: Dalits*, Delhi: ISPCK,1998, 122-133.
36. R. Thapar. *Ancient Indian Social History,* New Delhi; Orient Longman,1978, 141.
37. *ibid.* 142.
38. M.L. Sen (Tr): *Ramayana,* Culcutta, 1989, 699-702.
39. J. Gyandaka (ed.): *Snkhipat Mahabharate(Hindi),* Gorakpur, New Delhi, 69-72.
40. B. Kumarappa, *The Removal of Untouchability,* Ahmedbad: Navjivan Press, 1954, 158. Cf. M. Amaladoss, *A Call to...,*. 2-3.
41. Al-beruni, *India* (abridged edition of Dr. Edward C. Sachau's English translation and edited by Qeyamuddin Ahmed), New Delhi, 1988(revised), 46. Cf. Massey, "History and Dalit ....., 1995, 21-22.
42. J. Massey, "History and..., 1995, 22-23.
43. *ibid.* 23.
44. S. Kappen, *Jesus and Cultural Revolution,* 1983, 38.

45 *Dhammapda*, 393. Cf.M. Amaladoss, *A Call to..*, 22.
46 *Sutta Nipata*, Verse, 136. Cf. S. Kappen, *Jesus and...*, 40-41.
47 V.T. Samuel, *One Caste,...*, 1977, 85.
48 Cf. M. Amaladoss, *A Call to...*, 22.
49 Ayrookuzhiel, "The ideological notion of the Emerging Dalit Identity", in A.P. Nirmal (ed.), *Towards a common ideology, (n.d.)*, 92.
50 S. Kappen, "The Materialistic conception of Historyand the Indian Religious Traditions", *Negations*, 8(Oct-Dec 1983), 7.
51 M. Amaladoss, *A Call to...,*, 23.
52 E. Zelliot, *From Untouchables...*, 6.
53 M. Amaladoss, *A Call to...*, 24. Cf. J. Kananaikil, *Christions of...*, 1983, 98-114.
54 I. Ahmad (ed.), *Caste and Social Stratification*, New Delhi: Manahar Book Service, 1973.
55 Parvathama, in J. Kananaikil (ed.), *Christians of...*, 108-109.
56 *ibid.* 105.
57 Cf. V. Das, *Structure and Cognition*, New Delhi: Oxford University Press, 1982, 54.
58 J. Kananaikil, *Christian of...*, 23.
59 *ibid.* 106-107.
60 *ibid.* 104.
61 *ibid.* 106.
62 *ibid.* 110.
63 D.B. Forrester, *Caste and Christianity*, London: Curzon Press, 1980, 196.
64 *ibid.*
65 Cf. J. Silverberg, (ed.), *Social Mobility...*, 1968; M.N. Srinivas, *Social Change in Modern India*, New Delhi: Orient Longman, 1966.
66 M. Amaladoss, *A Call to....*, 19.
67 ibid, 20.
68 P. Kolenda, *The Caste...*, 1997, 96.
69 M. Amaladoss, *A Call to....*, 20-21.
70 P. Kolenda, *Caste in .....*, 99.
71 ibid, 100.

72 P. Kolenda, *Caste in..* 101.
73 *ibid*.102.
74 O. Lynch, *The Politics of* ...., 68-69.
75 P. Kolenda, *Caste in* ..., 103.
76 A. Beteille, *Social*...,1969. Quoted by Amaladoss, *A Call to*..,21.
77 R.L. Hardgrave, *The Nadars of Tamilnadu,* 1969.
78 M. Amaladoss, *A Call to*..., 21.
79 A. Beteille, "Caste in Contemporary India", in Fuller (ed.), *Caste Today,* 153.
80 M.N. Srinivas,1962, 15-41.
81 A. Beteille, "Caste in contemporary...., 153.
82 A. Pinto, *Dalits: Assertion for Identity,* 1999, 1. A.R. Thumma, *Voices of*..., 1999, ix.
83 *ibid.*
84 See V. T. Rajashekar, Dalit: The black Untouchables of India, Atlanta: Clarity Press, 1987.
85 Decan Herald, 3, July, 1997, 11.
86 J. Maliekal, *Caste in India Today,* Bangalore: CSA Pub., 1980, 4.
87 *ibid.*
88 AR. Thumma, *Voices of the Victims,* New Delhi, ISPCK, 1999,3.
89 M. Amaladoss, *A Call to*..., 4.
90 S. Manickam, *Slavery in the Tamil Country,* Madras: CLS, 1982; J. Silverberg, (ed.), *Social Mobility*..., *1968.*
91 A.R. Thumma, *Voices of*..., *1999, 3.* M.E. Prabhakar, *Towards a Dalit Theology,* New Delhi: ISPCK, 1989, 166-167.
92 *ibid.*
93 *The Week,* August 15, 1999.
94 A.R. Thumma, *Voices of*..., 1999, ix .
95 S. Kakar (ed.), *Identity and Adulthood,* 1979, 65-81.
96 M. Amaladoss, *A Call to*..., 5.
97 X. Irudayaraj, *Emerging Dalit Theology,* Madras: Jesuit Theological Secretariat, 1990, 13-14.

[98] M. Anand and E. Zelliot (eds.), *An Anthology of Dalit Literature,* New Delhi:Gyan, 1992.
[99] A.K. Ramanujan and Vinay Dharwadker, "Sixteen Modern Poems", *Daedalus,* Vol. 118, No. 4(Fall 1989), 325-326. Quoted by S. Clark, *Dalits and Christianity,* 1991, 1-2.
[100] Cf. John C.B. Webster, *The Dalit Christians, A History,* New Delhi: ISPCK, 1994, 210-211.The whole folk song contains 14 verses, it may have been recorded from oral singing.
[101] J. Maliekal, *Caste...,* 1980, 100.
[102] E. Zelliot, *From Untouchable....,* 1992, 212.
[103] A.R. Thumma, *Voices of...., 1999, 3.*
[104] James M. Freeman, *Untouchable,* 1979, 383-384.
[105] Bp. Nirmal Minz, "Dalits and Religion", *Dalit Solidarity,* Das and Massey (eds.), 1995, 141.
[106] J. Kananaikil, *Christians of Scheduled Caste Origin,* New Delhi: ISI,1983, 98-143.
[107] R. Deliege, "A Comparison between Hindu and Christian Pariyars", *IMR,* 1990. Cf. M. Amaladoss, *A Call to..., 9.*
[108] Antoniraj, 1992, 10-11. Cf. M. Amaladoss, *A Call to...., 9.*
[109] J. Thattumkal, *Caste and the Catholic Church in India,* 1983, 223-224. Cf. M. Amaladoss, *A Call to..., 9-10.*
[110] The Statement of the CBCI General body Meeting 21-28 March, 1988, Varanasi..
[111] Cf. S. Jayakumar, *Dalit Consciousness and Christian Conversion,* Delhi: ISPCK, 1999.
[112] ibid, xiii.
[113] Y. Singh, *Modernisation of Indian Tradition,* New Delhi: Thomason Press, 1973.
[114] *ibid.* 192.
[115] *ibid.* 203.
[116] M. Amaladoss, *A Call to..,* 27. Cf. P.A. Augustine, *Social Equality..,op. Cit.,* 108-128; D.B. Forrester, *Caste and..,* 155-172.
[117] M. Amaladoss, *A Call to..,* 27-28.
[118] E. Zelliot, *From Untouchables....,* 89.

119 J. Benjamin, "Social Mobility in Scheduled Castes in Bihar", *Social Action,* 41, 1991, 442-453. Cf. S.K. Sharma, "Social Mobility and Growing Resistance", *Social Action,* 41, 1991, 64-77.
120 M. Amaladoss, *A Call to..,* 28.
121 A. Beteille, "Caste in Contemporary...", in Fuller (ed.), *Caste Today,* 161.
122 *ibid.* 162.
123 S. Barnett, *The Identity Choice and Caste Identity...,* T.L. Dolgil et al (ed.), New York: Columbia University Press, 1997. Cf. M. Amaladoss, *A Call to...,* 28-29.
124 A. Beteille, "Caste in Contemporary...", in *Caste Today,* Fuller(ed.), 161-162.
125 *ibid.*167.
126 *Caste in Indian Politics,* New Delhi: Orient Longman, 1970, 240
127 A. Beteille, "Caste in Contemporary..., 167.
128 M. Marriot, *Village India..,* 36-55. Cf. A. Beteille, "Caste in Contemporary...., 168.
129 A.Beteille, "Caste in Contemporary.., 169.
130 C.J. Fuller (ed.),*Caste Today*20.
131 V. Singh, 1973, 190. Cf. M. Amaladoss, *A Call to...,* 29.
132 D.G. Mandelbaum, 1970, 487-520.Cf. M. Amaladoss, *A Call to...,* 29.
133 Gupta, 1991, 325. Quoted by M. Amaladoss, *A Call to..,* 29.
134 Y. Singh, *Modernization of Indian Tradition,* 168.
135 C.J. Fuller (ed.), *Caste Today,* 21.
136 S. Barnett, *Identity Choice...,* 279-289. By 'transactional mode' we understand the traditional set up of hierarchical inter-relational relationship that exists within different castes, with all transactions there. 'Substantial mode' is understood in the context of the modern changes that has taken place in the caste by way of group solidarity with the options of ethnic, class, cultural nationalist or racial bases.
137 M. Amaladoss, *A Call to...,* 30.

138 S. Barnett, 1975, 158-159. Cf. Fuller, *Caste Today*, 22.
139 C.J. Fuller (ed.),*Caste Today*, 22.
140 *ibid.* Cf. Searle Chatterjee and U.M. Sharma (eds.), *Contextualising Caste: Post-Dumontian Approaches*, Oxford: Blackwell, 1994, 19-20.
141 C.J. Fuller (ed.), *Caste Today*, 24.
142 E. Zelliot, 1972, 73.
143 C.J. Fuller (ed.), *Caste Today*, 24.
144 *ibid.* 25.
145 *ibid.* 26.
146 M. Amaladoss, *A Call to...*, 30.
147 S. Barnett, *Identity, Choice...*, 283.
148 K.L. Sharma, *Caste and Class in India*, Jaipur: Rawat Publications,1994, 1.
149 Victor D' Souza, *Inequality and its Perpetuation*, New Delhi: Manohar, 1981, 78-79.
150 J. Maliekal, *Caste in India...*, 91-98.
151 M. Amaladoss, *A Call to...*, 31; Cf. X. Irudayaraj (ed.), *Emerging Dalit...*, 34-38.
152 K.L. Sharma, *Caste and Class...*, 2-3.
153 *ibid.* 3.
154 *ibid.* 4.
155 M. Amaladoss, *A Call to....*, 32; Cf. Y. Singh, *Modernization..*, 214.
156 Masao Takenaka, *God is Rice: Asian Culture and Christian Faith*, Geneva: World Council of Churches, 1984, 27-72.
157 Cf. J. M. De Mesa & L. L. Wostyn in *Doing Theology*, Philippines: Claretian Publications, 1990, 25.
158 M. Amaladoss, *Beyond Inculturation*, 1998, 51.
159 F. Wilfred, "Politics of culture....", *Jeevadhara*, Vol XXII, 1992, 79-80.
160 M. Amaladoss, "Changing Culture and Religion", *Jeevadhara*, Vol XXII, 1992, 11.
161 Cf. Amaladoss, *Beyond Inculturation*, 1998, 51.
162 S. Kappen, *Jesus and Cultural Revolution*, 1983, 9-10.

163 M. Amaladoss, *Beyond Inculturation,* 1998, 51-52.
164 M. Amaladoss, "Hermeneutic of Tradition.....", 115.
165 *ibid.*
166 S.M. Parish, *Hierarchy and its Discontent,* Delhi: Oxford University Press, 1997, p. 6.
167 J.L. Segundo, *Faith and Ideologies,* New York:Orbis,1984.
168 M. Amaladoss, "Hermeneutic of....", 116.
169 M. Amaladoss, *Beyond Inculturation,* 1998, 54.
170 *ibid.* 55.
171 Ranjit Guha, *Subaltern Studies,* 1982, vii.
172 M. Amaladoss, *Beyond Inculturation,* 1998, 55.
173 S. M. Parish, *Hierarchy...,*6.
174 *ibid.* 6,7.
175 S.M. Parish, *Hierarchy....,* 1997, 2.
176 ibid
177 *ibid.*
178 *ibid.* 2,3.
179 Clifford Geertz, *The Interpretation of Cultures,* New York: Basic Books, 1973, 312.
180 S. M. Parish, *Hierarchy...,* 3.
181 *ibid.* 3,4.
182 *ibid.* 4.
183 Mary Pillai, "Cultural Hegemony: Its Traditional Roots and Present Manifestations", *Jeevadhara,* Vol. XXII, Jan. 1992, 36.
184 S. M. Parish, Hierarchy..., 7.
185 *ibid.* 9.
186 *ibid.*
187 M. Amaladoss, *The Fullness....,* 1993, 30.
188 S.M. Parish, *Hierarchy...,* 1997, 10.
189 *ibid.* 10.
190 O. Lynch, *The Politics of Untouchability,* 1969. Cf. Parish, 1997,10.
191 R. Williams, *Marxism and Literature,* 1977. Cf. Parish, *ibid.*

PART TWO

CASTE CULTURE: AN ANALYSIS

Caste has been a central preoccupation of anthropological studies in India and a social fact of great significance for millions of people. It has shaped their lives and fate. The ideology of caste apparently contrasts with moral ideologies of the West. Louis Dumont (1980) has especially given an image of the Hindu as *Homo Hierarchicus*. His account, which understands people existing in hierarchical interdependence, fails to give 'being' or value to individuals. Though it captures a central ideological note, it gives an incomplete image of cultural life. Such totalising one-dimensional interpretations dangerously obscure the actual diversity of human experience in Hindu culture.

My attempt here is not to make a detailed account of the analytical studies of the caste culture, nor is my effort to give a theoretical answer to the questions caste as a system of social stratification raises. But I do not mean to totally ignore the reflections and research done in this area by different people. My purpose is not to clarify or solve the issues that are raised by different experts from their own perspectives, but to have a sufficient and clear idea about caste culture, with a discussion of culture's discontents, of agency and resistance within culture, of the tensions and quandaries of cultural life, which will enable one to challenge and change it. I have given in Part One a brief survey of the caste system from a historical perspective, along with the contemporary experience of it. Now I shall move on to an integral analysis in a cultural framework put forward by M. Amaladoss.[1] However, before entering into the analysis, I like to put forward the relevant part of the description and analysis by Parish of the famous '*Chariot pulling*' in the spring festival in a Hindu city, Bhaktapur, Nepal. Parish analyses the caste culture with the focus on the cultural psychology of moral life, through some of its caste actors. Parish's analysis and interpretation are relevant in this thesis only because, unlike many other scholars, he discovered and put forward the idea that men and women in the caste cultural context were asserting and resisting hierarchy as the central social, cultural and personal reality for them. This I think, will serve as an introduction to the analysis of caste culture in its different dimensions.

CHAPTER IV
GOD-CHARIOTS IN THE GARDEN OF CASTES

Pulling the Chariot of the God during the Dussehrah festival is a common feature in many parts of North India. S.M. Parish involved himself in the lives of the people and cultures of the Hindu city Bhaktapur in the Katmandu valley of Nepal during the 1990s, and depicts the spectacular event of Chariot – pulling during the festival time that marks the turning of the year. The people of Bhaktapur pull two tantric divinities, god Bhairav and the goddess Bhadrakali. The Chariot is a mobile temple, a god-house on wheels, several times higher than the houses of the people who gather around it to worship. Parish sketches the kind of place Bhaktapur is, a Hindu city, a city of castes and divinities.

Bhaktapur is really an insignificant town packed into an area not more than half a square mile. In terms of meaningful human existence, it constitutes a world in itself. Parish describes it as a world built up by human imagination out of layers of religious and cultural meaning, constituting a whole intricate world. If you walk through the city with high caste persons, you may detect a flicker of disgust crossing their faces when you enter certain neighbourhoods. Glancing around they will say "butchers live here" or "this is where Untouchables live". Urban spaces and social emotions reinforce each other. Urban spaces are filled with images that invite and provoke religious feelings: with sculptures or myth–in–stone, memories, etc. In the festivals, the space fills in – the chariot festival is only one of many festivals. With the ritual dancers dancing and the devotees in the streets one can feel the presence of the divinity permeating the city everywhere. From its own religious perspective, Bhaktapur embodies Tantric Hinduism, as its inhabitants engage symbols and participate in rites that make up the religious conceptions of life, self and world.[2]

1. The Chariot and the Positions and Roles of Different Caste Actors

The priests do not have an easy drive through the streets during the journey with the gods. When the Chariots are pulled with different momentum and energy, and collide with houses making holes in the walls, the Chariots often get damaged as they cannot quite clear a corner in the journey. The priests will complain of the lack of decorum or discipline in the pulling of the Chariots; but one has to be mindful that god Bhairav is a dangerous god of force and motion; and the very movement of the Chariots through the streets seems somehow appropriate as a kind of metaphor for psychological forces, deriving from human emotions and dissatisfactions. These forces are sometimes capable of breaking through the superfluous construction of reality and common sense that help establish the political and cultural order of Bhaktapur.

Parish mentions that the symbolic representation of the priests who are in the apex of the festival celebration, shows the legitimacy of the special status the high caste generally enjoy in the caste system:

> The chief Brahman priest of the Taleju temple rides the chariot, carrying a sword that represents the royal power. This Brahman priest becomes a surrogate for the Newar's Malla kings; Brahman becomes King, for the purpose of the festival. Another Brahman rides with the king, representing the king's own Brahman priest and royal advisor, his *guru-purohit*. Thus, the apex of the caste hierarchy is represented in the (symbolic) persons of king and Brahman. They ride with the divinity:

their proximity to the god declares their status, and lends it an aura of legitimacy.³

Under the shade of a ceremonial umbrella accompanied by pomp and music, they solemnly march from the temple to the temple square where chariots wait for the ritual pulling and hauling. The priest-king commands the image of god Bhairav to be brought and placed in the chariot. The "king" worships it. Representing the king a Brahman takes a seat on God's right, and another Brahman representing the king's guru takes the seat on the left. Other caste members too take their respective seats thus reflecting hierarchical caste positions. Behind god Bhairav, a priest, representing non-Brahman priests and an astrologer take their seats. Four carpenters stand at the four corners. Representing the farmer's caste, who are the majority among Bhaktapur inhabitants, one takes the seat behind the royal Brahman priest. A kind of self-image of the Newar caste society is thus composed in the chariot and pulled through the streets of the city.

2. Men are Unequal

The traditional Newar society embodies the idea that men are unequal. Parish observes:

> The Newar cities grew to become extravagant flowers in royal gardens of caste, representing a cultural efflorescence of the idea of hierarchy, as caste practices were propagated and cultivated as the essence of the body politic. Taken up as part of the larger harvest of South Asian culture, the propagation of ideas and images of inequality as legitimate and the sacred values not only shaped the structure of society, of social relations, but also the intimate consciousness of men and women.⁴

As long as the rule of the king was there, the caste hierarchical system was legally supported even in the middle of the 20th century. The larger social and political context was quaking with radical structural change, but caste continued to be one of the key cultural axioms of the Bhaktapur local social existence even as the legal and political foundations for caste were being swept away.[5] Though in the early 1980s some castes had vanished or lost their symbolic and moral roles, the caste system survived in Bhaktapur and continued to grip people's minds, to define its social identity.[6]

The opposition between pure and impure, especially in the context of the sharing of food and other items is one of the basis with the caste hierarchy. The Untouchables or the impure cannot enter the upper stories of houses of the high caste. They are even barred from entering temples, though some Untouchables were accepted as attendants at certain shrines, as they perform stigmatising roles such as killing animals for a living, or handling excrement, accepting defiling offerings in death rites, etc.

The Untouchables were excluded by the upper castes in various ways. Mostly the higher castes lived in the centre and the Untouchables on the periphery of the city. The dangerously stigmatised sweepers, lived in a separate neighbourhoods outside the traditional boundaries of the city, in an area near the river, across one of the city's cremation grounds. This location symbolises their association with filth, decay and death. Education was limited to the higher caste members. Occupational mobility also was limited as certain occupations were reserved exclusively for certain castes. Distinctive ways of dressing, the limitation of construction to single storey buildings with thatched roofs were imposed upon the Untouchables. Entry to the city after sunset was denied to them. Accumulating wealth was also forbidden. Power and violence were used to keep the Untouchables in their places in the hierarchy.

Though the state no longer enforces such systems of exclusion, the pattern remains strong, showing the power of symbols and giving the message that it is not only the state and its actions that sustain the caste hierarchical system. Parish observes the situation in Bhaktapur:

> Untouchable sweepers still live outside the city. Untouchables now use water taps once reserved exclusively for use by the traditional 'high' and 'pure' castes, but may still be met with verbal abuse, made to feel unwelcome and inferior. Members of the traditional 'pure' castes of Bhaktapur object to untouchables entering the teashops in their neighbourhood.... They would risk being beaten if they did not accept the exclusions, if they did not conform to expectations held by members of other castes.... Practices that exclude or stigmatise people, that put or keep them in their place in the caste hierarchy, may no longer receive active support of the state, but groups, households and individuals remain under pressure to conform to such practices or else they may leave Bhaktapur altogether. Although legal and political constraints have eroded, the social and cultural constraints of caste life continue to have power, to be central to people's lives.[7]

Traditionally low caste people still perform traditional stigmatising occupations. There is change seen in the educational aspirations for children, in the improved economic circumstances of a few groups, in increasing tolerance among some members of other castes, and in the absence of explicit legal sanctions supporting the traditional caste order.[8] Instances of a few successful individuals in the modern sector can be seen and also rare cases of low caste solidarity that have brought success to a few. Even with such changes much of the life of the city still rests in its complex caste system; the caste system constitutes a division of labour, not only for economic activity but also for citywide ritual activities.[9] The essential roles connected with the temples of the cities rest on the Brahmans and other religious specialists. They officiate at some domestic rites of families. It is also admitted that roles that are stigmatising, impure and inauspicious, like sweeping, for example, are essential to the traditional social and symbolic life of the city. The impurities, misfortunes and sufferings of the city are conceived to flow into the Untouchables who live in a separate area outside the old boundaries of the city, for the sake of the purity of the city.[10] They have the 'nature' that suits them to their work of collecting dirt, feces and garbage. Conventionally the Untouchable castes are stigmatised as dirty, disgusting, impure, highly sexual and promiscuous, ignorant and lacking the discipline and mastery of language that would make them human. Parish summarises the caste conflicts thus:

> In total, they (the Untouchables) embody an 'otherness', for high caste actors, that is disturbing and yet reflects a moral order that is necessary, ordained by the very structure of the universe. High caste actors view low caste actors, individually and collectively, as deserving their fate. The low castes are polluted, that is, naturally defiled, a notion based on a complex physical theory of the flow of person-defiling substances; they are also viewed as realising the fruits of the sins of previous life times – their fate is justified by *karma* and ordained by *dharma*, the moral order of the universe, which caste society embodies.... In sum, a hierarchy constituted by power (the king and state) fuses in experience and in practice with a ritualised hierarchy constituted in terms of purity and impurity with a moral hierarchy of action and knowledge, of sin, virtue, and fate, and with a religious hierarchy of proximity to sacred values and access to spiritual power. In my view, caste hierarchy is all these, locked together in a dynamic propelled by struggles for domination and emancipation.[11]

Lower caste actors registered their resentment against the way they are subjugated, excluded and stigmatised. Formerly they were not able to do much with their discontents as they were powerless politically, socially, economically and culturally – the powerful could ensure that they were kept in their place. Though formally and legally the sanctions were removed, there were still not much they can do to escape being stigmatised. Parish points out the reasons and concludes that moral discourse in caste society does not alone reflect ideology but expresses profound ambivalence:

Overcoming the initial set of life–chances determined by their caste standing remains exceedingly difficult and for most perhaps virtually impossible. Since the invidious distinctions of caste are linked to subsistence and survival, the historical reality is that they could not really act on whatever analysis or critique of caste society some of them may have developed. Furthermore, since caste life generates a sense of moral community, shapes personal identity, and offers a number of meanings and satisfactions, it is not surprising that Newars are ambivalent about caste society. Moral discourse in caste society does not reflect ideology alone; it expresses profound, often self-shattering, ambivalence.[12]

Bhaktapur is more than caste hierarchy though caste has a central role in organising life. Parish points out how caste, with its central role in organising life, is deeply related with the psychological, social and cultural realms:

We should not identify Bhaktapur, or Newars with caste hierarchy, as if this is all they were - and not living human beings and a complex culture that is, and can become, more than any one anthropological study can describe. If we keep this firmly in mind, I believe we can explore caste life as central to the lives of people living in Bhaktapur, and examine Bhaktapur as a place where caste has a central role in organising life. But we must keep this tentative, not claim that it is the whole story, or the last word, on a community that has many aspects, and continues to form and transform itself...Caste practices are potent forms of life and thought: they help constitute psychocultural realities, lived worlds, for actors. As such, they pose quandaries for the moral imagination. Some actors find their social fate disturbing; find their powers or powerlessness disturbing. They are disquieted by cultural life, even as they live it.[13]

For many, especially the lower castes, the garden of castes mainly yields a harvest of discontent. However, ideally speaking to some extent in some sense caste practices are potent forms of life and thought that provide a sociological and psychological "home" to individuals and families as it in some way with its division of jobs in representative groups that can create a sense on interdependency which has a potency to organise life in common.

3. Journey of the Chariot

The ritual procession of Bhairav and Bhadrakali proceeds from the city's symbolic core as high caste people define it, through the two halves of the city. The chariot descends the hill, on which the major part of the city is built, down a steep, crooked street, and down to a wide field on the edge of Bhaktapur, near the river that passes through the city. All are swept up in the excitement of the festival, and are pulled out of their everyday lives and mundane selves. In a variety of ways festivals offer excitement, danger and stimulation, and generate palpable sacred thrills.[14]

At the bottom of the hill a crowd will have gathered to watch the chariot arrive. As the chariot arrives suddenly down the hill with great force and speed the crowd nearest to it scatters to avoid being run over. At the foot of the hill, in the field, the chariot rolls to a halt. For the smooth movement of the Chariot two special ruts have been built on stones in the surface of the street. Even with this, the Chariot can rush out of control, hurting bystanders. Untouchable sweepers, the Pore, stay segregated in a corner of the field. As the Chariot stops, men again pick up the ropes to pull it into position for the next stage of the festival. People who stand by as the Chariot moves make offerings tossing coins.

A few days before the chariot-pulling there is another ritual called god-pole raising and lowering. A goat is let loose in the forest to wander until it rubs its head against a tree. The goat is sacrificed to the tree. The tree is then cut down, clearing all its branches except at the very top. People call this tree trunk *yasin,* and consider it a deity. They visualise the tree-pole as a kind of body and ritually awaken divinity in it. The Chariot of the god and goddess are pulled and brought near the site where the god-pole is to be raised, so that the two deities can watch.[15] May be as tall as seventy feet, the *yasin* pole, with long ropes tied to it, is raised by the people, until it swings upright. The raising of the god-pole represents the old year and the lowering of it on the next day represents the New Year. The surrogate king and his royal Brahman were seated on the chariot while the pole is raised. Now they get down circumambulate both the Bhairav and Bhadrakali Chariots and also the *Yasin* pole, taking *prasad* at each, and then depart for the Taleju temple. People make offerings and sacrifices to the divinities.

After the ritual bath in the river people gather together for the taking down of *yasin* God. The king surrogate and his Brahman advisor, joined by the charioteers and musicians, return to the field and take up the seats in the chariot and watch the yasin-pole lowered.

Levy's account describes the process thus: "First the Yasin is rocked back and forth in the east-west direction, in a motion called "rocking to sleep". The god is said to be tired, for he has been standing all the year.[16] Symbolically the ropes represent the city's protective goddesses, and the god-pole is Bhairav himself and the goddesses his consort. Bhaktapurians understand the rocking of the pole and motion of the ropes as sexual intercourse between the god and the goddesses. When the pole falls, the New Year begins.

4. Festival and Socio-cultural Meanings

The festival has complex meanings. Parish writes:

> The festival is a ritual construction of order. The order it constructs has universal dimensions: it is social and moral, cosmic and sacred. These aspects of order are linked; the ritually declared connection to the cosmos and divinities helps give legitimacy to the royal and caste order. Human and divine actors witness the beginning of the New Year, participate in

it... This festival is among other things, a pageant of hierarchy and a spectacle of order.[17]

As Levy says, "the king and his entourage and the God Bhairav are moved by immemorial ritual order, as the sun moves through the year".[18]

In the festival, many activities take place not far from where the Sweepers, the Pore of Bhaktapur live. The question arises: What part do the Untouchables play in the festival? Or, what is the significance for them? There is the significance of dominance and subordination, inclusion and exclusion. Levy describes:

> Now some of the (Untouchables) take hold of the ropes at the back of the chariot, and other men, mostly Jyapus (farmers), take hold of the ropes at the front. Again a tug of war begins to determine the directions in which the chariot will move. The Jyapus are trying to pull the chariot back toward the city, while the Po(n) are trying to keep the deity in yasin field which adjoins the "Po(n)twa" (Sweeper word), the area where they live, just outside the symbolic boundaries of the city. This struggle does not lead to fights, and gradually the more numerous Jyapus with the advantage of the two extra ropes at the front of the chariot prevail.[19]

It is unlikely that the untouchables will ever win the tug of war as they do not come to the scene with the sufficient number and they have fewer ropes to pull. The ritual activity of the festival is to be seen as a ritual of social positioning that acknowledges their kind of existence and the assertion of their subordination and marginality. They were not allowed to take part in the other tug of war, the first one, in which only the men of higher caste are allowed to pull on the ropes. The chariots do not pass through their quarters, unlike the two halves of the city: they are symbolically "outside" the city. "The unequal contest asserts the power of the castes of the city over those outside the city, the Untouchables."[20] Finally god and goddess are taken away from the Untouchables.

5. After the Festival

The great event of the festival of the life of Newar people is over. Parish makes these observations:

> The god and the goddess return to their temples, the people return to their homes, the Chariot is dismantled and stored by the side of the Bhairav temple. The passing of the old year and the coming of the New Year have been celebrated. The order of life has been displayed. People have had their chance to come into the presence of divinity, and to view a kind of tableau vivant of the caste order, a living symbolic display of hierarchy in which members of certain castes get to pose as themselves. The tableau presents an eternal, unchanging image of the way things are – hierarchical, fixed, and sacred. It proposes that actual life is no different, that each actor is also a symbol in everyday life, an element in the cultural order. If this display cannot actually contain reality, if disturbing elements and ambivalence enter stage left, nonetheless life must go on. Having seen world – images and visions of themselves, people return to their routines, settle back into the habits of everyday life.[21]

Though it is a symbolic action the Chariot festival as it is celebrated at Bhaktapur gives anyone to think that the caste hierarchy is a living reality as a socio-cultural practice.

6. Some Caste actors

Parish sketches some of the individual actors in order both to convey the way they are positioned in caste society and to acknowledge their individuality. In Newar culture the upper stories of a house are considered purer than the ground floor. Parish explores the kind of conflicts in the understanding of purity-pollution position among persons of low and high castes by presenting different actors representing different caste roles. Parish gives an example of how the different actors of different castes show characteristic behaviour patterns:

I had two friends who would sometimes come to see me, to help me by talking about their thoughts and experiences, by discussing a variety of cultural topics. They had very different ways of making their presence known when they arrived at my house, and I believe that this expresses, in a small way, the reality of caste differences. Shiva Bhakta, a high caste man, would run confidently up the steps, pound vigorously on the door, call out my name in a loud voice. Kancha, an untouchable, would come into the tiny courtyard of the house and sit down on a stack of lumber. He would quietly smoke a cigarette, waiting until I come down or poked my head out the window to see if he was there. I asked him to come to the door and knock, so that I would know that he was there, but he refused. He did not refuse directly – he always bobbed his head affirmatively when I explained to him that he should do this – but he would not make the journey to the top of the stairs. I would poke my head out the window next time we had arranged to meet, and would find him sitting at the bottom of the stairs, smoking. [22]

Kancha – an Untouchable

Kancha is a middle-aged man, a lower caste actor, an Untouchable, the Pore who cleans the streets of the city and the courtyards and latrines of private householders. He shows the characteristic behaviour, wearing dirty, ragged clothes; carries the tools of his trade as he goes around as an Untouchable. Kancha exists on the margins of society, on the underside of hierarchy, in its stigmatising depths. Sweepers live in separate quarters, outside the city, with their houses mostly in thatched roofs. Kancha knows he is marginal, his work stigmatises him, his work is what he is. To survive he feels he must live his life on the terms given in the caste system, and this shapes his view of his world. Parish narrates further his character, revealing his psychological and personal traits:

> He struggles to reconcile a sense of self with the burden of his social identity. He recognises that he is stigmatised, rejects

some of the implications of hierarchy for himself, but knows too, that his survival and that of his family depends on his relations with high caste people. Kancha undergoes a social metamorphosis as he leaves his home and goes up "into" the city to work, walking up the same street the god-chariot came rolling down and "out" of the city during the festival. In the social gaze of high caste actors, who bring a hierarchical sensibility to what they see, he undergoes a "transformation"... At home, he finds meaning in domestic life, finds a measure of psychological security – "my caste is good for me", he will tell. There, he sees himself as a good father, a husband, a head of household, and a person with aspirations for himself and his children... As he enters the city, he enters a world where his presence and being have other meanings... He simply exists for others as living symbol of hierarchy. High caste people "know" and experience him as a member of a functional category that performs needed, but degrading work. They see that his hands and clothes are dirty from contact with feces and filth.[23]

Kancha represents in caste culture a source of impurity, a polluting presence. The representation given by the caste cultural set up is of a person who absorbs or soaks up the most dangerous and disgusting residues and effluents of higher caste bodies and themselves: he is most unbecoming. He is a receiver of impurity, of inauspiciousness, of what others reject and seek to keep away from them. Kancha does not seem bitter about his status; at times, he defends the caste system. He doubts whether he will survive without it. His heart wants something else for his children; still there are moments when he approves and justifies the caste hierarchy.

Shiva Bhakta – a high – caste

If Kancha is drawn as a man living at the margins, Parish depicts Shiva Bhakta as the one who occupies the centre, in a physical and social sense. Some of Shiva's many centres, his personhood and status, his prospects and possibilities, his class and caste position, are partly defined in sharp contrast with that of Kancha's existence, way and style of living. Shiva, a city dwelling Brahmin, belongs to a big household and is its head. Shiva dresses neatly and wears a black hat, befitting his status. He is a relatively prosperous merchant. He lives in a larger social world than that of Kancha occupying a more central position socially and economically and he feels life is getting better. In line with this philosophy he makes all efforts to generate wealth and through it prestige. He is also centered in a moral world, in the traditions of family, religion and city, which he identifies with the *dharma*, the moral order and rightness. His confidence in his sense of self comes not just out of money and power, but also from the caste status and family history. This ordering core of Shiva is socially and psychologically attuned to the moral order of his city, his family line and significant others, integrating past and present; all these are for him agents to integrate self and culture. *Dharma*, the Hindu moral order, gives Shiva the moral insights for living his life; which at the same time helps him to constitute a society that oppresses others, such as Kancha.

Kesar – a Jugi

Kesar, a courageous and at the same time angry man, voiced his rage and contempt; he also expressed at times his sense of powerlessness at the caste system for he sees much bad faith involved in it. He straightaway rejects caste for its oppressiveness. He often spoke with irony and sarcasm, pointing out the bad faith and hypocrisy at the root of caste. His goal was clearly freedom; he wanted to break himself from caste dependency, to become a man of independent means. He takes pride in the business of selling chickens and goats, which he manages for himself. This makes him relatively free of his group's dependency on caste roles. As a result of this feeling of independence, he is not worried about the powerlessness he feels in the face of the realities of caste, and even he takes courage to scorn the caste system. Parish expresses thus his state of mind, "in his 'inner' world he imagines and strives to create himself over against the caste system. By claiming that he did not make the world of caste, he emphasises that he did make himself, in defiance of the caste system and the place it allotted him. He values his hard-won, relative independence, the freedom of choices he has earned".[24]

The description of the chariot festival celebrated by the Newars of Kathmandu Valley and some of the caste actors is aimed at the exploration of the some aspects of everyday moral discourse and of the social criticism directed against caste. This is to understand the caste cultural dynamics and to analyse it in view of a countercultural interpretation.

CHAPTER V

CASTE CULTURE IN DIFFERENT DIMENSIONS

The caste system is a complex phenomenon. Besides the historical and contemporary perspectives of the caste reality shown in the Part I, I have tried to present the same through the festival, with its spectacular event of Chariot – pulling by the Newar people along with the depiction of a few characters representative of some of the castes, as introduced by Parish. In all these, we notice the complex nature of caste culture with the interplay of its different dimensions, especially the interplay of ideologies like equality and hierarchy, which direct the struggle of the people to find meaning for themselves in the culture they are in. For the integral understanding of the caste system Amaladoss introduces a grid made up of six elements: economics, politics, society, the individual person, culture and religion. He explains:

> *Economics* indicates who owns the means of production, how wealth is produced, who produces it and how it is distributed. It deals with labour and commercial relationships. We speak of capitalistic and socialistic systems. *Politics* deals with the realities of power and its exercise. We talk about democracy and dictatorship, relationship of participation and dictatorship, relationships of participation and domination. *Society* is a network of relationship based on family and kinship, race and caste, culture and social status. A variety of human groups are structured into a society in a perspective of equality or hierarchy. The individual *person* is socialised into a group. The person can freely and creatively interact with society,

though both freedom and creativity may be conditioned in many ways. Hence such interaction depends upon each one's personal resources and the social context. *Culture* is made up of the world view, the system of values and attitudes and a way of life and relationship that are expressed, affirmed and transmitted in myths and symbols, social rituals and celebrations. Language too plays an important role. *Religion* is part of culture and is at the same time the heart of culture in so far as it answers ultimate questions. It speaks of origins and ends and is open to the Transcendent.[25]

He further elaborates how these six elements interact with each other integrally in a dialectical framework of symbolic or meaning structures and ideological structures in the process of interpretation for transformation and change:

Political power often goes with economic power. Economic and political power determines social relationships and gives substance to inequality. While society conditions the individual, a person with leadership and commitment can change society. The symbolic world of culture reflects social conditions and experience. Ideology can produce social change. Culture conditions religious experience and expression and religion tend to legitimate current socio-cultural structures. However, in the context of the Transcendent, which it experiences, religion can also be prophetic and challenge culture and society to change, imagining a new future and providing motivation and inspiration to achieve it. The central element of the whole structure is the person in society. The person in freedom and fellowship with others can creatively reinterpret cultural and religious tradition and transform the social, including economic and political structures.[26]

1. Caste Culture and Economics

A recent social survey has identified 4635 separate castes in India, defined by occupation, ethnic characteristics, etc.[27] In the analytical grid, economics comes first for analytical understanding of the caste system. Economics normally means the production and distribution of goods and services, which presuppose relationship with nature and people themselves in society. Harmony in relationship between the people and the nature in the production and the distribution of goods is an important factor in normal life. The first relationship is between the producer and the consumers of the things produced. Harmony involves here a sufficient, not excessive, production and a cost of production proportionate to the satisfaction the goods produced. There is also the harmony between those who own the means of production and those who work for it, which depends on the kind of relationship existing between them in the material basis of life, production and distribution. Production and using goods are there either in harmony with nature or in domination and exploitation of it. Science and technology can be used either to help increase production and control or, with its commercial interests, be used to exploit nature alienating the humans more from it.

Economically, the caste system is seen as a network of services and obligations both in the rural and urban, agricultural and industrial situations. Amaladoss elaborates the mutual relationships in the way of services and obligations existing in the context of caste explaining the term *jajman* and the different connotations the term has in the mutual relationship existing between different castes:

> The kingpin of the system is the group that owns the land and controls the production of food. While the Brahmins provide intellectual and ritual services, other castes provide other services like agricultural labour, working the metals, cleaning, barbering (barber's trade), trading, shoemaking, etc. Each group is given a certain amount of agricultural produce every year for its service. This is known as *Jajmani* system, the *jajman* being the one who owns the means of producing food. The term also has a ritual significance in so far as the *jajman* is the one who sponsors sacrificial rituals for his own and the

community's benefit. Scarcity of land resources can lead to occupational mobility. The advent of money economy may loosen up contractual relationships. The addition of industry to agriculture only adds the owners and entrepreneurs of industry to the landlords in the dominant group. In our industrial setting the workers may get together on the basis of class, going across caste lines.[28]

On the question of economy and production Kancha Ilaiah describes and contrasts the Dalitbahujan (a term used by Ilaiah for Dalits which means 'the people and castes who form the exploited and suppressed majority') with Hindu high castes: the way they behave and show themselves in the daily work programmes. He says:

> A Dalitbahujan couple rises every morning at *koodikuuta* (cockcrow). The man enters directly into his agrarian tasks; the woman begins immediately on her household activities. Bath and prayer have no place in their lives at that juncture. The man has to feed his cattle and clean the cattle shed... A Goudda gets up and straight away puts on his toddy-climbing clothes and goes to the toddy tree rows... The Malas and Maadigaas rise from their beds and begin either to clean and cure skins or prepare the leather for shoemaking. In the majority of cases, they then go to their master's fields to cut the crop or bundle it up. In these families what they must do every morning is not decided by them, but by their masters. The women in these families get up and go to the master's cattle sheds to clean them, or to sweep the surroundings of the master's houses. The women must rush because they must reach the working point in the fields much before the dawn breaks.[29]

He further says:

> A Hindu — a Brahmin, Baniya or Kshatriya — on the other hand, gets up to take a cold water bath and then still clad in wet clothes picks up his book — the Gita — and begins to relate to God. He or she asks God for the day's food, the

day's *Gyana* (knowledge) and the day's *sheela* (character). God for them is a stud-bull that can produce everything. All difficult and delicate tasks can be taken care of by him. The priest therefore, leaves everything to him... A Hindu relates in prayer and meditation to this God and thereafter he changes from the *tadivastram* (wet cloth) to a *pattuvastram* (silk cloth) which, of course, no Dalitbahujan can ever dream of wearing.[30]

The Baniyas are known as *koomaties* or *shahukars*, who in spiritual terms relate to the Brahmins. Their children's consciousness formation is similar to that of Brahmins. In the centrally located house a Baniya establishes a structured shop, which provides the mechanism for the buying and selling. He communicates with the Dalitbahujan not in Sanskrit language but in language of the people, and meets them individually when they come for buying and selling; that is the way he chooses for the business manipulation, yet he ensures that the manipulation is not apparent to the collective consciousness of the masses.

Globalisation and Brahminism

Globalisation can be approached and understood from a different perspective. Though economic globalisation that seeks to bring the whole world under one market system with free movement of capital and products seems to be understood as the basis of globalisation in the present times, the term globalisation can be understood in different dimensions, such as political, cultural, religious, etc. In the context of caste culture in India and the cultural domination, Brahminism could be termed as a form of globalisation which has its roots in economics, politics, culture and religion. M. C. Raj opines "the ideology that promotes globalisation is Brahminical: its roots are in the domination through Brahminism".[31] Undoubtedly, the Dalits and the tribals will be the victims of globalisation. Kancha Ilaiah comments on how globalisation corrupts the ethics of production, market, communication and economy:

Caste Culture in Different Dimensions 93

The globally processed commodities are entering into the Indian market with a Brahminical cultural coat. In all advertisements Brahminical temples, Brahminical modes of man-woman relationships (wife-offering coffee to husband in turn a husband presenting a washing machine to wife) have become the favoured cultural idioms. At least at the time of the green revolution, several agrarian tasks relationships, work ethics came on to sign boards, but now even that has gone out of fashion mode of communication. Like in a classical ritualistic *pooja* where either a temple or a closed house were centres of culture, even in the present phase of globalisation, commoditised home, vehicle borne street, nuclearised family settings, which in no way relate to production, get constantly projected. Nowhere one sees a shoe-stitching Madiga (Chamar), a sheep breeding Golla-kuruma-kuruba (Yadav), a pot-making Kunumari, a cloth weaving Mala (or Shala), a face-shaving or hair cutting barber, and a cloth-washing Chakali acquire respectable advertising space in the globalised market. Whether eating a modern packet food item, or drinking a Coca-Cola, these professional producers do not become subjects of communication. The market, the knowledge systems, the communicative channels do not consider that producers in the fields in the household industries, both in rural and urban settings have a right to consume the products of globalised markets.[32]

Government policies and projects have mostly in view the dominant caste people, for politicians, businessmen and bureaucrats come mostly from such groups. Harish Khare reports in *The Hindu* newspaper commenting about the *Budget 2000* with the heading "Out to please the computer class ". He writes:

> Mr. Yashwnt Sinha's budget has done little for, if not betrayed outright, the core of the BJP's political constituency — the middle classes. Nor has he done anything for the larger BJP constituency, the just-above-the-poverty line masses, who all these years have been waiting for a 'hindutva' regime to bring

them bliss and prosperity. Instead the finance minister has opted to provide the breaks for the upper slice of the upper income groups, the "computer *wallahs*" and "mobile" class.[33]

Ambedkar in one of his speeches against Brahminism and capitalism, gave a new interpretation of Brahminism:

> There are in my views two enemies which the workers of this country have to deal with. The two enemies are Brahminism and capitalism.... By Brahminism I do not mean the power, privileges and interests of the Brahmins as a community. By Brahminism I mean the negation of the spirit of Liberty, Equality and Fraternity. In that sense it is rampant in all classes and is not confined to the Brahmins alone though they have been the originators of it.[34]

In the caste cultural conflict the economic disparity that has its roots in the caste norms concerning occupation and the production and distribution of material goods, plays a great role in the discontentment of the caste cultural life.

2. Caste Culture and Politics

By politics we understand the power relationship in society. It is exercised for the well being of society, especially for the defense of the people, maintaining law and order and for the protection of the poor and weak. The village is a political power centre, which operates at the micro-level and macro-level. Politically there are two spheres of power: traditionally the Brahmins and the Kshatriyas, Brahmins in the religious sphere and the Kshatriyas in the secular sphere. Land ownership is a decisive factor in the political dominance by the dominant castes. But this is an inadequate understanding. Ilaiah explains how the caste system paves the way for the inner dynamism of power relationships. He also brings out the mentality of different caste groups in the exercise of power, relating each other in a given framework:

> Power relations cannot be discussed merely in terms of institutions that relate to the state. The Dalitbahujans live very

much within a certain framework of power relations. First and foremost the caste system itself sets up a certain type of power relations. The Malas and the Madigas, right from childhood, are trained more to obey and to listen than to command and to speak. Starting from the early age one learns to listen and to obey or to speak and to command depending on the status of one's caste. The lower the caste of the person, the higher will be the level of obedience, and the higher the caste of the person, the stronger will be the motivation to speak and to command.[35]

As the power relations between castes are so structured, the self-respect, which is of critical importance in developing the personality of Dalitbahujan women/men, is affected:

> In all South Indian villages (this may be true of North India too), the Kshatriya caste, which handled the institution of state power, has become dormant, and a neo-Kshatriya force from the Shudra upper castes have begun to emerge. In Andhra Pradesh, for example, the Reddis, Velamas and Kammas are increasingly coming to believe not only that they form a part of the Hindu religion but also that they are castes who have the right to insult others. In ritual terms they are not *dwijas* or twice born, but today in political terms they are attempting to play the role of the classical Kshatriyas by establishing their hegemony in all structures in which power operates.[36]

These neo-Kshatriyas, the new caste based power, are becoming the patrons of Hindutva. If Brahmin-baniyas are manipulating the Dalit-consciousness in the areas of spirituality and economy, the neo-Kshatriyas taking the role of 'classical' Kshatriyas, manipulate relations at various levels: Hinduism believes in the theory of co-option and exclusion.[37] The neo-Kshatriyas are co-opted and those who are below them are excluded. The neo-Kshatriyas are attempting to acquire for themselves a new cultural status. Their ambition is not to dalitise or democratize human relations but to brahminise them. Their domination is explicit in every sphere of life. Seemingly they have made politics and power obvious aspects of life. Yet because of their roots in agriculture and their ambiguous non-*dwija* spiritual status, they hang between democracy and dictatorship as their political form.[38]

Who is ruling India?

Politically, we have two spheres of power, the secular and the religious. In the secular sphere the groups that own the land and head the states mostly come from the dominant castes. And the dominant castes, the Kshatriyas, neo-Kshatriyas, etc., who are at the top own the land and are politically dominant. In the past this dominant status was related to the King, to him they paid tributes or supplied soldiers to his army and in turn they dominated and exploited the others. Today we see politicians mostly belonging to the dominant castes use their positions to grab power and privileges, and accumulate wealth and profit with the patronage of the State. In the religious sphere the Brahmins dominate as they are the ones who mediate in ritual matters. They are fit for that as they set themselves apart from others by their purity, essential for their dealings with the gods.

This ruling class forming around 10% of our population controls the whole country and its government, and the rest are puppets in their hands. The main concern of the politicians and the ruling political parties seem to be the survival in power and so they indulge in the electoral malpractices with money and muscle power and even trade with legislators and parliamentarians. As a result people lose the trust in the Indian state and its agents: the military, police, parliament, bureaucracy, judiciary, etc. "There is, therefore, a sharp decline in the legitimacy, authority and credibility of the State as an agent of liberation and transformation, an instrument of law, order and security, and a mediator in social conflicts." [39]

Socio-political inequalities are as before. The leadership in the political parties shows the fact that any kind of political identity and political assertion is not easy for the Dalits.

Democracy of Dalits

Among Dalits normally a democratic kind of political relationship exists in the family and community settings. In terms of the parent-children relationship, politics works as a democracy that could be qualified as 'patriarchal'. The Dalit household is not essentially private: the sense of private does not exist in the Dalit consciousness. What prevails in these castes, as far as the house is concerned, is the social unit. Wife-beating as a patriarchal practice is not found among the Dalits. The problems and disputes between man-woman, inter-family, intra-family, etc., are taken to caste panchayat and are solved in the open. In the caste panchayat everyone who is present has a right to be involved in coming to a judgement. Among the Dalits, law does not emerge from authority, but from the community. Since it is open in its function, it can check injustices.[40]

Even if it is open and the notion of private does not exist, violence does take place. The positive aspects here are when the brutality takes place the Dalit law will prevail and the public outrage becomes an instrument to bring normal situation. One of the important mechanisms of this public outrage is found in the congress of women's deliberations popularly known as *Ammalakkala Muchchatlu* (the deliberations of the mothers and sisters).[41] They are open deliberations, political and juridical in nature, which evolve a feminine consensus for settling problems. Such debates take place in variety of places and various times, inside the village or else in the fields in the mornings or in the evenings. Concerning the kind of relationship among the Dalits and concerning the notions of private property and communal property in different castes Ilaiah observes:

> Every personal relationship among the Dalitbahujans is both social and political.... Here the human bonds are structured in terms of "we" but not 'I'. Even if the concept 'I' exists; it does not have the same meaning among the lower castes as it has among the upper castes. The individual here is a part

of a collective. And that collective is both social and political. For the Dalitbahujans individualism is an expression of negative will. There is nothing like 'mine'. Everything is ours... In terms of consciousness we might say that most of the Dalitbahujan castes keep struggling between the notions of private property and communal property. Higher up in the caste hierarchy the notion of private property becomes greater... Preserving for the next day, for the next month and for the next year has not yet become part of the consciousness of scheduled castes. By and large scheduled castes have retained the tribal notion of property as 'public' for thousands of years.[42]

Against the high caste and state agencies' critique of the culture of dispossession of the scheduled castes, Ilaiah shows an affiliation and commitment to the cause of Dalitbahujans of which he is a part and suggests the ideal that the future of India lies in such a culture:

The state agencies and also the Indian 'upper' castes have been criticising the culture of dispossession among the scheduled castes as 'spendthrift'. These groups speak of the latter as 'lazy fellows'. An incessant discourse among the so-called upper castes, often expounded in abusive language is that these lower caste bastards should not be given anything, as they do not know how to retain or invest it. But the upper caste criticism is absolutely wrong. The Dalitbahujan culture that India has is a remarkable legacy. The Dalitbahujans never believed that power is embodied in property. The 'upper' caste condemnation that the scheduled castes are unworthy of possessing property is actually turning the Dalitbahujan philosophy upside down. A community that has lived for thousands of years with no notion of private property will quickly dispossess themselves of it, even if it is given to them in charity or by welfarism. The notion of private property goes against its philosophy. It is not the weakness of a people but their strength. Actually this is where the future of India lies.[43]

Patriarchal Authoritarianism and Brahminism

A change can be noticed in the notions of power and property (private, public, personal, etc.) when we go upward from neo-Kshatriyas to the Brahmins in the caste hierarchy. The caste *panchayat* is slowly disappearing giving in to hierarchy, which slowly enters the homes of higher castes. There is a struggle among the high castes on the question of power because of the emergence of the neo-Kshatriyas, while the notions of power undergoes change. Ilaiah observes:

> As their homes move from the secular to the spiritual domain, their notion of power revolves round divinity, and human beings begin to look like non-entities. The homes of neo-Kshatriyas are split between a divine and Brahminised femininity and an aggrandised masculine power structure which appears at times divine and at times secular. Neo-Kshatriya masculine power hobnobs with Brahminism, as it is perfectly well suited to the philosophy of casteism. At the same time, however, it wants to displace the Brahmins and the Baniyas physically from the hegemonic locations of political power and of the market.[44]

On all India level, in the post independence period the Brahmins and the Baniyas have acquired dominion both in the fields of politics and economy. Side by side the neo-Kshatriyas emerged, and established their social base, aligning with the Brahmin-Baniya ideology. The alliance of Brahman-Baniya and the neo-Kshatriya is being projected as a sort of modernity in India. In the First Part where the contemporary understanding of caste system was discussed, we had some discussion along these lines. Hinduised modernity is an antithesis of Dalitbahujan assertion. It aims at the destruction of the political assertion of the Dalitbahujan castes, which form the democratic and secular social base of India. The capture of power by the dominant castes in the secular domain will be a threat to the emergence of the democratic forces. To keep up this trend the upper caste combine, i.e. Brahmin-Baniya and neo-Kshatriya, mix spiritualism and political power. This has its roots in their caste based patriarchal authoritarianism. The country today is not governed by the laws of Manu, but by a Constitution which guarantees freedom, equality, fraternity and justice to every citizen.[45] In terms of power relations Brahmin families are anti-democratic. This notion of patriarchal authoritarianism reflects in the Brahmin family set up. Ilaiah explains:

> The male patriarch establishes his authority over the entire family - particularly over the women. The manipulation of the consciousness of the family members takes place in terms of projecting the patriarchal God's all powerfulness. This power is demonstrated not in terms of the God's ability to sacrifice, but in terms of their power to manipulate, defeat and kill... Brahminism not only excludes masses but also delegitimises their languages. In other words Brahminical patriarchy operates by conditioning two kinds of mentalities. On the one hand, it creates a mind that controls, manipulates and finally structures: the male mind. On the other hand, it forms a mind that can be manipulated, controlled and structured: the female mind.[46]

In contrast Dalitbahujan patriarchy is completely antithetical to Brahminical Patriarchy, though the notion of men being superior and women being inferior does exist. However, there is a great difference. In Dalitbahujan patriarchy the woman is an agent of both production and reproduction. There is no total bifurcation of the domains of man and woman both at home and field. Man-woman relations are far more democratic in Dalitbahujans. Dalitbahujan patriarchy is a loose structure which can be demolished with counter-cultural movements more easily than Brahminical patriarchy, which is rooted in a spiritually underwritten authoritarianism and which can be therefore easily turned into fascism.[47]

Hindu Political Institutions and Dalitbahujans

In the state institutions where power begins to operate the Dalitbahujans are systematically excluded, especially in the three main institutions: Police, Patel and Patwari (village police, administrative official, and revenue official), though these institutions are slowly being replaced with *gram panchayats*. Ilaiah explains this bringing in more related aspects:

> Hinduism runs as a thread in a garland in sharing all institutions as 'upper' caste preserves. Given the authoritarian patriarchal home life of the Hindus, whether it is the Patel Patvari institutions or modern institutions like gram panchahyats, which combine liberal-democracy with authoritarianism, in essence they are embryos of 'upper' caste dictatorship. Elections become a form that can be used to retain real power in the hands of Brahmins and neo-Kshatriyas. By and large the Baniyas operate only within the domain of the market, but the extraction of surplus in the market is closely related to these power structures. Even in the national context Brahmins have the monopoly over power structures in every sphere. The most powerful position in the village, that of the Patwari, is even now a preserve of the Brahmins. The institutions that handle law and order are left to the neo-Kshatriyas. They use the power to acquire control over the land. However, the emergence of the neo-Kshatriya political power did not in any way undermine the hegemonic control of Brahmins and Baniyas.[48]

The domination of these modern institutions by the upper castes was possible because the British colonialists themselves saw that they could manipulate institutions, parties and organisations if they remained in the hands of the so-called upper 'castes'. The Brahminical *bhadralok* (upper caste elite) and the colonial rulers both wished to preserve the status quo. The British propped up even the so-called democratic intellectuals like Raja Rammohan Roy, Rabindranath Tagore, Ranade and Nehru. Consciously or unconsciously the British themselves helped to construct a 'brahminical meritocracy' that came to power in post-independence India.[49]

In the postcolonial time, two kinds of political parties were known generally: democratic and communist. The main political force that represented a liberal democratic political ideology was the Congress, which was systematically molded into a *bhadralok* party. Ilaiah observes:

> The Congress party, as a liberal democratic party, began structuring itself in a Hindu fashion. The Congress 'upper' caste leaders lived a Hindu life. If there were a Congress Brahmin leader, even at the village and town level, one of his relatives would be the priest in the temple while mother's relative would be an officer in the government. These people had common political aims and interests at various levels. The nexus between them was total, and they were able to manipulate the system. But the Dalitbahujans who by imitating them were trying to get assimilated into this politicised Hinduism or Hindutva, were never allowed to be equal partners.[50]

The second major political movement that acquired a social and intellectual base is the communist movement, which notionally was trying to portray itself as an integral part of the masses and as not different from the people. Ilaiah clarifies :

> In reality the Dalitbahujan masses and the communist leadership remained distinctly different in three ways: (i) the communist leadership came from the 'upper' caste - mainly from Brahmins; (ii) they remained Hindu in day-to-day life styles; and (iii) by and large the masses were economically poor but the leaders came from relatively wealthy backgrouds. The masses came from Dalit-bahujan castes, and these castes never found an equal place in the leadership structures. Even in states like Andhra Pradesh and Kerala, where non-Brahmin movements were strong enough to influence society, the pattern held good.[51]

Ilaiah critisises the Indian communists whose leaders mostly hail from the Hindu upper castes and share their ideology in the power management sector. The counter-culture they talk about is not capable of bringing any solution to the social, economic and political problems of the Indian caste-based society, due to the nexus with the high caste ideology- especially of its leaders:

Even as the communists talked about the counter-culture, their counter-culture never distanced itself from Hindu notions of life. This is a unique characteristic of Indian Communists, and it is the result of the caste that the leaders belong to and the Hinduism of which they are a part. They may say that they do not go to temples as ordinary Brahmins or Baniyas do, but they simply forget the fact that they have converted their central committees into Hindu power management centres. They converted Marx, Engels and Lenin into Communist Gods where people were supposed to find solutions in their theories for every social, economic or political problem that Indian casteist society was suffering from.[52]

In general, in the caste cultural situation, political power is exercised not on behalf of the community at large and in defence of the poor and weak, but to defend individual and collective selfishness and to dominate and exploit others. The democratic sense of community participation is not considered at all as a value.

3. Caste Culture and Society

Every person is not only the member of a particular family but also of a community, and shares the network of social and cultural values in the process of socialisation. We have different communities and groups with separate identities in different castes and cultures. The Hindu society is historically marked by a rigid form of social stratification, the *varna-jati* model of social organisation, in which the Brahmanical religious principle, namely purity and pollution, plays a central role in defining social hierarchy and separation.[53] As a result there arose many social inequalities characterised by social oppression. The caste, a hierarchically organised complex of small communities, is self-sufficient in itself for internal life. Their separation from other groups is marked by meal and marriage taboos. Amaladoss elaborates:

Even when there is a common village banquet on the occasion of a religious or social festival, each caste will sit separately as a group. The groups higher in the hierarchy will not take cooked food from those who are lower. Some exceptions are made for food cooked with ghee. There is no intermarrying. The only exception is that sometimes a bride may be given in marriage to a person above her caste. The contrary is strictly forbidden.[54]

Though marriage is important both for Dalits and caste Hindus, it is important to note that socio-cultural differences in its form and content exist between them. Ilaiah explains:

> For us Dalits, marriage is a human and a worldly affair that performs the human functions of procreation. For Hindus, marriage is a sacred ritual divorced from all kinds of productive activity even notionally. Even in procreation the main intention is to produce a son who can pave the father's way to heaven.[55]

In the villages different groups have separate living space. The untouchables are living outside the village. At the administration level too, the different castes have their own council of leaders who are in charge of seeing that every member of the caste observes regulations. The elders of the dominant caste have the final say when inter-caste disputes are taken up. The caste system provides autonomy to diverse cultural groups in an atmosphere of community, mutual dependence and security without competition. The Dalits though they are the work force and therefore the producers, are at the services of the society, and hence outcaste. Bhagvan Das narrates their plight:

> They are outcaste and treated as untouchables and forced to live outside the villages, which were inhabited by 'pure' people... They were counted as exterior castes or menial castes. They were given different names, recognising their disability and sometimes on the basis of their occupation or profession, at different times, by the rulers or priestly classes. For administrative convenience the Census Commissioners

clubbed them under one title, e.g. the Depressed Classes... Untouchables worshiped their own gods and goddesses, relished beef and pork besides carrion, and buried their dead. Neither Hindus owned them, nor did they follow Hinduism.[56]

Fuller brings out well the life of the Dalits always at the periphery of the social world of the village:

> In constituting the village unity at a temple festival, the division of ritual labour requires Harijans to participate. In that way, the hierarchical design of the village community is forcefully displayed. Harijans must also be present as symbolic denizens of the exterior, in opposition to which the village is represented as a civilised centre. From the latter perspective, Harijans are included precisely so that they can be portrayed as excluded, and the ambiguity of their role is intrinsic to the ritualisation of village unity.[57]

The Harijans were distanced earlier in a very rigid way in the social space in the village set up, and it was stronger in the South than in the North.[58] Beteille refers to one such instance in Kerala, which will seem ridiculous to us today: "A Nayar must keep 7 feet from the Nambudiri Brahman; an Iravan must keep 32, a Cheruman 64, and a Nayadi 74 to 124. The respective distances between these lower castes are calculated by a simple process of subtraction: the Iravan must keep 25 feet from the Nayar and Cheruman 32 feet from the Iravan."[59]

Though the lower caste people are socially much distanced from the high caste people, they perform the polluting traditional works for them. There still exist perspectives based on equality, capable of challenging and subverting the dominant construction of reality. The caste hierarchy is a way of life for certain social practices, and not based on the difference of nature. Parish[60] refers to Hari of the Jugi caste in Newar, who does a traditional stigmatising work. He defends his duty, rebukes his adult son and daughter when they turn away high caste people who come seeking his services. He says, "Our caste has done this from long ago". He has his own way of seeing people as both the same, and different. He says, "People are the same in essence; what makes them different is their role in society". Parish reports Hari's answer to his query: "How are Jugi (or Kapali) and other castes different?

> "As people there is no difference. Our rules and our practices are different. Looked at in terms of what we do and the rites we observe, – this is a Barber, this is a Jugi, so it is said. We need the Barber caste to purify us by cutting our hair and nails, and we need a Brahman to perform our death rites [*Sraddha*]. And so it comes to be [that social life] was organised in this way." ("Humans are not different, their work is different.") "Their work is different, but men are nowhere different. They have a nose, they have legs, they have eyes. When any one is cut, when you are cut – then you bleed blood, and I bleed blood too. You do not bleed milk. If I say you are a great man, still you will bleed blood. So will I. But here we have the order of high and low. People must worship, and so they need Tantric priests. The auspicious times for worship and ritual must be found. Therefore, the caste of Astrology is necessary.... To create order, the system of high and low arose."[61]

The low caste respondent sees that people are essentially the same. He does not see that the caste hierarchy expresses natural differences, differences in the substance or moral "being" in people of different castes. He perceives that as human, we all are same, even if we are belonging to different castes. Hierarchy is understood only as a way of life, a division of labour necessary for the performance of rituals. That is, this is a matter of social practice, not of nature or substance. Castes develop because of pragmatic social needs. Since there is no difference among people in nature, the social differences are only for the social ends, to create functional inter-dependence. He rejects the stigmatising implications of his position in the caste hierarchy, and neutralises hierarchy. Thus, he does not see his essence, his ultimate identity or being, as constituted by the caste hierarchy; he rejects the implication that it constitutes him (or anyone) as a "person".[62] Social pressures to continue to perform the polluting functions have been radically reduced, which is clear from the attitudes in Hari's own children, their resistance to participate in such stigmatising roles. He is prepared to find the meaning of the differentiation in ritual work and social practices.

Equality in Newar Moral Discourse

The words Newars normally use for 'equality' are *samantha*, *barabar,* etc. They also make common propositions about mutual recognition in the form, "I too am a person, you too are a person", to undermine hierarchical constructions of difference. Here they try to establish that the distinctions of caste or wealth are not the only relevant factors in relationships. This view where they distinguish the category of "person" or "people" from caste roles, economic status, etc., substitutes undifferentiated humanity for hierarchical differences. "Some Newars evoked equality through the imagery of "blood" and "flesh". Blood and flesh of the people are the same, not different. Others advanced the idea of a kind of transcendent spiritual equality".[63] Assertions that "all are equal" or "the same" are made by low caste Newars who will, in the next breath, assert their superiority to other low castes groups who are just as stigmatised as they and suffer the same disabilities. From the responses of the Newars that show a kind of ambivalence, Parish concludes:

> It would be wrong, I believe, to interpret this as a commitment to a shared ideology of caste hierarchy. The vacillation and equivocal values of low caste men and women reflect the ambivalence of cultural experience, not the structuring of mind by ideology... Assertions that all are equal, or "the same," are equivocal in this regard. Hierarchy is likely to be cancelled in an upward direction and maintained in a downward one. High caste individuals may defend hierarchy, or take inequality for granted – several informants reported they had never considered the point of view of low caste

individuals – but some express sympathy with ideas of social equality. Informants are aware that law has established equality. Some modernised Newars did make statements judging the caste system based on such contemporary innovations.[64]

Equality of Moral Worth Versus Social Equality

Dharma Raj, a Brahmin who was interviewed by Parish, was making some points about hierarchy and equality stating that the *dharma* of the god Vishnu-Narayana does not make hierarchical distinctions. He maintains that the 'way' of Vishnu-Narayana does not divide people into 'high' and 'low' but rather makes it possible for people to transcend hierarchical social distinctions by acquiring "inner knowledge" of Narayana through devotion. His focus was not on the differences in the rituals or myth, as Parish was expecting, but on the ethic of spiritual equality. Parish makes an assessment saying that the dissenting minority view is capable of becoming a counter ideology to the dominant one:

> This argument represents a kind of dissenting minority view in Newar culture, which in practice is organised in terms of hierarchical values. A concept of equality is often expressed by asserting that the god Vishnu (Narayana) dwells inside each person... The implication is, I think, that every person has moral worth regardless of empirical individual differences. Empirical differences co-exist with an image of the way people are alike... This kind of notion of spiritually grounded equality of moral worth has the potential of being used to attack class and caste differences; it could be used as a "levelling" ideology.[65]

Kesarlal, of the 'impure' Jugi caste makes a sharp contrast to the kind of equality that having God dwelling within confers. Envisioned as an "ultimate" reality, this view is not able to do away with the injustices and inequalities of real life, as experience shows. Kesarlal, responds to Parish's question: "you speak of a 'heart God' don't you?":

"Narayana. Narayana is with you too, is the same. He is with me too, the very same." (the same for all). "The very same" (he pauses). "If he is the same then the Narayana that dwells within wants to be rich too. The God that dwells within you is the same God that dwells within me, but you have wealth, and if you must say or do something, you can quickly do it – you are ready and able. I do not have wealth. Because I am not rich, even the Narayana that dwells within me is of one mind, even if I want to do something, I cannot".[66]

Here Kesarlal was ironic. The irony is clear: people are the same because God dwells in each of them, but their life situations are different. Parish draws some conclusions saying that the expressions of frustrations of people like Kesarlal are capable of bringing a moral tension between the ultimate moral equality and the hierarchical social equality, integrating divine and human:

> The idea of spiritual equality is other – worldly, concerned with ultimate reality; Kesarlal wants to reverse this, and make the God within the source of desires and needs in this world, where inequalities rule – this highlights injustices. Kesarlal's words are energised by anger and bitterness. He contrasts the immanence of Narayana in each person with the social reality of unequal access to the resources needed to act. People are equal but their freedom of action is limited by poverty in the social world... Kesarlal's words play on deep frustrations, and give form to an essential moral tension: the idea of ultimate moral equality cannot easily be reconciled with hierarchical social reality.[67]

The social disharmony existing in the caste cultural life caused by the social inequalities characterised by social oppression has its main root in the socio-cultural and religious principle of purity and pollution maintained by the dominant castes in Hindu society. Such dehumanising and conflicting situation necessitates the lower castes, the victims, to think differently and come out with leveling discourses.

4. Caste Culture and Person

Psychologically, social identity seems prior to the identity of the individual.[68] The human person, the subject who experiences, is in reality a part of an existing culture and society and not an abstract individual. The person lives and grows up in a group. Therefore, each individual is born into a particular system of thought, attitudes and action. Individuals in human groups are understood according to the particular traits they show, within a particular caste, ethnicity or culture. Amaladoss elaborates:

> Anthropologists have noted that the people in the villages, when questioned, identify themselves in terms of their caste, rather than in terms of their persons. The individual never feels alone. He can always find support in the group in times of crisis of whatever kind. On the other hand the individual is expected to be loyal to the group and its culture: that is, the individual is forced to socialise into the caste community. The ties are so much the stronger, because they are not merely social but through kinship.[69]

The question of superiority or inferiority comes from childhood experiences and the individual interiorises the experiences, good or bad; the individual is not seen as person in isolation. He/she is a person in relationship. He or she is part of the tradition and culture. So the personal (psychological) dimension is important in the caste-culture analysis.

The Distorted Dalit Psyche

The very utterance of the word caste tends normally to make us think in terms of the victims, the Dalits. That does not mean that we overlook nondalits. As Jerry Rosario says, "Liberation is urgent for the victims, the Dalits and ultimately for others, the dominant groups".[70] The caste reality is to be seen in its totality. Dalits are the "depressed class" for the British. They are named "Harijans" by M.K. Gandhi and the Congress Party, "Schedule castes" in the Constitution of India. Now they have given a name for themselves, "Dalits".[71] The Sanskrit term

"Dalit" has several related meanings.[72] A.P.Nirmal, a Dalit theologian explains: "The term "Dalit" means (1) the broken, the torn, the bent, the burst, the split; (2) the opened, the expanded; (3) the bisected; (4) the driven asunder, the dispelled, the scattered; (5) the downtrodden, the crushed, the destroyed; (6) the manifested, the displayed."[73]

All these meanings reveal the reality of Dalits who were deprived of their humanity and treated as "non-persons and "no people".[74] Kancha Ilaiah narrates his own childhood experiences as a school child:

> As the first generation in Dalitbahujan history to see a slate and a pencil, we jumped straight out of the jungle into school. Even there, what was in common between Hindus and us?.....Our school teachers' attitude to each one of us depended on his own caste background. If he was a Brahmin he hated us and told us to our faces that it was because of the evil time – because of *kaliyuga* – that he was being forced to teach "Sudras" like us. In his view we were good for nothing. That wise teachers used to think of us coming from s*uudari* families (families of field hands). Working in the field in his view was dirty and unaesthetic... But who, according to the teachers, were the 'great' ones? The children who came from Brahmin, Baniya and the upper caste landlord families. These were the "great" ones... It is not merely the teachers, even 'upper' caste schoolchildren think about Dalitbahujan children that way.[75]

Again he painfully reports that all such childhood experiences distort the very formation of the consciousness in the early days of life, and the scars and wounds in the mind will continue to hurt till the end of life.

> What was arrested and what was stifled was that consciousness. The consciousness of 'us' and of 'our' culture was never allowed to exercise our minds. Childhood formations are important for a person – female or male – to become a full human being. But our childhoods were

mutilated by constant abuse and by silence, and by a stunning silence at that. There was the conspiracy to suppress the formation of our consciousness. For hundreds of generations the violent stoppage of the entry of the written word into our homes and our lives nipped our consciousness in the very bud. Even after schools were opened to us because of independence or *swaraj,* a word which even today I fail to understand, the school teacher was against us. Our homes have one culture and our schools have another culture...The gap between the two was enormous... In fact these two cultures were poles apart.[76]

He continues:

In the olden days after such initiation (*upanayana*) the so-called upper castes used to send their sons to *gurukulas* (brahminical schools). Now they send them to English-medium convent schools; the same schools that were hated by the same Hindus during the freedom struggle. Even in the 1990s Hindutva ideologues condemn such schools as 'anti-Hindutva' schools – of course, only to send their children to the same schools promptly after the *upanayana*. The Hindus condemn English, yet they sent their children to English-medium school. We have not yet acquired the consciousness to condemn the complete domination of Telugu-medium schools by the Hindu scriptures. Having had no alternatives we send our children to schools that teach only Puranas or the epics in every textbook. This is a paradox, and we live with many such paradoxes.[77]

Generally speaking the social and cultural identity seems to be sought after prior to the identity of the individual. People when asked about their identity identify themselves with their caste identity than in terms of their persons: individuals socialise themselves to the caste community. The individuals interiorise the values from the concrete experiences in the growth process from the early stages of life. Some interiorise the superiority feeling and others the inferiority feeling. The struggle is on for the Dalits to become free from the psychic distortedness seeking human dignity and freedom.

I am a Person, you are also a Person

The stay and acquaintances with Newar people helped Parish to become conversant with their life and culture. Listening from some of his informants the phrase "I am a person, you are a person" startled him. Taken out of context the phrase will simply mean the self-evident, but in the context of their lives and struggles the phrase could signify and constitute a whole mode of moral discourse of Newars. It was a declaration of equality, an invocation of mutual recognition, voiced by high and low caste Newars alike. This for Parish was not the *Homo Hierarchicus* image at all, but something of equality 'I am a person, you are a person'. Parish says that from such assertions we are led to understand the ultimate basis of justice is equality and it starts from mutual recognition:

> For the Newars I conversed with, invoking this principle of equality was usually a prelude to speaking of treatment experienced as unfair – of being coerced or ordered about in a peremptory way, of being insulted, cheated, or exploited. By declaring the moral equivalence of human beings my Newar acquaintances asserted their conviction about the ultimate basis of justice; if persons are alike, if they are the same in morally relevant ways, then they deserve to be treated the same. If I am a person, and you are a person, if we are interchangeable, then if you should actually be transposed with me, placed in my life and circumstances, you will feel what I feel, know what I know, and suffer what I suffer. What harms me would harm you, and you would reject treatment that I reject, for we are persons. Since we are alike, you would want to be treated in the same way I want to be treated. Thus, for Newars, invoking the moral equivalence of human beings constitutes and deploys a sense of justice. Moral discourse, Newars were telling me, begins with mutual recognition.[78]

The question is how to reconcile this affirmation of equality with the image of *Homo Hierarchicus*? The ideological constructions of hierarchy fail to do justice to the range of ways that men and women in South Asian cultures know themselves and evaluate their society. There exists ambivalence in the people of Newar when they relate themselves both to caste hierarchy and to equality in their personal and social life. Parish explains:

> Many Newars have doubts about the ideology of caste hierarchy, about what it means for themselves and others. Some of them find meaning in concepts of equality and solidarity, asserting that these, not hierarchy, are the ultimate moral grounds of social life. They use concepts of human equality and solidarity to resist some of the implications of hierarchy. They identify themselves with society, and commit themselves to social practices, on the basis of these ideas, not exclusively on the basis of concepts of hierarchy. Sometimes they justify hierarchy as a functional expedient, or reject it as an imposed order, ultimately encompassed in higher order solidarities.[79]

The Dalits' world is not only one of discrimination, but of intimidation, affecting their psyche deeply. The moral intuitions coming from them will have its origin in their psyche along with other cultural aspects.

In the moral life and practices Dalits consider hierarchy as something dominant, at the same time they see the existence of equality: thus both hierarchy and equality exist in a dynamic, uneasy complementarity. Parish makes it clear:

> Let me re-emphasise the values of hierarchy, not equality, shape Newar inter-caste social relations. Hierarchy is the dominant value because it is enacted with respect to other castes, and because it frames and gives meaning to equality within caste and kin groups. Yet equality is present, felt, and significant in a number of ways. My argument is not that equality has equal place with hierarchy in Newar culture – that would be a false symmetry – but that the

values of equality and hierarchy exist in dynamic uneasy complementarity.[80]

The ambivalence that exists between hierarchy and equality is a clear sign of the struggle for justice and equality, implied in: "I am a person, you are a person". Parish elaborates:

> For many Newars the hierarchy of purity and impurity is merely one way of viewing self and society. They play with the idea of alternative hierarchies, based on other principles, which, if enacted, would give them a different place in society. The relationship of Newars to the dominant caste hierarchy – and to equality as well – is perhaps best described as one of ambivalence. In action, in terms of actual social practice, hierarchy is dominant. This dominance, I think, can only be fully understood when we see it as the outcome of a long-term struggle to overcome the sense of justice and equality evoked by mutual recognition. The ideology of hierarchy itself bears the marks of this struggle.[81]

Inequalities in the context of caste hierarchy are a complex issue. This issue is to be addressed in an integral manner, in its different dimensions: economic, political, social, personal, cultural and religious. The inabilities imposed by the inequalities on the victims tend to be cumulative. The economically poor Dalits tend to be politically poor. In the same way, social equality could be hoped for and achieved only when efforts are taken to promote equality in other spheres. The legal approach and action envisaged in the Constitution goes towards this direction, taking all factors into consideration. However, the realisation of such formal and legal equality envisaged in the Constitution and elsewhere is not free of threats even in the participatory democratic setup of India. Vested interests politicise the caste issue.

Though hierarchy is dominant, there are voices heard evoking sense of equality and justice that come from the struggle to shape a culture that is more humane seeking the fullness of personhood. Though voiced by a few the self-affirmation and socio-cultural resurgence of native peoples and subaltern groups show a struggle to bring development and change by upholding the value of the person within the caste cultural society where relationship between persons is mainly conceived as domination and submission.

5. Cultural Dimension of Caste

Culture is at the service of the well-being of people. People are the creators of culture and not passive recipients of it.[82] To study the contemporary caste culture, it is important to learn from the problems and perspectives of those who have been the classic example of social deprivation and oppression. To get these experiences and perspectives one has to turn mainly to the Untouchables, the victims.[83] Amaladoss speaks about the formation of the caste culture by different groups structuring society in a hierarchy of socially and culturally superior and inferior:

> Each caste group may acquire through the years its own way of speaking and behaving so as to develop its own sub-cultural identity. This specific identity may be shown for instance in dress and food habits, in language and in the gods one worships. This separateness may further be strengthened by real or imagined ethnic/racial differences – for instance Aryan, Dravidain, Tribal, etc. Given the central importance of sharing food in the caste system, food habits acquire an important place. Vegetarian food is considered socially superior to non-vegetarian. Among non-vegetarian foods, the downward hierarchy is as follows: fish, chicken, mutton, pork, beef. An important way in which the separation between castes is signified and maintained is through the giving and receiving of brides.[84]

Taking some texts as the basis some say that among Hindus the man–woman relationship is conditioned by manipulation and deceptivity. The text of the law of Manu makes it clear the instrumentalisation and domination of women by man: "In childhood subjected to her father, in the youth to her husband, and when husband is dead to her sons, she should never enjoy independence"[85]. Among the Dalits the man-woman relationship on the other hand is based on openness. Ilaiah is very sharp in contrasting the man-woman relationship among the caste Hindus and the Dalits as he remarks:

> A Dalitbahujan woman does not have to perform *padapuja* (worshiping the husband's feet) to her husband either in the morning or in the evening. She does not have to address her husband in the way she would address a superior. In a situation of dispute, word in response to word, and abuse for abuse is the socially visible form. Patriarchy as a system does exist among Dalitbahujans, yet in this sense it is considerably more democratic.[86]

Both the protection of the sexual purity of the women to conserve the purity of caste and the sexual exploitation of the Dalit women are signs, not only of physical, but also of cultural domination.[87]

Interplay of Hierarchy and Equality

The self-image of people has much to do with their cultural experience of hierarchy. From the testimony and behaviour of the Newar people, Parish notes that the image of *Homo Hierarchicus* does not fit them. It is not a self-image but an image fashioned by others.[88] These images of India as "other", as what the West is not, springs from the assumption of the nature of reality. Parish explains:

> Deeply imbedded in recent Western thought is the idea that the thing posseses an inherent basic nature, an essence of some kind that constitutes what they are, constitutes their irreducible identity. This guiding idea shapes thought about other cultures, not just things and persons: each civilisation must have a basic nature, a stable essence that defines it, as if cultures are natural kinds, like species – or as if they embodied a master principle, a principle that makes them what they are. Inden (1990) argues that "India" and the "West"

have dialectically constituted one another... In this imagining of India and West, hierarchy fuses with holism, equality with individualism, to yield diametrically opposite values: the dominant principle of "India" is hierarchical interdependence, while the essence of the "West" is egalitarian individualism. Once again, India is "Caste", the West is "the individual".[89]

Challenging Dumont's image of India as *Homo Hierarchicus* Parish points out the distortion of the complex histories, cultures and selves that issues from a reification of the concept of hierarchy. Important as the concept of hierarchy is, it co-exists with concepts of equality, solidarity and justice. This co-existence of hierarchy and equality, was referred in the previous section, in the discussion on the personal dimension of caste culture. People invoke multiple models in cultural life and in moral discourse. What people know and feel does not reflect a cultural consensus based on a single model.[90] Our area of interest is the mental foundations, the pre-conditions of practice. How are people capable of reflecting critically on cultural formations that have a bearing on them, to re-imagine "forms of life" in which their lives are basically conceived? What is the way a critical tradition develops within a culture which enables people to evaluate and re-imagine social and political life? Parish observes:

> Ranking groups or individuals requires a cultural code, some principle of inclusion and exclusion, superiority or inferiority – a hierarchy-making principle. Yet there is no single principle of hierarchy in Newar culture. Multiple, overlapping symbolic frameworks organise inequality... I do not think that the ideology of caste hierarchy "encompasses and thereby situates all aspects" of South Asian culture, even where caste is a dominant social form. In making hierarchy the central principle of Indian life, the principle that gives an identity to India, I think Dumont's paradigm has substituted a part (the opposition of pure and impure) for the whole (south Asian life as dynamic moral and political ecology).[91]

Caste Culture in Different Dimensions

At the same time one should not fail to recognise Dumont's contribution. Dumont has gripped a part of reality, the reality of caste, to draw the image of India. For the full understanding of India, it is crucial to approach caste hierarchy through its multiple ideologies. I doubt any culture can be understood in its totality with a single ideology or value. To skip from surface to deep structure without pausing to contemplate other and more concrete aspects of meaning and experience can obscure much of what caste means to self, its political value, its quandaries and ambivalences.[92] The low caste actors may further the interests of the high castes by way of replication. That is to say the lower castes enact caste relations in a different spirit, may be for the purposes of their own. They seem to constitute a intentional world that is both like and unlike the world of caste of the dominant castes. The over-extension of exploitative relations helps to validate the entire system so that the lower castes remain entrapped in the total system. This ignores their critique of the caste system. Dissent exists. A process of re-imagining occurs, often private, sometimes public. This struggle goes on within the cultural order and within individual hearts and minds, and this is part of the cultural order. As Parish says about the cultural dynamics:

> In complex societies, at least, cultural subjectivities stand not fixed and encompassed in a single ideology but move fluidly in the mutually entangled webs of meaning that are ideology and critique. Each of these unravels the other and each requires continual maintenance and reweaving. Thus what I would term "the critical self", itself diverse and positioned, is an integral part of cultural life, a mode of thought and action that men and women can animate. Interpreting and acting persons are not so absorbed in ideology that they vanish, disappear into the culture they internalise: nor do ideas and critiques or the process of thinking and re-imagining exist apart from cultural meanings, experiences and practices.[93]

The different actors from Newar were doing the same when they spoke of caste life: they evaluated it, defended it and criticised it. They worked at re-imagining the caste system, proposing alternative forms of hierarchy and equality. About this interplay between hierarchy and equality Parish elaborates:

> The relationship of hierarchy and equality is dynamic, not static and passive; if they imply each other, then both are available for use in moral rhetoric and each can be used to resist and place limits on the other. The hierarchical concepts of Hindu cultures reflect this. If hierarchy implies equality, and equality can be used to subvert hierarchy, then the cultural construction of hierarchy will involve efforts to prevent this subversion to counter egalitarian ideas. Therefore, the relationship of a dominant ideology of hierarchy with egalitarian concepts will never remain one of absolutely passive implication, but will always involve an active animosity. This antagonism inspires rhetorical actions, efforts to undermine the opposing value. This will develop into a more sustained political polemic; this can lead to further elaboration of an ideology. The rhetoric and argumentation developed out of this ideological work constitute tools in struggles - however glacial they may be – to shape and control the social order; ideology, rhetoric and polemic may be mobilised to help *overcome* egalitarian thinking... Thus equality blossomed in the poetry of *Bhakti* devotionalism and is voiced passionately today in critiques that Untouchables make of the caste system.[94]

Though in their minds the Dalits are outraged at the social order, to stand up against the caste hierarchy is difficult, as it involves challenging the high caste actors, and speaking against the ways the caste hierarchy has constructed them, excluding them and confining them to a stigmatised social identity.

Confrontations

Opposing the dominant groups low caste actors create cultural forms for themselves juxtaposing their own central intentions about themselves with the constructs derived of the high castes. The low caste actors are not living in total isolation from the high caste in a self-contained culture, at the same time they do not share fully their culture with that of the high caste actors. Parish mentions the way the low caste actors struggle for themselves for the development of their identity and culture.

> Low caste actors may continue to live in the gap between cultural perspectives, while they may resent the way they are stigmatised, it is hard to be "at home" in their own self-contained cultural perspective, because it is neither wholly self-contained nor unaffected by high caste values and judgements. They have to live defending and affirming themselves.[95]

A Dalit movement song where equality is evoked confirms this:

> Rise, People, rise up now, break the chains of caste
> Throw off the corpse of slavery, smash the obstacles,
> Rise, People –
> We may be Maratha, Brahman, Hindu, Muslim, Christian,
> Humanity is all one, all are brothers.[96]

The message is clearly resistance to and a protest against all forms of discrimination that the dominant cultural tradition perpetrates, and the identification and destruction of all such forced domination, which in a way has become the 'eternal culture' that was offended even by the touch of their shadow. The lyric forcefully speaks against all that stands for socio-cultural oppression and inequality. But confrontations seem to have relatively little impact on the caste system with out the change of mind.

6. Caste Culture and Religion

Religion, which is part of the tradition of interpreted human experience we call culture, is also a human product. It is a cultural response to an ultimate reality. The religious response also flows out from the individual's reactions to social facts in a common cultural, historical and ecological context. An original religious experience of salvation and well-being, which is at the root of religion may become impossible within a fossilised religion of doctrines, rituals and laws, oppressive of the human search for fulfillment.[97] From the religious point of view Amaladoss points out the oppressive ideology of purity and pollution connected with the caste system:

> This purity can be seen at two inter-connected levels. Actions like sexual intercourse, events like death or menstruation in women and gestures like contact – touch — with dirt, can pollute someone. This pollution can be got rid of through bathing. Castes also can be seen as polluting in so far as they are more or less in permanent contact with polluting objects. Purity acquires a ritual connotation because it is seen as essential requirement for approaching the deity for worship or sacrifice. Thus the sacred-secular differentiation strengthens the purity-pollution complex. The Untouchables are seen as permanently polluted people, whereas the Brahmin tries to remain in a state of purity as far as possible, the others being at various stages of purity.[98]

The many symbols of the caste-culture like purity, sacredness, diet, dirt, sexuality, religious power, etc. are perceived and practiced by different actors differently. While the low caste actors react to the dominant ways and practices out of their existential pragmatic necessities, the high caste ones with the support of the religious ideas like *dharma* and *karma* try to make hierarchy seem natural and necessary.

Deity of Caste Hindus and Dalits

Along with the caste hierarchy there are gods and goddesses both for caste Hindus and Dalits. The manipulation of the consciousness of the Dalits by high caste Hindus takes place systematically through socio-economic and cultural designs. To sustain this hegemony by the brahminical forces, Hinduism has created many institutions. According to Ilaiah it is done in two ways (i) creating a consent system which it maintains through various images of Gods and Goddesses, some of whom have been co-opted from the social base that it wanted to exploit; and (ii) when such consent failed or lost its grip on the masses, it took recourse to violence.[99] Hinduism, in fact used violence as the principal mechanism of control. No other religion has introduced such variety of Gods who use both violence and consent to force the masses to submission. The relationship between the Gods of Hinduism and Dalits has been that of oppressor and oppressed, manipulator and manipulated. Ilaiah refers to a theory of consciousness constituted to maintain such relationship:

> Brahminical theoreticians have constructed their own theory of consciousness with a specific notion that the majority (bahujan) consciousness is confined to one specific activity and that consciousness has to be constantly monitored in order to arrest its further growth. If a consciousness is manipulated to become and remain the slave of another consciousness, some day or the other it will rebel. These revolts are mostly suppressed. All religions have worked out strategies to manipulate and contain such revolts by teaching the slaves a so-called divine morality. But no religion has succeeded in suppressing the slaves forever.[100]

Differing from other religions, Hinduism has institutionalised all the Gods and Goddesses and modified and contextualised them in an anti-Dalit mode. Though there is the claim that Dalits are Hindus, in actuality their gods are set against the Dalits. "As a result, this religion, from its very inception has a fascist nature, which can be experienced and understood only by the Dalitbahujans, not by Brahmins who regard manipulation and exploitation as systemic and not as part of their own individual consciousness. The reality is that every upper caste person takes part in that exploitation and manipulation and contributes towards the creation and perpetuation of such cultures in the Indian context".[101]

The Brahminical forces were ever trying to suppress the consciousness of the Dalitbahujans by the way they institutionalise the images of God. Ilaiah points out some characteristic features of the Dalitbahujan Gods \Goddesses:

> The consciousness built around Dalitbahujans Gods/ Goddesses images is rooted in production processes. Though the Dalitbahujans imagination has played a role in institutionalising these images it is also important that those images find their centre in human existence and in the relations between productive forces and nature. In this sense, the philosophical parallelism in which Goddess/God images are developed among the Dalitbahujan masses is different. Deities do not function as means to subdue a section of society; they are not designed to exploit a section within the community; they function to create a common cultural ethic, one that re-energises the masses so that they can engage in productive activity.[102]

Amaladoss also gives some of the differences between caste Hindu and Dalit Gods and Goddesses:

> Within the pantheon the Gods worshipped by the lower castes have servant roles in relationship to the higher Gods. The ways of worship too are different. While the higher gods require only vegetarian offerings given by brahmin priests, the lower gods prefer blood sacrifices. While the higher castes worship Vishnu and Shiva and their avataras and manifestations, the lower castes are devotees of lesser divinities like Hanuman who have a servant role in relation to the higher Gods.[103]

Dumont has examined the complex relationship between Aiyanar, the Lord and Karupan, the servant, in the South Indian village shrines.[104] Fuller too points out a symmetrical relationship between Sundaresvara (Shiva) and a local Goddess Chellattamman.[105] Sundaresvara is God in his own right, whereas Chellattamman's divinity is relational and totally dependant on Sundaresvara. This is a typical cultural model of caste system:

The contrast between Sanskrtic and village deities therefore reveals a symbolisation of the social order that generates a double process of legitimation. Sanskritic deities symbolise the Brahmans's ideal, a world where highness ceases to depend on the existence of lowness. The representation of their divinity legitimates the Brahmans' superiority in society by denying relationship with inferiors. In opposition to this, village deities symbolise the hierarchical interdependence of caste, the mutual though asymmetrical dependence of the high on the low and vice versa, and the indispensability to society of the low castes. But their representation again legitimates the Brahmans' social superiority by stressing their apical position. Thus it is not Sanskritic, but village deities – mainly worshipped by low castes – who provide the model of and for a hierarchical world. When such a model issues from the religion of inferiors instead of superiors the legitimation of hierarchy surely attains its apogee.[106]

Ascetic and Householder

The contrast between householder and ascetic is sometimes used as a moral control. Parish elaborates this point from the acquaintances he had with Newar people:

> A brahman told me that Newars should not become world-renouncers; rather, a Newar must bear the burdens of the life of the householder, which he said were very hard, and involve many religious and social duties. A Brahman, he added, who complained excessively about the hardship of the householder (*kuldharma*) might be told: "If you feel the life of a householder is too difficult you can become a renouncer. Who is stopping you from being an ascetic? But if you don't want to be a renouncer, then you have to do these things"... This statement plays on the contrast of ascetic and householder, splitting them into separate and opposed realities... When informants get the life of the ascetic and of the householder in opposition, it is possible to speculate that the rejection of renunciation is tantamount to a rejection of equality and anti-structural dissent. This follows from the

identification of self and hierarchy: to reject hierarchy is to reject "self".[107]

"Equality" as an ideal radically would demand from the householder to distribute wealth, prestige, and freedom of action, which is something that cannot happen in his life. Equality is an ethical goal that could take place only in the world of the renouncer. So, equality is an "otherworldly" mode of being, totally different realm from the social world. This means that equality, as principle of subversion of hierarchy or as abolition of differences, is a theoretical spiritual possibility. A non-hierarchical way of life is just a religious idea, but bringing no meaning to ordinary people. Parish concludes:

> The world of the renouncer exists on the other side of a chasm from ordinary values. The freedom that the renouncer has from the restrictions of hierarchy presupposes withdrawal from society, family and kinship, from the domain of political action, of social esteem, of prosperity and pleasure... The world renouncer is the "other" who defines the self of the householder.... Furthermore, certain of the general values of transcendence (although not of equality) associated with asceticism (especially religio-magical power) are duplicated within the social system and monopolised by priestly Hindu Brahmans who have a vested interest in sustaining the hierarchy.... The contrast of renouncer and householder poses a psychological dilemma for high caste persons who are ambivalent about the hierarchical life of the householder... To reject hierarchy in this way is to lose "self". But efforts to rebel against hierarchy in other ways, while attempting to remain part of the social world, invite social and economic sanctions, even the use of force or violence... The Western sense of "equality" is wholly obviated in the process.[108]

From the point of view of the householder, a person may not coherently lead an ordinary social life that avoids or levels hierarchy. It is not possible to reconcile the life of the householder and the life of the renouncer. This disharmony and the consequent ideological structuring allow the defenders of the normative order to divert or undermine challenges and keep the hierarchical social system in its place, secure from any danger.

Karma and Hierarchy

The concept of *karma* is also used to explain and support caste system. It provides a means by which a concept of justice that applies to individuals – the idea that people should get what they deserve – can be evoked in a social context, where the issue is distributive justice, and used to justify the unequal distribution, misery and opportunity, reward and hardship.[109] M. Amaladoss refers to the concepts of *dharma* and *karma* and explains how these concepts were used to explain and support the caste system:

> Each person is involved in a cycle of births. The status that one will have in a particular birth is determined by one's past actions. The fact that one is born a Brahmin or an untouchable in this birth is not accidental or arbitrary, but is a consequence of what one had done in one's own previous birth. Thus caste is not only a ritual hierarchy, but a moral one. I think that this is not so much an explanation of the caste system, as a justification of it. Once one is born in a particular caste the only way of progressing in the journey towards *moksha* or ultimate liberation is to do one's duty, which is the duty of one's caste, in the community. Each caste has its *dharma*. It is by doing it faithfully that one attains a better birth in the next life and thus progress in the way of liberation. The caste then is also a spiritual hierarchy. By being faithful to one's *dharma* one is also contributing to the well being of the entire world.[110]

Mostly people with low caste status do not attempt to reconcile the idea of spiritual equality with the concept of *karma*. However, a few attribute low caste status to the action of *karma*. Birth in a particular caste demands the performance of duties prescribed by that caste. Each caste has its *dharma*, and doing it faithfully one progresses in the journey towards *moksha*. Doing the duty prescribed by the caste one belongs to, is in a way the contribution one makes to the betterment of the world. The world community is seen as a network of different castes with different functions and relationships, but the concept of *karma* rationalizes inequalities. The coming together or crossing together of two kinds of justice, the distributive justice and the one framed in terms of what an individual deserves, makes *karma* a powerful political concept.

What makes this concept culturally distinctive and psychologically powerful is not the coupling of two types of justice, i.e., the demand of social equality and the principle of personal actualisation, but the idea of transmigration that clarifies the concept and acts to establish, maintain and validate the link between these two justice concepts. Parish explains:

> According to *karma* theory the sins (*pap*) a person commits are punished in this and subsequent lives while acts of *dharma* are rewarded... The conditions of life of high and low castes are thus the just desserts for actions for which persons were morally responsible; they got what they deserve, and statusquo is justified... Some suffer without seeming to have done wrong in any tangible sense; others enjoy privileges despite the fact that they did nothing evident to deserve them.... What appears to be a gratuitous distribution of good fortune and misery becomes intelligible when seen in terms of the ideas of transmigration and the *karmic* conservation of the moral consequences of individual actions. Newars retain the doctrine of *karma* as one of several explanations of why low castes have their present position in the society. The theory of *karma* seals status boundaries, just as the idea of the presence of God in each person tends to make them permeable.[111]

Karma is another cultural system that neutralises equality. The rhetoric of *karma* is also capable of displacing equality from a potentially politically charged discourse to a moral discourse. Then equality continues to reappear in thought forms, as voiced by householders, Brahmans and Untouchables alike.

The caste system exerts a lot of influence in the lives of many Indians. Its complex nature demands one to enter into its cultural roots. The authors, whom I frequently quote in this thesis like Parish, Amaladoss, Ilaiah, etc., take us in different directions in analysing the caste system in the cultural framework. Parish takes us to the caste culture into the roots of its dynamics and to its external expressions, bringing into focus the life and consciousness of the people of Newar, through their festival celebrations and through different actors representing different castes. Correcting the one-dimensional approach to the caste culture he emphasises the dialectic approach by pointing out the politics of consciousness in the caste cultural conflict. Any critique one makes on the caste culture should take into account the interplay between caste ideologies, hierarchy and equality. Parish sees ambivalence of different actors while they deal with hierarchy and equality.

Amaladoss gives a framework of culture in its six-fold dimensions. He insists that the caste system has to be approached and analysed culturally, and enters into the dynamics of culture. Conversant with the caste cultural practices he puts forward the different cultural expressions in different dimensions and gets a holistic understanding. Ilaiah, too, from his rich experience in the caste life in cultural conflicts, puts forward the different cultural expressions vividly, from a victim's perspective. Caste cultural analysis according to him should enter into the consciousness level and find out the aberrations and correct them. He is very strong in his critique on the upper caste ideologies, the oppressive character of which he sees as responsible for the stifling and subjugation of the consciousness of the Dalits. He writes with passionate anger, laced with sarcasm, on the caste cultural situation of India. He looks at the socio-economic and religio-cultural differences between the Dalits and the caste Hindus entering into his own experiences in the family life, market relations, power relations, relations with Gods and Goddesses, etc., and presents his own vision of a just society.

From the brief analysis of caste culture in its six dimensions I would like to enter the interpretative level to attain a clearer view, though analysis and interpretation cannot be separated in water tight compartments.

NOTES

PART TWO

1. M. Amaladoss. *Towards Fullness.* Bangalore: NBCLC, 1993, 30; M. Amaladoss. *A Call to Community.* Gujarat: Gujarat Sahitya Prakash, 1994, 34.
2. S.M. Parish. *Hierarchy and its Discontents.* Delhi: Oxford University Press,1997, 23.
3. *ibid.* 24.
4. *ibid.* 25.
5. *ibid.*
6. *ibid.*
7. *ibid.* 27.
8. *ibid.*
9. R. Levy. *Mesocosm: Hinduism and the Organisation of a Traditional Newar City in Nepal.* Berkeley: University of California Press, 1990. Cf. S.M. Parish. *Hierarchy..,* , 28.
10. S.M. Parish. *Hierarchy….,*28.
11. *ibid.*
12. *ibid.* 29.
13. *ibid.*
14. *ibid.* 30.
15. R. Levy. *Mesocosm:......,* 476. Cf. S.M. Parish. *Hierarchy....,* 31.
16. *ibid.* 485.
17. S.M. Paish. *Hierarchy....,* 32.
18. R. Levy. *Mesocosm:.....,* 493. Cf. S.M. Parish. *Hierarchy....,* 33.
19. *ibid.* 486.
20. S.M. Parish. *Hierarchy.....,* 33.
21. *ibid.* 39-40.

22 *ibid.* 34.
23 *ibid.* 35
24 *ibid.* 37-38.
25 M. Amaladoss. *A Call to Community..*, 34.
26 *ibid.* 34-35.
27 Reuters, New Delhi, June 13, 1993. Cf. M. Amaladoss, *A Call to....*, 35.
28 M. Amaladoss, *A Call to....*, 35-36; The *jajmani* system is a system of distribution in Indian villages whereby high-caste landowning families called *jajmans* are provided services and products by various lower castes such as carpenters, potters, blacksmiths, watercarriers, sweepers, and laundrymen. Purely ritual services may be provided by Brahman priests and various sectarian castes, and almost all serving castes have ceremonial and ritual duties at their *jajman's* births, marriages, funerals, and at some of the religious festivals. Important in the latter duties is the lower castes capacity to absorb pollution by handling clothing and other things defiled by birth or death pollution, gathering up banquet dishes after the feasts, and administering various bodily attentions to new mother, bride or groom. Cfr. Pauline Kolenda, Caste, Cult and Hierarchy, Meerut: Ved Prakash Vatuk, 1983, 10-67. Also Cfr D.G. Mandelbaum, *Society in India*, Vols1 and 2, Bombay: Popular Prakashan, 1972, 161-178.
29 K. Ilaiah, *Why I am not a Hindu,* Calcutta: Samya, 1997, 24-25.
30 *ibid.* 25.
31 M.C. Raj, *From the Periphery to the Center*,Tumkur: Reds, 1998, x.
32 K. Ilaiah, "Globalisation and Hindutua", in *Globalisation,* R. Vishvanath (ed), 1998, 35.
33 *The Hindu,* Wednesday, March 1, 2000.
34 Reported in *TheTimes of India*, 14 February, 1938, annotated by Gail Omvedt, in *Dalits in Modern India*, S.M. Michael (ed), New Delhi:Visthar Pub.,1999, 35.
35 K. Ilaiah, *Why I am....,* 36-37.

[36] *ibid.*
[37] *ibid.* 38.
[38] *ibid.* 39.
[39] J. Desrochers, "The role of social movements", in J. Desrochers, Bastian Wielenga, Vibhuti Patel, *Social Movementets, Towards a Perspective*, Bangalore: CSA, 1991, 10.
[40] K. Ilaiah, *Why I am...*, 40.
[41] *ibid.*
[42] *ibid.* 41.
[43] *ibid.* 41-42.
[44] *ibid.*
[45] M. Amaladoss, *A Call to...*, 80.
[46] K. Ilaiah, *Why I am...*, 44.
[47] *ibid.* 47.
[48] *ibid.* 48.
[49] *ibid.* 49.
[50] *ibid.* 58-59.
[51] *ibid.* 60.
[52] *ibid.* 61.
[53] S. Selvam, "Sociology of India and Hinduism", in *Dalits in Modern...*, 167.
[54] M. Amaladoss, *A Call to ....,..*, 36-37.
[55] K. Ilaiah, *Why I am...*, 20.
[56] Bhagavan Das, "Socio-economic...", in *Dalit Solidarity*, Das and Massey (eds), 1995, 35.
[57] C.J. Fuller, *Flame. Popular The Camphor Hinduism and Society in India*, Princeton: Priceton University Press, 1992. 148. Cf. M. Amaladoss, *A Call to....* , 37.
[58] *ibid.* 148.
[59] A. Beteille (ed) *Social Inequality*, Hammondsworth: Penguin, 1969, 268. Cf. M. Amaladoss, *A Call to....,* 37-38.
[60] S.M. Parish, *Hierarchy......,* 53.
[61] *ibid.* 53-54.
[62] *ibid.* 54.

63 *ibid.* 45.
64 *ibid.* 46.
65 *ibid.* 47.
66 *ibid.* 48.
67 *ibid.*
68 M. Amaladoss, *A Call to....,* 38.
69 M. Amaladoss. *A Call to....,* 38. Citing M. Marriott(ed), *Village India. Studies in the Little community*, Chicago: University of Chicago, 1955, 102-144..
70 In one of the talks of Jerry Rosario at Samanvaya, Bhopal, March 8, 2000.
71 J. Massey, *Roots*, Delhi: ISPCK, 1991, 9-10.
72 *ibid.*
73 A. P. Nirmal, "Towards a Christian Dalit Theology", in *A Reader in Dalit Theology,* Chennai: Gurukul, (n d), 139.
74 A.R. Thumma, *Springs from the Subalterns,* Delhi: ISPCK, 1999, 1-2.
75 K. Iliaiah, *Why I am ....,* 12.
76 *ibid.* 14-15.
77 *ibid.* 15-16.
78 S.M. Parish, *Hierarchy....,* 41-42.
79 *ibid.* 42.
80 *ibid.* 44.
81 *ibid.* 42.
82 J.M.D. Mesa & ..L.L. Wostyn, *Doing Theology* , Philippines: Claritian Publications, 1990, 28.
83 R.S. Khare, *The Untouchables as Himself,* ix.
84 M. Amaladoss, *A Call to......,* 38-39.
85 C.J. Fuller, 1992, 20. Quoted by M. Amaladoss, *A Call to...,* 39.
86 K. Ilaiah, *Why I am..........,* 34.
87 M. Amaladoss, *A Call to..,* 39. Cf. C.J. Fuller, *The Campher....,* 21.
88 S.M. Parish, *Hierarchy...,* 66.

[89] *ibid.*67.Cf. R. Inden, *Imagining India*, Oxford: Blackwell, 1990.
[90] S.M. Parish, *Hierarhy*.... 69.
[91] *ibid.* 70-78.
[92] *ibid.* 80.
[93] *ibid.* 80-81.
[94] *ibid.* 82.
[95] *ibid.* 55-56.
[96] Quoted in Joshi (1986:97), where it was translated by Gail Omvedt.
[97] De Mesa &L.L. Wostyn, *Doing* ....., 30-32.
[98] M. Amaladoss, *A Call to*...., 39-40.
[99] K. Ilaiah, *Why I am..*, 71.
[100] *ibid.* 72.
[101] *ibid.*
[102] *ibid.* 91.
[103] M. Amaladoss, *A Call tro*...., 40.
[104] Lessa and Vogt, 1965:189-195. Cf. M. Amaladoss, *A Call to*......., 41.
[105] C.J. Fuller, 1988:19-37. Cf. M. Amaladoss, 1994:41.
[106] C.J. Fuller, 1981: 35. Cf. M. Amaladoss, 1994: 41-42.
[107] S.M. Parish, *Hierarchy*..., 49-50
[108] *ibid.* 50-51.
[109] *ibid.* 51-52.
[110] M. Amaladoss, A Call to..., 40. *Karma*, an important tenet of Hinduism, is a concept that includes actions, causality and destiny. Action being inevitable, it is said, the human individual is bound by the results of his actions, pleasant fruits flowing from good deeds and unpleasant consequences from evil ones. What we are today, is the result of our past deeds. At the same time we are makers of our future as per our actions at present. The Hindus believe in reincarnation with the soul being reborn in a long series until the attainment of liberation.

The different caste actors take different stand in the understanding of concepts like transmigration, *moksha* and *karma*. When the high castes (mostly Brahmins) mostly give a traditional stand in interpreting the above mentioned concepts the middle castes (mostly jat farmers) deny belief in reincarnation, *moksha*, or an afterlife and emphasise life on earth, claming that heaven and hell are to be found on earth. If the low caste actors like Sweepers accepted the full *karma* theory, they could be expected to explain their low-caste status as the result of the sinful past lives of the members of their castes, but they do not draw this conclusion. Rather they ignore all but gross differences in caste rankings. They do feel compelled to explain their low rank, but they do so by different set of theories, which seem to say," We originally had very high rank, but were tricked out of it", or "We should have high status, but others do not recognise our claims". In the case of *karma* theory, low status is not admitted, and in the case of the alternative theories, high status is claimed.

[111] S. M. Parish, *Hierarchy*...., 52.

PART THREE

TOWARDS A COUNTER-CULTURAL INTERPRETATION

We see, from the caste cultural analysis, people struggling from the ambivalence and discontent the caste system that fills life with injustice and yet is viewed as the moral basis of the traditional society, and as part of the natural order. For many who are at the margins, the caste system is not just an objective social fact but also a disturbing social fate, a problem of meaning, and a matter of survival. The crisis demands at once a counter-cultural interpretation and a movement marked by a change in the perspectives and understanding of the society. These alone are ultimately capable of bringing change and transformation in the self and in the world. Rather than listing the elements of the counter-culture, my effort, is to approach here the question of caste cultural crisis theologically and pastorally, highlighting some perspectives and pointing out the need for a fresh interpretation. Many prophets and movements in this direction have made many heroic efforts in the past and the present time. It will not be possible to present them in a detailed manner. After mentioning a few of them I shall go on to a theological and pastoral response.

CHAPTER VI

COUNTER-CULTURAL VOICES AND MOVEMENTS

Working for a counterculture or an alternate culture is made necessary by the conflicts of race, caste, class, gender and language. The awareness of the suffering caused by the caste cultural conflict is the starting point of a way to a liberation process for all members of the caste-ridden society, especially the Dalits, the most affected ones. Such a goal of liberation may be achieved through efforts of self-discipline and through the mediation of a saviour figure, as seen in major liberation movements. In this section my objective will be to explore some of the counter-cultural trends and prophetic voices and movements of the Indian caste cultural scene.

1. Counter-culture in the Buddha's Dissent

Early among the protest movements of India we find the Buddhist revolt against the Brahminic domination based on purity and pollution. The ethical outlook developed by the Buddhists served as an antidote to the Hindu religious arrogance. Buddhists conducted their propaganda in a variety of forms and spread the message of social revolution in the hearts of the people.

As an alternative to Sanskrit, Buddha used *Magadhi*, the language of the people to spread his message. His teachings were first gathered in the *Pali* language of the North-West region of India and in this language the teachings of Buddha, the *Tripitaka*: *Vinaya Sutta* and *Abhidamma*, are preserved. The teachings of Buddha that served as the foundation of the movement, developed as an alternative culture in the Brahmin society. K. P. Rao gives some of the traits of this new culture:

> This movement initiated six centuries before Christ tried to develop as an alternative culture. Culture is generally something which reflects the life-style and thought pattern of the individual and society. A change in a continuing culture implied a comprehensive change in the education, art, literature and philosophy of the society concerned and in their inter-relations. The Buddhist *Jataka* stories, which are very well known, are different from the tools of Hindu culture.[1]

Buddha saw the totality of human alienation in sorrow (*dukha*), the source of which is craving – the craving for pleasure, for life, for power. Only elimination of all craving can ensure complete emancipation.[2] The approach and diagnosis of the human predicament and the means for liberation as put forward by Buddha are not restricted to a few but open to all without distinction of caste and gender. One can detect elements of universal humanism in Buddha's teachings and his understanding of the way of final emancipation. The ultimate goal *(arahatta)* consists in the absence of acquisitiveness (*alobha*), absence of oppressiveness and hatred (*adosa*) and freedom from illusory knowledge (*amoha*).[3] The monastic community that embodies this ideal is also a symbol of religious communism: they are called to share all things in common, even the morsel of food falling into the begging bowl, as Buddha declared.[4]

Mutuality or reciprocal dependence of the metacosmic (*lokutara*) and the cosmic (*lokiya*) or the dialectics between withdrawal from the world and involvement in the world, or contemplation and action, is so clearly attested as in the political role that spiritual persons played in the Buddhist culture.[5] The Buddha gives more importance to right means than to conceptualising the end of human striving. The eightfold path that consists of right vision, right aims, right speech, right action, right livelihood, right effort, right mindfulness and right meditation sum up the right means.

Gautama affirmed the centrality of friendliness (*maitri*) and compassion (*karuna*), which, along with joy and equanimity, go to form the four cardinal virtues of his religion.[6] The centrality of love, not the cosmic order (*rta*), is stressed when he says: "Never in this world is hate appeased by hatred; it is only appeased by love – this is eternal law (*sanatana dharma*)".[7] On the basis of the principle of moral righteousness and social security, the king's main function is to see to the establishment of equality and justice. Buddhism went beyond the equality based on work and declared that by birth all human beings are equal. It was the duty of the Buddhist state to ensure that there is no crime, and the state should also adopt means for the acquisition of wealth on the part of those devoid of wealth.[8]

According to Buddha righteousness is something to be found in every person regardless of his/her birth or social status. *Varna* or *jati* is understood in Buddhist texts as mental or spiritual ways of behaviour, and not in the traditionally accepted meaning. Thus the characteristic mark of a Brahmana, as described by the *Dammapada*, is that he is not easily recognisable to the external eye. This particular quality is to be found in every verse of the '*Brahmana Vagga*' of the *Dammapada*, and indicates that any righteous human is a potential Brahman[9]. We see many examples for the rejection of the existing caste order in the Buddhist literature, for example, in the story of Ananda and Chandala maid.[10] Ananda accepts water from her, demonstrating the irrelevance of class or caste for him, despite her protestations. Eventually this so-called low-caste Chandala maiden is admitted into the order of Bhikunis, much to the disgust of the nobility of Sravasti.

The Buddhist culture made an impact even on the leaders of the later Bhakti movement, like Kabir, Guru Nanak, etc., because of its humanist note.

2. Bhakti Movement and Counter-culture

The Bhakti movement was a protest movement against the cultural domination by the dominant castes. The leaders of the Bhakti movement made an impact on social rather well beyond the religious sphere.[11] They proposed a humanism that served as an alternative to the views of religious orthodoxy. The Bhakti movement originated in Tamilnadu and spread to other states like Karnataka and Maharashtra and eventually to the whole of North India. It repudiated Vedic sacrifices and the practice of ritual purity as Buddhism had done. The *Bhaktas* saw no meaning in devotion divorced from neighbourly love and the practice of justice as may be seen from the following passage from the commentary to *Bhagavata Purana* which Basava wrote in the 12th century:

> I am always present in all beings as their soul and yet, ignoring Me, mortal man conducts the mockery of image-worship.... Good behaviour is what pleases God.... Kindness is the root of all righteousness.... The man who is kind and who practices righteousness, who remains passive amidst the affairs of the world, who considers all creatures as his own self, he attains the immortal Being, the true God is ever with him.[12]

The Bhakti movement has links with Sufism within Islam and finds expression in Kabir, Guru Nanak, Tukaram, etc.

Sufism

Sufism, a reform movement in Islam, arose to bridge the conflict between the *Sunnis* and Shias. The *Sufis* dissociated themselves from the established centres of Islamic orthodoxy as a protest against what they believed to be a misinterpretation of the Quran by the *Ulema*. They strongly protested against combining religion with politics, cooperating with the Sultanate and deviating the community from the original democratic egalitarian principles of the Quran. The Sufis preached the concept of *equality of all men* and tolerance and harmony among the followers of all religions. K. P. Rao sums up the main points of the Sufi teachings:

God is only one; all men (and women) are his children;

1. All men (and women) are equal. Differences based on caste and *varna* are manmade, artificial.
2. Love of God and man is superior to sacrifices and other rituals.
3. The individualisation of the supreme Soul results in individual souls; who again merge with the Supreme. The Sufis were not afraid of God. That is why they were able to love God and man. They followed the Buddhist teachings in practice, which influenced the Indian society.[13]

Sufism, inspired by the Buddhist teachings, had an influence on the people of the time, in their literature, culture, ideas, language and actions. Its humanist ideal and appeal were powerful counter-cultural elements to challenge the combined forces of orthodox religion coupled with state power.

Though in the thought and practice Sufism and Bhakti fuse together in many aspects, they differ in one thing, i.e., the Sufis are secluded from society whereas the Bhakta saints are very much available to the common people, even to simple minds.[14] A special feature can be noted in the rise of Bhakti movement, that is, the majority of the Bhakti saints hailed from either artisan or the class of less prosperous cultivators, and from them there arose preachers, singers and poets. This background contributed to their attack on the institutionalised religion and objects of worship; caste distinctions were disregarded; women were encouraged to join gatherings; and the teaching was entirely in the vernacular language. Kosambi points some of the political and economic reasons for the plight of the peasants which might have provoked the counter offensive from their part:

> With the recurrence of the foreign invasions, the centralised state power had weakened, and a loosers, feudalistic form of political organisation had come into being. On the economic level, taxation weighed heavily on the peasants, whose surplus

was expropriated for the construction and upkeep of temples and palaces.[15]

The forerunners of the Bhakti movement in North India were Kabir (1440-1518) and Guru Nanak (1469-1539). Kabir hailed from a lower caste artisan community. His guru was Ramananda, who put great emphasis on the spirit of equality in his teachings. He had disciples both from Hindus and Muslims. More than just a religious reform, he wished to change the society. In a very intelligible manner he expressed his ideas in couplets with full of imagery. He was against caste, idol worship and religious bigotry, and stood for non-violence, morality and devotion. K. P. Rao gives in summary the vision of a society and culture Kabir upholds as a challenge to the existing one:

1. Sanskrit is like the water in a well; the people's languages are like flowing rivers;
2. If it is possible to see God by worshiping stones, I can worship mountains;
3. If salvation can be attained by bathing, frogs should get it first;
4. If one can reach God by being naked, the deer deserves it;
5. One doesn't become a scholar by reading hundreds of books; the one who understands the two syllables of "*prema*" (love) is a true scholar;
6. Live truthfully and naturally, truth alone is natural;
7. Understand truth with your heart;
8. Whoever denies truth will be the origin of religious conflicts.[16]

Influenced by Kabir's teaching, Guru Nanak started a Bhakti movement of his own. He was born in the village called Talwandi, in Punjab. He was educated by the generosity of a Muslim friend, who later employed him as a store-keeper in the Afghan administration. He belonged to the *Khatri* caste. He left his family and friends and joined the Sufis, but after a while he left them and travelled through the length and breadth of the country, and finally rejoined his family and settled in Punjab.

His teachings are found in *Adi Granth*, which challenged the untouchability and other oppressive and dominant traits like *karma*, etc. in Hinduism and were capable of awakening the people of the lower castes. He taught his disciples the path of truth, universal brotherhood, collective life and dignity of labour. His main teachings are:

1. Devotion cannot be achieved by wearing Kundalas (ear ornaments), or shaven heads or daily baths;
2. Doubts are cleared only by a real Guru; and the mind is at peace;
3. God exists wherever his name is recited;
4. The mind must be pure; there must be good behaviour, and a simple, exemplary life; Men must love one another.[17]

Free from caste feelings, his teachings are of a great value in contemporary society which is dominated by religious orthodoxy and bigotry. Sikhism, the main religion in Punjab was evolved by his followers after his death. It mainly propagates a philosophy of humanism, which made lasting impression on Indian society deeply troubled by the caste-cultural conflicts.

There are similar prophetic interventions made by other Bhakti saints in different parts of the country, sometimes even before Kabir and Nanak. The Bhakti movement in general was charismatic and so the rise and fall of such movement was roughly connected with the saints who propagated it. Though Bhaktas initiated a process of change, not all of them were able to sustain it and often acted rather as agents of stability. Kappen points out some of the characteristic teachings of the Bhakti movement, which have counter-cultural traits:

> Before the divine lover there is no distinction of sex, wealth, caste or colour. According to *Bhagavata Purana*, the main

scripture of the movement, access to God is not considered upon birth or social status. If God has any partiality, it is for destitutes and those persons without wealth, the Shudras and the outcastes. The favourite of Krishna is a low caste woman. Though the *Bhagavata Purana* does not denounce the caste system outright, it rejected the notion of determining a person's status by birth. In fact the poorer classes formed the bulk of the followers of the movement.[18]

Not all leaders of the bhakti movement were, however, radical, or could withstand the high caste strategy of subjugation by co-option.

3. Mahatma Phule and Counter-culture

Jotirao Phule was born in Pune in 1827. He belongs to the *Malis*, a sub caste in Maharashtra, which formed part of the larger '*Kumbi*' or agricultural cluster of castes in the Western part of India. He was considered by Ambedkar as the greatest of the Shudra of modern India, who made the lower classes of Hindus conscious of their slavery to the higher classes. He preached the gospel that for India, social democracy was more vital than the independence from foreign rule.[19] It was his vision to free the Shudras and Ati-shudras by cleansing the minds of his fellowmen and women from the outdated belief/system that denied equal status to all human beings. To achieve this aim, he first engaged in rewriting the history that had been incorrectly recorded and reinterpreted the religious symbols redefining their cultural script from the viewpoint of the Shudras and the Ati-shudras. Secondly, he envisaged an action-oriented approach by establishing the institutions and organisations that would translate the new cultural script into practice.[20]

Phule rejected the Brahmin version of the caste division. He described the Brahmins as usurpers who destroyed the golden past of the Kshatriyas. For Phule the Aryan Brahmins came from a region beyond the Indus, and defeated, seduced and destroyed the peaceful situation that existed among the Kshatriyas, who were the original cultivators of the land. The terminology that is used to represent the lower castes gives hints to this struggle. The term Shudra was used to mean 'low and insignificant', those who were defeated, while the term Mahar probably derived from the phrase *Maha-ari* meaning 'the great enemy'.[21] The Mahars and Mangs put up fierce resistance against the invaders, and as a result the Brahmans thrust upon them the punishment of untouchability.[22] In order to fulfil the plan that Kshatriyas, Shudras, Mahars, etc. should remain perpetually in slavery, and that they themselves should be able to live comfortably on what others earned by the sweat of their brow, the Brahmins created the fiction of caste divisions and compared books on this.[23]

Another strategy Phule used to reinterpret culture and history was to give a collective identity to all agriculturalists by assimilating their Shudra status to that of the Kshatriya status. This is supported by the interpretation given to the term Kshatriya. The origin of the term is seen from the Marathi word *kshetra*, means a field.[24] Interpreting religious symbols with new meanings was another proof of his genius. One example is the interpretation of the myth of King Bali. There is a common Marathi saying, "May all sorrows and troubles disappear and the kingdom of Bali come." This saying has its origin in the defeat of the king Bali, the protector of the low castes, by King Vaman, the upholder of the Brahmins. So on the Dassehra day the women prepare images of Bali and repeat the eschatological blessing, "May all evil disappear and Raja Bali's empire be restored." It is generally said that the Shudras are fond of King Bali because he took their part against Vaman and the Brahmans.[25] Thus Phule strategically exposed the Brahmins, their association with corruption, bribery, etc.

In his collection of ballads he makes people disbelieve the necessity of a Brahmin to carry out the religious rituals. Such belief does not aim at having access to divine power but is the result of an urge to dominate and rule. The ballads give a powerful message to the victims of manipulation and oppression, and challenge the oppressors to conversion and change.

Phule not only reinterpreted but also translated his counter-cultural messages into action by devoting himself to a variety of social reform campaigns. He established several schools for the low caste people. Through education he intended to inject into low castes a sense of power so that they come to positions of power at different levels, which he thought would destroy the poor self-image they possessed.

The Satya-shodak Samaj was an institution directed against the religious and cultural domination of the Brahmin priests. It was started in Pune in 1873 in a gathering of sixty important men, where Phule was elected its first president. The object of the Samaj was to redeem the Shudras from the influence of Brahminical scriptures, under which the Brahmin priests fleeced them, and to make them conscious of their human rights, and to liberate them from their mental and religious slavery.[26] The Samaj conducted many marriage ceremonies without calling and paying Brahmin priests.

By different ways of reinterpretation and cultural activity Mahatma Phule empowered and liberated the lower castes from the socio-cultural shackles of oppressive caste cultural structures.

4. The Challenge of Periyar E. V. Ramaswamy

Periyar E. V. Ramaswamy was a fighter from Tamilnadu who led the anti-Brahmin Movement. He is known in Tamilnadu as *Thandai* Periyar, which means 'Father', 'the Great One'. At the age of forty he became the Municipal Chairman of his native town Erode and involved himself fully in the public life. He entered the freedom movement in the year 1919 by joining the Congress Party. He focussed mainly on the recovery of the self-respect lost by the Dalits and the other weaker sections in Hindu society. He was the leader in the *satyagraha* for the abolition of untouchability at Vaikom in 1924. When the commemorative stamp was released at the centenary of his birth, there was this mention in the citation: "Ramaswamy preached inter-caste marriages and re-marriage of widows. It was his firm conviction that orthodoxy, superstition, social discrimination and other evils which persisted in the society should go."[27]

When he started the self-respect movement the Tamilnadu situation was always in his mind, and he worked for the collapse of the false structures built by the Brahmins. The false structures of caste culture, Periyar declared, were for the Brahmins' own livelihood. He asks the question: While fire, water, air, and earth were elements of nature, how can these be touchable for some and untouchable for others? He registered his protest by resigning as the secretary of the Tamilnadu Congress Party when he saw manipulations in the running of a hostel founded for the weaker sections by the Party itself. He resigned from the Party when its policies were against the Dalits, especially on the question of Reservation. To counter the Brahmin domination he gave shape to the Self-Respect movement. He promoted self-respect marriages and inter-caste marriages without Brahmin rituals. In view of creating an alternative to Hindu Braminic culture, like Phule and Ambedkar, Periyar publicly and severely criticised the Ramayana, Manusmrti, Mahabharata, and other *Sastras*.

Periyar's antagonism to the Brahmanic Hindu culture has helped the socio-political emergence of non–Brahmin castes. His approach has helped to create more awareness among people about inequality and other social evils that are systematically promoted by the dominant caste.

5. Ambedkar and his Interpretation of Caste Culture

Born a Mahar, on April 14, 1891 at Mhow in Madhya Pradesh, Bhimrao was the 14th child of a British Army Major Ramji (1848-1913) and Bhimabai (1854-1896). Ambedkar popularly known as Babasaheb, had his early studies in India. Later he went to Columbia in United States and to London in England

and came back to India as a Barrister-at-Law with a double doctorate, in 1923. He gave up his job in Baroda State when he was insulted in the name of untouchability, for he was a Mahar. He settled down in Bombay, taught as professor at Sydenham College. He contributed significantly to the political and constitutional development of independent India, paving a strong foundation for secularism, socialism and democracy. K. P. Bhagat shows that Ambedkar's vision of and mission for a cultural alternative emerged from his life experiences and took shape in a creative outpour of writings:

> As regards his Socio-Politic-Religio-Economic thoughts it must be pointed out that because he himself suffered from childhood poverty, inequality, injustice, exploitation, tyranny and oppression, and untouchability as a Dalit his main mission in life was to uphold the right of human dignity, liberty, equality and human relationship (fraternity) and to appeal and arouse in humankind the underlying passion for right relations and discard and destroy the caste system and the human curse of untouchability. Therefore, he wrote books in connection with these subjects such as: "The Untouchables, Who are They? And, why have they become Untouchables?" "Caste in India their origin, Genesis and Mechanism", "Who were the Shudras and how they came to be the Forth *Varna* in Indo-Arian Society", "Annihilation of Caste", "Mr. Gandhi and the Emancipation of the Untouchables", "What Congress and Gandhi has done to the Untouchables?"[28]

He started the *Bahiskrit Hitkarini Sabha*, with the motto: "Educate, agitate, organise", at a conference at Barshi in 1927 with the purpose to promote education, culture and economic development of the depressed classes.[29] Like Lord Buddha, Ambedkar, rejected the theory of *Chaturvarn,* and demanded liberty for the downtrodden and the oppressed and the servile classes because they were treated by the caste Hindus as sub-humans worse than beasts.[30] Ambedkar presents his philosophy of an ideal society based on liberty, equality, and fraternity, with indigenous roots in the teachings of Buddha:

> Positively, my social (and political) philosophy may be said to be enshrined in three words: liberty, equality and fraternity. Let no one; however, say that I have borrowed my philosophy from the French Revolution (1789). My philosophy has roots in religion and not in political science. I have derived thus from the teachings of my master, the Buddha.[31]

Ambedkarism is today a living force in India. It is a Dalit movement; in a broader sense it is an anti-caste movement. There are some major themes in Ambedkar's thought that stand out, as enumerated by Gail Omvedt:

> First an uncompromising dedication to the needs of his people, the Dalits, which required the total annihilation of caste and Brahminic superiority it embodied; second, an almost equally strong dedication to the reality of India — but an India whose historical cultural interpretation he sought to wrest from the imposition of a Hindu identity to understand it in its massive popular reality; third, a conviction that the eradication of caste required a repudiation of Hinduism as a religion, and an adoption of an alternative religion which he found in Buddhism, a choice which he saw as not only necessary for the masses of Dalits who followed him but for the masses in India generally; fourth, a broad economic radicalism interpreted as 'socialism' ('state socialism' in some version; 'democratic socialism' in others) mixed with and growing out of his democratic liberalism and liberal dedication to individual rights; fifth, a fierce rationalism which turned through his attacks on Hindu superstitions to interpret even the Buddhism he came to in rationalistic 'liberation theology' forms; and finally, a political orientation which linked a firmly autonomous Dalit movement with a constantly attempted alliance of the socially and economically exploited (Dalits and Shudras, 'workers' and peasants in class terms) projected as an alternative political front to the Congress Party he saw as the unique platform of 'Brahminism' and 'capitalism'.[32]

Around the idea of the individual and his rights Ambedkar built his theory of social and political organisation. The state is the human organisation to encourage the good of the individual, who is considered the centre and the highest value. Ambedkar wrote: "The main purpose behind state socialism is to put an obligation on the state to plan the economic life of the people on lines which would lead to the highest point of productivity without closing any avenue of private enterprise, and also provide for the equitable distribution of wealth."[33] Ambedkar aims at the emergence of a new economic order of the common good and welfare of all, and insists on the need for the implementation of mixed economy, a restructuring of the classes, etc.

Ambedkar rejected not only the Marxist "class theory", but also the kind of "caste theory" represented by the Non-Aryan identity claims of the other Dalit radicals of his time. The two books published in his lifetime, namely, *Who were the Shudras?* And *The Untouchables* and the unpublished manuscripts such as *Revolution and Counter Revolution in the Ancient India*, *The Untouchable Children of India's Ghetto,* show the breadth of his attempt to articulate a historical theory. Ambedkar considers the irreligious and the anti-religious outlook and way of life advocated by Marxism inferior to the Buddhist way. K. P. Bhagat points out the main reason for the preference of Buddhism over Marxism thus:

> Marx advocated abolition of private property through violence, dictatorship of the proletariat (worker) and the withering away of the state, whereas Lord Buddha for social and moral emancipation of humankind staunchly upheld the eightfold path — right view, right mindedness, right speech, right action, right livelihood, right endeavour, right thought and right concentration.[34]

In some of the famous writings such as, "Annihilation of Caste (1938)", "The Buddha and the Future of his Religion (1950)", and "The Buddha and his Dhamma" Ambedkar tried to give his own understanding of religion and its relation to politics and power. Ambedkar pointed to a 'true religion' based on principles replacing the religion of the rulers, and was convinced that the 'true religion' is the foundation of society. The criteria of this kind of religion he put forward, "rests on a view of religion which is somewhat different from the ordinary view according to which religion is concerned with man's relation to God and all that it means. According to this view, religion exists not for the saving of souls but for the preservation of the society and welfare of the individual".[35] Ambedkar bases his concept of religion on a contrast and analysis of two sets of values, the Western democratic principles and Hindu caste cultural principles. The democratic values are universalistic and the Hindu values are particularistic. In a democratic kind of society, freedom of the individual implies a new kind of freedom, the freedom to choose one's religion. The principles of equality, liberty and fraternity can be practiced in a secular society in which religion becomes a matter of personal commitment, whereas in a caste Hindu society the religion is not something which anybody chooses but is set by rules codified in texts like the Manusmrti, which apply to particular people in particular situations. Different categories of people marry only into specific sub-caste, must have different occupations, must live in different parts of the village, and so on.

In *Buddha and the Future of his Religion*, Ambedkar gives an analysis of the ethical principles of Buddhism, Christianity, Islam and Hiduism, and opts for Buddhism. He explains the reason: "I prefer Buddhism... because it gives three principles in combination, which no other religion does. Buddhism teaches *prajna* (understanding as against superstition and supernaturalism), *karuna* (love), and *samata* (equality). This is what man wants for a good happy life. Neither god nor soul can save society".[36] In his interpretation of Buddhism Ambedkar turns to the original teachings of Buddha and Dhamma, and to the social order advocated by him. He prefers the original

Theravada to the *Mahayana* form. His Buddhism can be and is called Neo-Buddhism. Its essence is morality. Its mission on earth is the establishment of the kingdom of righteousness.

6. Gandhi and Interpretation of Caste culture

Gandhiji's perception of the problems surrounding the caste cultural conflict is very complex. He was totally against the untouchability and was committed to its abolition. But at the same time, he wanted to keep the caste system. Ravinder Kumar explains this uneasy and complex attitude:

> Gandhiji's perception of the Dalit location within Hinduism was radically transformative so long as it is remembered that it represented an upper caste solution to the problem. The *varna* system, so the Mahatma argued, was originally based upon a division of labour without being tied to any hierarchical scale of society. The dignity of the artisan or the peasant, for instance, was no less than the dignity of the warrior or the merchant. Over the centuries, however, a social order which extended a status of equality to all those who contributed to the labour that sustained society, changed into one in which there prevailed the grossest form of hierarchy.[37]

As the leader of the Congress Party Gandhi declared: "Swaraj is unattainable without the removal of untouchability as it is without Hindu-Muslim unity".[38] He showed disgust over the evil of untouchability: "Untouchability is not a sanction of religion; it is a device of Satan".[39] He declared untouchability a sin, and there is need of a conversion or change of heart on the part of the upper caste Hindus. He calls for the expiation of such sins:

> To remove untouchability is a penance that the caste Hindus owe to Hinduism and to themselves. Hindus will certainly never deserve freedom, nor get it, if they allow their noble religion to be disfigured by the retention of the taint of untouchability. As I love Hinduism dearer than life itself, the taint has become for me an intolerable burden. Let us not

deny God by denying to a fifth of our race the right of association on an equal footing.⁴⁰

The renaming of Untouchables as *Harijans* was a step forward in his struggle to bring about a social revolution. Gandhiji preached the moral responsibility of every member of the society to get rid of all sins against *Harijans*. Jesudasan clarifies:

> First, it was a sin of disbelief in God, his goodness, and his Fatherhood, making him an "Untouchable". Second, it was a sin of irreligion, a prostitution of religious principles in the name of a satanic institution made by human beings. Third, it was a sin against Hindu religion in particular, spelling the death of Hinduism, since the two could not long survive together. Last, it was a sin against the Harijans, the children of God, the special servants of God, in whom he was especially present.⁴¹

Mahatma Gandhi defended the caste system even as he worked for the transformation of Hindu society. He defended caste system because he found occupational diversity essential in any society, but in his heart he smashed untouchability. E. Stanley Jones reports, perhaps, with a bit of overemphasis, Gandhiji's commitment in this respect: "No one has been a greater force in the breaking of caste than Mahatma Gandhi; caste as a system is crumbling and the Mahatma, by his insistence on getting rid of untouchability, was the greatest in causing it to crumble. For when untouchability goes, caste goes. It is not possible to get rid of one and hold the other. And yet for a while Mahatma tried it."⁴²

Even when Gandhi defended the fourfold division in the caste system, he says that this division is not vertical but horizontal:

> For me *varnashrama* does not mean a graded system of untouchability... It is not a vertical division. It is a horizontal one. In my view all *varnas* stand absolutely on the same plane, i.e., of equality. Hence, there can be no question of

untouchability... I have sufficient warrant in Hindu scriptures for saying that the Brahmins and scavengers are absolutely on a par in the eyes of God.[43]

It is well-known that in the question of Dalits and the caste cultural conflict there were differences in the approach and the method between Gandhi and Ambedkar. Yet they had the common mission: the emancipation of human beings and the country. The main difference between Gandhi and Ambedkar in removing untouchability was in their approach and in the line of action - one was evolutionary and the other was revolutionary says J. R. Kamble:

> Both stood against social evils. Both wanted to reform a corrupt society. But their line of action was different. One was revolutionary and the other was evolutionary. One wanted to reform the existing institution of Hindu society; the other wanted to create a new order based on the concept of justice and equality of all men. To Dr. Ambedkar the institution of untouchability was a sin and was to be destroyed the sooner the better, and, therefore, the *chaturvarna* system must go, and the Hindu society must have a platform shorn of all inequalities. To Mahatma Gandhi it was a religious question. He upheld the *chaturvarna* dharma and proposed gradual changes in it so that in the course of time Hindu hearts would be changed.[44]

The contemporaries of Gandhiji and Ambedkar and all those who witnessed the great deeds done by both the leaders will agree that they have contributed greatly to the nation and the people. The manner of their contributions and sacrifices may be different. Ambedkar, perhaps via Buddhism (and Western influences) stood for the dignity of each individual and the individual's right to *mukti*, while Gandhiji remained an inheritor of the Brahminic philosophy where not the individual but the *genus*, the *jati*, the social order was primary.

In his writings in the thirties and forties Ambedkar rejected the perception of Gandhi surrounding the caste cultural conflict as one compounded with faulty history and a deeply flawed romanticism. The organic linkage of the Dalit communities with the Hindu society, according to Ambedkar is something morally and socially repugnant. The relation between the Dalits and the upper caste Hindus came to a crisis situation in the course of the Constitutional debate in 1932. Ambedkar demanded at the Round Table Conference in London, in 1931, that the Untouchables be considered a minority and granted separate electorate. When the request was granted in August 1932, Gandhi went on an indefinite fast as a protest against such arrangement. Gandhi argued:

> The British proposal was a device designed to condemn the Dalits to a permanent state of political serfdom. We do not want on the requests of our Census Untouchability classified as a separate class... Will Untouchables remain Untouchables in perpetuity? I would foresee rather that Hinduism died than that Untouchability lived.[45]

R. K. Sidhwa said in a meeting in Delhi, "Truly speaking, Gandhi was influenced by Ambedkar to do something for the political rights of the Untouchables. Ambedkar was the liberator of the downtrodden and was a great seer as well."[46]

7. The BSP Movement in North-West India

A characteristic trait of the dominant culture is to impose its ideas and will on the dominated. The dominated or subaltern culture either accepts or rejects the schemes of the dominant. But the generally accepted traditional forms and norms of dominance are getting blurred by the forces of democracy, politics and economics. The resurgence of the Dalits in independent India, with a new political identity is in a way the strength of the weak and the weakness of the strong. The Dalits are mobilised politically, in the urban situations more than in remote villages. The resurgence of the weak Untouchable threatens the dominant. To illustrate the change taking place in the Indian political scene in the milieu of caste-culture carrying the sign of a counter-culture, it will be useful to have a glimpse of the way the Bahujan Samaj Party under the leadership of Kanshi Ram and Mayavati, has emerged as a force in the North-West India.

The Emergence of BSP Movement

The consistent and clear political direction of Ambedkar, though passing through many changing circumstances, gave way to different political formations. In the 1930s Ambedkar formed the Independent Labour Party (ILP) including peasants and workers with a bold peasant-worker action programme. In 1942 the Scheduled Castes Federation (SCF) was formed as a Dalit Party. The political aspirations of Ambedkar to develop a broader movement led him to declare his willingness to work with the backward castes and scheduled tribes and to accept a federal merger with the Socialists, the Justice Party and the Kisan Mazdur Party, without jeopardising the SCF's autonomy. Before his death, Ambedkar finally gave a call to form a party representing all the exploited groups, which resulted in the creation of the Republican Party.

In the 1970s in the Western and Southern parts of the country there emerged many Dalit organisations like Dalit Panthers in Maharashtra in 1972, the Dalit Sangharsh Samiti in Karnataka in 1974 etc., representing a new generation of educated the Dalit leaders. They protested against the failure of the state to eradicate caste oppression and untouchability. Drawing upon the Marxist and Ambedkarite traditions they tried to form a broad coalition of Dalits, non-brahmins, middle and low castes, peasants and workers.[47]

The Bahujan Samaj Party (BSP) movement that was concentrated in the Northern and Western India and proposed "Bahujan" as the new cultural identity of the Dalits.[48] Its emergence was the culmination of an evolutionary socio-political process started in Dec. 6, 1978 by Kanshi Ram and his colleagues with the establishment of the BAMCEF (Backward and minority community Employ's Federation) for the Scheduled Castes, Scheduled Tribes, Other Backward Classes and Minorities. The primary objective of the organisation was: "to subject our problems to close scrutiny and find out quick and equitable solutions to the problems of injustice and harassment of our employees in general and the educated employees in particular.[49] Kanshi Ram belonging to a Sikh Chamar background from Punjab employed in a Pune laboratory resigned his job in 1964 following a long-drawn dispute on caste issues. He spent time to discover Ambedkar and determined to dedicate his life to the movement. Dissatisfied with the way the Republican Party's was working, after seven years of committed service he decided to have a different kind of organisation which we call today the BSP. It represents a new political assertion by the Dalits, that comes after a long period of fragmentation and absorption/ cooperation by or with the Congress.

Through the BAMCEF Kanshi Ram established a network of the educated employees first in Maharashtra and then in Central and North India. He also mobilised other sections of society that resulted in the creation of a well-disciplined cadre, which helped the organisation of what is called, in BAMCEF's terminology, "Man, Money and Mind Power".[50]

Kanshi Ram's socio-political thrust and rhetoric gave birth to the DS4 (Dalit Shoshit Samaj Sangarsh Samiti) on 6th December 1981. Many Dalit conscientisation programmes were organised under this banner. Some such programmes were: "Poona Pact Denunciation Programme", "Miracle of Two Feet and Two Wheels", "People's Parliament", "Social Action for Equality and Self-respect", "Baraiely March against Liquor Sellers", etc. The focus of all these programmes was the problems of the Dalits in the whole of India.

Evolving a Political Base

From social awareness programmes Kanshi Ram moved quickly towards political action in Northern India. It is necessary to see this political phenomena in its specific socio-historical and geographical contexts. Gail Omvedt observes while saying that Kanshi Ram has an appeal to Dalits in an all India basis, his political base is limited to the North-West of India, that too in the Chamar-caste group:

> Though Kanshi Ram has an all-India appeal to Dalits, and though his root organisation, BAMCEF, is all-India in scope, so far the political base of the BSP has been limited to Northern India, North-West India, to be more accurate. In spite of the genuine ability to appeal to other backward and minority communities, the main social base has been the large Chamar caste-group, just as that of Ambedkar and the Replublican Party today whose social base is the Mahars of Maharashtra.[51]

Kanshi Ram criticised the political reservation for Dalits (Art. 330 and Art. 332), telling that it is only a means to produce stooges who serve the upper castes by speaking the language of their political party. In his book *The Chamcha Age,* he argued that combined electorate gives only symbolic, not real representation to Dalits.[52] In what it called "limited political action", the DS4 put up forty-six candidates for the assembly elections in Haryana in 1982.[53] It was quite astonishing that the position of the DS4 candidates in terms of percentage of votes polled was very satisfactory and in fact better than many other established political parties.[54] The Bahujan Samaj Party was launched on April 14, 1984, on Babasaheb Ambedkar's birth anniversary. The new name of "Bahujans" that Kanshi Ram gave for Dalits, OBCs and Minorities helped to create a new identity for these sections of people.

Soon after its foundation the BSP put up candidates for the Lok Sabha elections of December 1984 and the U. P. Vidhan Sabha elections in March 1985. Though it lost all the seats contested in both elections, it won over a million votes in the Lok Sabha elections, and in the Uttar Pradesh Assembly elections it was thought to have played a decisive enough role in drawing votes away from the Congress, giving fifty one seats to Lok Dal and Janata Party candidates.[55] According to Kanshi Ram, in line with Ambedkar's description, the Congress Party is a unique blend of 'Capitalism' and 'Brahminism'. It has been responsible for a pattern of development in which despite considerable progress after independence the benefits have not reached the weaker sections.[56] In the Punjab Vidhan Sabha polls also it was thought to have played a decisive role in turning the tide of the Akali Dal. In the Bijnor Lok Sabha by-elections in December 1985 the ruling Party's prestigious candidate Meera Kumar (daughter of late Jagjivan Ram) just managed with a meagre margin of five thousand votes over the BSP candidate. The Allahabad Lok Sabha by-election in July 1987 was the crucial one, where along with V. P. Singh of the Opposition and Sunil Shastri of the Congress, Kanshi Ram contested. Kanshi Ram managed to get eighteen percent of the total votes compared to Sunil Shastri's twenty four percent and V. P. Singh's fifty two percent. Here Kanshi Ram emerged as a national figure and the BSP as a new political force on the national scene.

The ideology of the BSP aims at replacing the Brahminical political rule by that of the Dalit Bahujans, to provide the latter with better and faster economic advancement. 'Political Power', according to Kanshi Ram, is the key by which any lock (obstacle) can be opened.[57] Another central tenet of the Party's ideology is the concept of retributive social justice which, it is argued, would correct historical wrongs and provide the Dalits with their right socio-economic and political place in the society.[58] The slogans of the Party are very clear: *Jiski Jitani Sankhya Bhari Uski Utani Bhagidari* (Everyone should get representation according to the strength), *Mat Hamara Raj Tumhara, Nahi Chalega Nahi Chalega* (Our vote and your rule, no longer, no longer).

Politics of Alliance

The Bahujan Smaj Party entered into alliance with Mulayam Singh Yadav's Samajwadi Party (SP) in the Uttar Pradesh

Assembly elections in 1993. Nobody expected that the BSP-SP alliance could keep the Bharatiya Janata Party (BJP) away from power, after it attained the "martyrdom status" at the *Babri Masjid* and *Ramjanma Bhoomi* tangle reaching its climax on 6th December, 1992 and its government was dismissed by the President on the same day. The BSP-SP alliance created a vote bank which comprised the Dalits, the Muslims and the backwards. Though the BSP benefited from this alliance in spreading its base with 67 seats in the assembly, the alliance could not last long as it was not natural.

The alliance broken with the SP, the BSP supremo accepted the offer of the BJP to support unconditionally the BSP. This was just an *ad hoc* arrangement to avoid the split in BSP, though many criticised the leadership. The rift between SP and BSP was exploited by BJP.[59] The BJP had clear designs to split the BSP by supporting the first ever Dalit government to get the sympathy from Dalits and making inroads to them. When the BSP did not accept the plan of the BJP, out of frustration the leadership pulled down the BSP government.

In a similar way, with minor changes, an alliance was formed between the BSP and the BJP. This coming together of the two parties without much ideological agreement – agreeing only that each party having the Chief Ministership for six months. In the tenure of Mayavati, the BSP Chief Minister, and her government lead by the BSP, tried for the first six months to implement the party's programmes and policies of social transformation, injecting a lot of enthusiasm among the Dalits. The alliance could not stand long as the *Hindutva* forces continued to harm the Dalits. It culminated in the split of the BSP, engineered by the BJP.

Pursuing the goal of the party Kanshi Ram entered into alliance with Congress (I) in 1996 assembly elections. Though the BSP played a decisive role in forging the alliance relegating the National Party, with 110 years of history and the legacy of the freedom struggle, to a minor partner, it did not benefit much from this. On the other hand the Congress Party could consolidate its lost ground.

In the February 2002 Vidhan Sabha elections in UP the Bahujan Samaj Party performance surpassed all predictions and it emerged as the second largest party in the assembly. About the upsurge of the underprivileged in the North India referring to the UP elections the *Hindustan Times* reports:

> If the last decade of electoral politics in UP has a place in history, it is not for its unstable governments and strange coalitions. It has a special place as a political laboratory, where the new social equations of North India were fashioned, through the democratic upsurge of the underprivileged. The big question in this election was: has the transition from a regime dominated by upper castes and upper classes to one dominated by Dalits and members of the *Bahujan Samaj* been completed in UP? Intertwined with this question was another issue: will the hold of the caste over the political imagination of the voters become weaker? The defeat of the BJP in this election does not look like a simple anti-incumbency verdict..... At stake is a social order that has worked to the advantage of a few and against the majority. That is why political fortunes have been deadlocked in the last few elections.[60]

Though the Samajwadi Party emerged as largest party in the hung assembly, with a tally of 143 seats in the assembly of 403 seats, the animosity of the BJP and the BSP towards the SP brought together the BSP and the BJP with its allies in the coalition government in which Mayawati was sworn in as Chief Minister on May 3, 2002 for the third time. This time Mayawati managed to govern the state as Chief Minister one year and few months. When the BJP withdrew its support to the government, the largest party headed by Mulayam Singh Yadav managed a split in the BSP and with the support of this split group and with that of the smaller opposition parties like the Congress formed the government. The BSP-BJP coalition governments proved short-lived due to the differences in the socio-cultural polices the partners had.

Achievements of BSP Movement

The achievements of BSP in a short span of its existence are significant. With political mobilisation and assuming state power, though for a brief period, first for four months in June 1995 and then for six months in March 1997, and finally for one and a half years in 2002, the BSP has contributed to the construction of a new history for the Dalits. Mayawati is the first Dalit woman in the independent India to become the Chief Minister of a state, with an independent Dalit leadership. To become the Chief Minister of UP. thrice is a great achievement for a Dalit woman in a male dominated Indian society. Mendelshon and Vicziany rightly say:

> Mayawati has been able to bring a charisma and liveliness to the hustings.... She has represented a novelty — a direct and forthright Dalit woman with courage sufficient to run hard against powerful institutions that so suppress poor Indians. In short, Mayawati has become both considerably popular and also a force to reckon with.[61]

The BSP tried to popularise the legacy of the Dalit prophets like Mahatma Jyotibha Phule, Chhatrapati Sahuk Maharaj, Periyar, E.V. Ramaswamy Naikar, Sri Narayana Guru, Babasaheb Bhimrao Ambedkar, etc. Through the creation of the pantheon of the leaders and referring to their teachings, especially of Buddha, Balmiki, Ravidas, Swami Achootanand etc., the party tried to mobilise different sections of the society, especially the most backward sections.

To concretise the identity of "Bahujan Samaj" along with the construction of a new history, and the evolution of the pantheon of leaders the BSP tried construct physical symbols. Examples are the construction of "Ambedkar Park", "Parivartan Chouck", "Ambedkar Village Development Scheme" etc. The creation of physical symbols contributed in raising the self-esteem and self-respect of the Dalits. Along with the physical symbols cultural symbols also were created for the speedy mobilisation of the Dalit masses. *Jai Bheem* became the symbol of greeting with in the Bahujan fraternity. The BSP organised meals and fairs which became the cultural symbols of the Dalits and OBCs. It organised the Ambedkar Mela, Periyar Mela, Sahuji Maharaj Mela etc. to mobilise solidarity among the Dalits and to develop the consciousness among them for their own cultural traits.

With the evolution of different identity and the construction of cultural and political symbols the BSP has created a distinct socio-political grouping. This is in contrast with and opposed to "Homogenised Hindu Majority" as propagated by Hindutva forces. It has necessarily created some tensions, as Vivek Kumar observes: "With this independent Dalit leadership and BSP's expansion of base, tensions with dominant castes and Dalits on the one hand and state institutions on the other have increased. This can be proved by the increase in atrocities against the Dalits by the upper castes and breaking alliances first with the OBC (Samajwadi Party) and then the upper caste dominated party, the BJP".[62]

Sudha Pai mentions the significant achievements of the BSP in the recent past in the Dalit culture in its different dimensions:

> This has created a new identity and counter ideology to the *varna* system.... It has succeeded in removing the hold of Brahminical ideology and the submissive attitude of the Dalits, providing them with a new confidence, self-respect and hope of freedom from oppression, together with economic development... In politics these achievements have helped break down the vertical pattern–client relationship with the upper castes and constructed new solidarities on horizontal dimension. The BSP has made good use of the political space available to it following the decline of the Congress system to emerge as a strong political party in U. P.[63]

The rise of BSP in UP. has great political significance, and speaks volumes about the Dalit mobilisation. Kanshi Ram's vision and strategy, and his understanding of social change proved fruitful. The BSP entered into the politics of alliance, because he believed in the primacy of capturing political power as a means of social reform. The progressive broadening of the political base and the political assertion by the Dalits and the underprivileged in the North West India is certainly creating ripples in the socio-cultural and caste cultural scene of contemporary India. It is a crystalisation of the vision and strategy of Kanshi Ram, which he inherited from the great visionary Ambedkar.

CHAPTER VII

THE INDIAN UNTOUCHABLES' CRITIQUE OF CASTE CULTURE

It is difficult to live in a cultural world where people detach themselves from the life and the problems surrounding the "culture" and reifying it and go for a one arid and one-dimensional discourse of it, under the hold of power and domination, as is seen generally in the caste cultural world. Untouchables, who live mostly in such a caste milieu with its socio-culturally determined and religiously sanctioned way of life thrust upon them, find it difficult to cope with life. Human values like justice, equality, fraternity, community, etc. are the focus of the critique one has to make in such a conflict situation. Conflict is basically a part of any life process. The term 'conflict' is derived from Latin root *con-fligere* to mean 'to strike together' which implies "fight, clash, sharp or mild disagreement or even antagonism". Conflicts vary:

> Sometimes they are constructive, some times destructive. Whenever human agency is alive and active, they appear rather clearly, in a positive or negative manner. They are found at the intra-personal, inter-personal, intra-group and inter-group levels. In the conflict between disempowered subalterns and the ruling elite, we choose to side with the disadvantaged. In the struggle, we become aware that the tensions visible at the public realm (in social, political, economic transactions) and those invisibly operative at the interior realm (psychological sediments from nature and nurture, religio-cultural world-views, personal and collective preunderstandings) are interrelated.[64]

For those who are struggling to feed themselves, to satisfy their hunger and thirst, it is impossible to live. For them it is not the intellectual coherence or consistency that reigns supreme but pragmatic necessity. Let us have food first, they think, even if it is dirty or waste from the one who stigmatises. This stamps one's identity with the seal of inferiority, and deforms the self.

1. The Untouchables' Critique – indigenous and integral

Plurality is a fact which poses a challenge to any univocal, uni-dimensional approach to any kind of reality. "Any kind of homogenisation of the subalterns by putting together various categories of differentiation (like caste, gender, class, age, status, office, power, forced migration, ethnic origin, linguistic identity etc.) fails to attend to the uniqueness of each brand of subalternity."[65] A. Thumma observes: "Plurality, the hallmark of Indian reality, is multi-lingual, multi-religious, multi-ethnic, multi-regional and multi-cultural."[66] So a pluri-dimensional, integral approach is called for in the understanding and interpreting the caste reality with its many dimensions: economic-political, psychological-social and religio-cultural. The Untouchables, the victim of the caste cultural life with its sharp division of self and the other and scattered into the boundaries, seem to occupy the centre-stage in the critique of caste culture that is indigenous and integral.

Facing each other, the Untouchable and the caste Hindu elicit a characteristic relationship of the dominated and the dominant. The dominant castes impose their ideas and will on the dominated, constructing a "crushing objecthood"[67] for the Untouchables by excluding, distancing, stigmatising, and subordinating them. We see in the ideology and attitude of the high castes a case of constructing a nature for the Untouchable: dirty, filthy, impure, depraved, people who "must have" sinned in a past life. The dominated normally take one of the two courses: either accept the schemes put forward by the high caste actors or reject them in a way suitable to the social situation.

Although this has been the standard social script for the Untouchables, there is a marked change in contemporary India. The modern Indian State marked by a liberal democracy, parliamentary system, general elections and egalitarian socialist ideals, has found it hard to inculcate the values of equality and liberty among the Indian masses, shaped by a hierarchical social structure and benumbed by a caste ideology.[68]

In this changed situation, the Indian Untouchables register their dissatisfaction and affirm that they deserve a higher position and role than the one given to them by the caste Hindus. They challenge: Why should high caste Hindus have precedence in the social set up? They begin to insist that they are there not merely as signified; they do signify too.[69] They have become more and more alert and sensible to the problems they face, despite the fact that they were dependent on the dominant others, they seek survival from their problems with dignity. The Untouchables today see change from earlier times, and challenge the tradition and test the promises of Indian democracy. But those changes are hardly enough, Khare cautions, and he suggests the necessity to have an effective cultural critique and an ideology for the Indian Untouchables:

> The issues of the positive self-image, social fairness, and practical effectiveness engage the contemporary Untouchable in India. The changing politics of culture, especially in this century, shape his expectations and strategies. To survive in today's political culture, therefore, the Untouchables must have not only a positive cultural ideology but also an ideological voice; he must have an effective cultural reasoning and not merely tenacity for daily survival.[70]

Today the urban Untouchables express resentment of their traditional deprivation and dependence and turn to democratic politics and its version of social justice for support and direction. It is true that a fundamentally positive ideology and assertive identity are the most urgent needs of the contemporary Untouchables. From the research and study Khare has made in this respect, he observes that these positive attitudes are much harder to achieve. But he affirms the need to go along with the indigenous thought and experience in the method of interpretation:

> Yet as certain civilisational categories provide genuine value formulations, the categories do not stop there; they also evade static value oppositions to raise a truly Indic - holistic and cosmological - lexis and praxis. As Derrida has said, "To deconstruct the opposition is first.... to overthrow [*renverser*] the hierarchy." The construction and deconstruction of differences actually go hand in hand in indigenous thought and experience; each must not only culminate in the other but also transcend itself and the other. As indicated in the text, a Derrida-style erasure, dispersal, and indeterminacy may help capture the presence and meaning of such "differences" within the Indian scheme. Obviously all such interpretations refer to a configuration of critical Indic notions (*i.e., dharma, karma, maya*, and *samsara*) that guides the recognition and passage of all distinctions and differences between self and society.[71]

The Indian Untouchables, though estranged from the caste Hindus, continue to share the same civilisational framework of them. They also dispute the cultural basis of the identity thrust upon them by the high caste actors to exclude, distance, stigmatise and subordinate them. It is a debate "whether it is a social personality mentally leveraged into social existence by the opposition of the pure and the impure, or an identity framed conceptually by ideas of a biomoral nature of coded-substance, or a typification of the "other" scraped off the concrete surface of the stigmatising roles they play in cultural life, or all of these, but agrees that it is an identity culturally constituted."[72] If the identity given to the Untouchables by the high caste embodies the other, the identity the Untouchables take upon themselves culturally will be both the other and the self. That is to say the Untouchables project themselves into the opposites, the other and the self.

The Low caste actors express a kind of self-contradiction in the way they reject and affirm the hierarchy, place themselves within and beyond it. They often have an ambivalent multiple consciousnesses of the self and the world due to the acceptance and rejection of the dominant culture that constructs them as "other". So they fall into the trap of embodying the other in their own eyes. They allow the high caste ideology to form their own self–concepts. The question is: if the Untouchables are constituted out of a culture, can they reject this second nature and construct the self and society differently, reform culture and emancipate themselves externally and internally?

Parish clarifies that Untouchables are not that passive always but in deep dialogue with culture and redefine and reimagine culture and self:

> These are key questions: people do not magically stand free of the cultural attitudes that stigmatise them, but respond to the threat, the challenge, posed. Confronted with the images others hold of them, they do not just internalise, or just resist: they internalise and resist. Rather than seeing the untouchable as born a creative resister in the cradle, or passively created by the dominant culture, we need to see how they struggle to achieve identities and open up cultural spaces for themselves. Almost unavoidably, any untouchable as an individual self is inhabited, haunted, subverted, by the high caste, collective version of himself, even if, even as, this image of self is rejected. This is the dialogue with culture that untouchables are — it defines them as other to caste Hindu and other to self, and they respond, re-defining themselves, reimagining culture and self.[73]

2. The Articulation of the Untouchables in counter-cultural discourses

Many movements and action groups identifying with the subaltern groups like Dalits have developed ideologies and theologies on the issues concerning the meaning of life, the significance of their struggle, their value system, ultimate goals, faith vision, understanding of justice, etc., flowing from deep commitment and reflection.[74] They come to interpret life and events subjecting the dominant ideologies to severe critique. Parish points out the dynamics, relationship and the interaction between ideology and critique, a process taking place within the self:

> The Untouchables identify with and struggle against meanings they embody for others; they project themselves into ideology and into critique, finding identity in both. However, whatever critique of caste ideology the Untouchable makes, that critique develops within a cultural self that ideology helps constitute and shape, or that it subverts and threatens, perhaps having all these relations to self at once. The critique is critique from the inside, from within self, from within a culture, in intimate ways.[75]

While pursuing the enquiry into the Untouchable's critique of caste-culture one has to reflect both on the way the Untouchable is made to embody the other in the "Indian caste culture" and understand the way the Untouchables treat the caste Hindus as their other. The Untouchable critique can be found recorded in many important works like Parish's (1997), in the discussion we had about his encounter with the low caste Newars, and in Khare (1978, 1984), Feeman (1979), Mahar (1972), etc. In most of the above-mentioned works the method of interpretation used is deconstruction. Parish explains the method and its dynamics in the Indian context:

> Like many others exasperated by this term's [deconstruction] misuse and by excesses associated with it, I have at times wished it would go away — but I find I need the concept, or something like it, to sustain a necessary project: to conduct multiple interpretative readings of multiple indigenous "readings" of Hindu-Indian culture, where such indigenous "readings" radically contradict each other, while also suffering from radical self-contradiction. In a certain sense, the Untouchables I seek to understand have a deconstructive

stance towards "Hindu" culture. Untouchables often subvert normative and dominant interpretations of culture. They question the ethical, ontological, and existential status of key cultural constructs, they endeavour to examine the way these are produced and understood, taken up in life and put into practice. They take the pieces of culture apart and reassemble them, amending, and supplementing culture in the process, giving a "spin" to symbols and meanings that they lack in the dominant community.[76]

As moral and political discourses such readings sometimes contradict each other. I here visualise culture both as contested and shared, for the grounds on which the Untouchables dispute the dominant ideology are often equivocal. In the caste system, a person does not want to be lower than others, and at the same time he/she wants to be higher. In the same way a person who resents the superiority of the higher caste may resent efforts by those lower to claim equality. People are both for emancipation and domination.

The Critique and its Language

A critique becomes an alternative ideology or "counter-ideology,"[77] which too is subject to critique. Parish points out the problem in conceptualising non-dominant meanings. For what the low caste actors formulate the "culture-as-critique" generating a discourse is in turn critiqued by the high caste in their language, to defend their own position in the culture. There are two sets of discourses constructed by two sets of actors seeking contradictions in each other's cultural productions. The analysts who seek to construct coherence for a culture that may not possess it the problem consists in conceptualising non-dominant meanings that may co-exist in the same mind with the dominant ideology. The temptation may then be to overlook them or dismiss them, or not to conceptualise their significance. Since "conflicting" schema and "non-dominant" ideology can have sociological and psychological significance that may be used by different actors from the one culture they share to produce different "readings" from different understandings, this is not justified.[78]

In India many different cultures co-exit. There is sharing of certain aspects and resistance in others. Parish observes the mutuality and the difference between them:

> The caste Hindu and the untouchable may "have" the same culture, but "read" it in different ways, and animate it as a vehicle for thought and life in radically different ways. Their readings overlap, but also diverge. Shared concepts have contested meanings in "Indian" culture; we need to explore both, the shared forms and their disputed significance. We should certainly not dismiss the untouchable's point of view or fail to assess its sociological and psychological significance because it is self-contradictory and equivocal, or because it is often restructured "back into" the hierarchical institution and ideology from which it emerged, reflected on, criticised and resisted more or less strongly. [79]

The world of caste is a world of oppression. It exposes people to deprivation, and produces a situation where life is surrounded by fear. Caste is a world of dissimulation or distorted communication based on denial of mutual recognition. Parish writes about how the distorted communication takes shape when the different caste actors try to communicate in the context of caste cultural conflict:

> The world of caste is a world of violence and deprivation. In this context, the language of hierarchical models is often used to articulate not the consensual grip of hierarchical models, but the experience of domination, violence, deprivation those models formulate, organise and legitimise, because it is the only language permitted, and the key to surviving. I would argue that low caste people often appropriate the language of hierarchy, give it a different "spin" in their own minds, define how it is to be interpreted with tacit or explicit metacommunications - ranging from an exaggerated obsequiousness to a fatalistic shrug and declaration that "we

have to eat" to irony - and so inflect the idioms of hierarchy to express their sense of deprivation, powerlessness and resentment. [80]

There are other ways the low caste individuals and communities show their dissatisfaction and protest against the stigma and oppression they face, and against the dominant ideology of hierarchy. Khare (1984) does this by distinguishing the role of the Untouchable ascetics vs. caste-oriented renouncers as a way of "liberation" in some of the root concepts of South Asian cultural tradition. By assuming the key symbol of "renouncer" the Untouchables work out a critique and counter-ideology. "In response to their systematic and effective marginalisation by the sacred tradition of the elite in each culture, subalterns create pragmatic and constructive counter-symbols that uphold the values of protection of life, production for livelihood and procreation of new life."[81]

Sathianathan Clarke speaks about the production of a cultural world of the Dalits and other counter-ideologies and the dynamics involved that serve as the resource for peoples' emancipation. There are two ways in dealing with the Dalit culture: the first one is self-affirmation. It consists in the understanding the complexity and richness of the production of the cultural world of Dalits embedded in their cultural and religious world and accepting it wholeheartedly. The second way emerges from the fact that the survival and the promotion of the particularity of the Dalit cultural identity depends on the successful resistance to dominant forces that seek to obliterate, co-opt and demonise it. "The resistive dynamic to counter such dominating tendencies is subsequent to the act of claiming the self-identity of Dalits. In other words, the self-actualising and self-expressing dimension of Dalit communities, which can be grasped through the variety of their cultural representation, must be reasserted; after which the countering tendencies of resistance and rebuttal can be incorporated. An examination of the motifs of self-projection and self-promotion, however discriminatingly and subtly they may be exhibited in the culture of Dalits, precedes an analysis into its counter-hegemonic and anti-*status quo* tendencies".[82] The Dalit culture is both self-affirmation ('yes') and rejection ('no').

The critique and counter-ideologies are not outside the culture but a dynamic aspect of it. Another language the Untouchables make use to arrive at a critique is the sexual politics of caste. We see an inter-connection between the gender hierarchy and caste hierarchy. For many not the opposition between pure and impure or the upper caste and the lower caste, but the opposition between male and female is the most basic prototype of the hierarchy. Their opinion is that God created only two castes – male and female. Caste hierarchy can go but the gender hierarchy will remain as natural and necessary.

The Untouchables make use of a language of necessity that disputes with the language of hierarchy, as it comes out of the pragmatic strategies of life which Khare terms the "pragmatic ethos". Kancha and other low caste Newars used to say: "We have to eat". Whatever they do is not from their free will, but forced on them as they have to eat. This expresses the coercion they are in that robs them of their freedom.

It is clear, therefore, that the Untouchables make use not of only a single language, hierarchy, based on the opposition of pure and impure, but a cluster of languages with which the actors interpret reality in a variety of ways. The privileged and the dominant ones use mainly the language of hierarchy in their cultural productions. The language of hierarchy is a veiled language of power in its effort to assert and justify domination, and is connected with politics and history.

3. Counter-ideologies through Dissimulation

To explain and explore the actions and experience of the actors who make a critique on dominant ideologies we make use of the concept of the dissimulation. Parish gives many examples of dissimulation where efforts are often made to conceal one's caste background by taking high caste names and other tactics and explains how dissimulation can occur differently in different contexts of hierarchical interaction and practice:

> Dissimulation does not always have to represent a conscious policy; sometimes dissimulation is deliberate, and other times represent the activation of cultural knowledge in frame-sensitive or context sensitive ways. In these frames, as actors participate in hierarchical interactions and practices, they may accept the structuring of behaviour and the disciplining of consciousness entailed by the context. Doing so actors may not always actively "know what they know" — that is, they are not acting on knowledge and values they possess consciously ...in other settings, where they may be overtly critical of caste, but on the basis of knowledge and values relevant to the particular hierarchically structured context with which they are engaged. Other knowledge and values are kept "out of frame" and perhaps "out of mind" - for the duration of the interaction.[83]

We have an example in James Freeman's volume, *Untouchable: An Indian Life History*, an intimate and disturbing life history of an Indian Untouchable, named Muli. He belongs to the *Bauri* caste, lives in a village on the outskirts Bhubaneshwar, the capital city of Orissa. He lives in a segregated ward, apart from the high caste neighbourhood. As Muli belongs to the *Bauri* caste, the bottom of the caste system, he belongs to the 20 percent who continuously face the threat of starvation. Only 20 percentage of the village live comfortably according to Freeman.[84] Muli starved in his life quite often he recalls his childhood "as a time when he was always hungry."

The high caste villagers stigmatise the *Bauri*, and justify their caste rank with the usual concepts: untouchables must have done something wrong in previous lives, are inherently polluting, are polluted because of their occupation.[85] As low castes, the *Bauri* resent ill treatment and reject the dominant ideology.[86]

They act in conformity with the higher caste rules; there are times when they confront and challenge high caste actors. "A *Bauri* insultingly tells a Brahman who cheats him that if he is so greedy for the *Bauri's* property, why doesn't he also eat *Bauri's* excrement?" They are not ready to accept any differences in cultural terms for the caste differences (as the separation of the pure and the impure). The only difference they will attribute to the high caste is that "they have more money".

Freeman gives the description of Muli when he first met.[87] A "gaunt forty-year-old with betel blackened teeth" Muli was "sitting in the dusty road in front of one of the small thatched roof tea shop in the village, with his glass and saucer placed conspicuously beside him a silent signal to the shopkeeper that an untouchable wants to buy some tea." Three men were on the bench, taking tea and gossiping. The servant boy does not attend Muli, instead ignores him, even pours on him insults. Muli "dropped two coins into the boy's outstretched arm". He drinks his tea obtained through the ritual of abasement. And when he leaves, he has to perform the ritual that defines him. "Suddenly he stood up and shuffled off, crouching to show respect, so that as he passed by the men in the teashop his right hand trailed in the dust." This he does to show the established pattern of displaying one's status. Sometimes, elsewhere, he mocks high caste pretensions, which are not worthy to be respected. He sometimes ridicules the high caste people and devises strategies to make them dependent on him.

Freeman writes on the scepticism of Muli concerning the purity-pollution complex:

> Muli's belief in the concept of ritual pollution, applied only to limited situations. While he believed that a corpse polluted immediate relatives, he ridiculed the idea that *Bauris* pollute high castes, and he even questioned whether higher caste people themselves really believe it, since he saw them disregard such notions when they became inconvenient.[88]

Parish highlights some of the values and attitudes and images the Untouchables capable of providing counter-ideologies, posing some questions:

> Such attitude towards high castes and the images and experiences that nurture this scepticism, represent knowledge and values; but not the knowledge and values expressed in crouching in front of high caste actors. Does Muli experience but conceal this other knowledge of caste life as he crouches before the high caste people? Is this knowledge active in his mind as he drags his arm in the dust to show respect? Does he conceal his attitudes towards caste in the way he might conceal amusement by putting a hand to his month to cover a smile or laughter? Or, does he conceal his knowledge also from himself and practice a form of self-deception?[89]

The answer may not be of course either-or. Man has the capacity for doing things with irony. The Untouchable may be stooping down; at the same time he knows how much he needs to resent the caste system. Dissonant and dissident knowledge may be active in the way an actor experiences or evaluates a situation, may inflect the meaning of an interaction.[90] The Untouchables might not act and interact as the high caste actors do, since it might expose them to violence and deprivation. Despite changes in law, despite modernisation, despite reform movements, the world of caste continues to be a world of violence and deprivation for the multitudes of Untouchables; it means not only a state of discrimination but also of intimidation. Where high castes have power over low castes, caste relations are ultimately enforced with beatings or economic sanctions and in extreme cases by murder or massacre.[91]

4. Practical ethos of Living: The idiom of Necessity

Among the Untouchables whom Parish encountered, many said often like Kancha; "We have to eat." Both literally and critically, this defines the idiom of necessity. This is a fact that they have to eat, and so are forced to do many things that they do not want to do. There is a coercion that robs them of their freedom.

Freeman describes the plight of the family of Muli. At one time, they were eating only one meal every other day. No one even gave a loan of rice to them. They used to dig up roots and steal *yams* from the fields to satisfy their hunger. Muli's wife took to "selling" berries, which Freeman observes as a slightly distinguished way of begging. "Buyers exchanged rice for berries, knowing that the seller was poor and probably starving."[92]

There is a complementarity between the idiom of hunger and idiom of purity in India. It is not possible to have structures based on the opposition of pure and the impure to be practiced in India without power and desperation. "The primal language of this concrete world is hunger, spoken before, and around, and through the idiom of purity, which is — for many — only a supplement, a deformation, of the idiom of necessity."[93] Untouchables like Kancha, challenge and invite us to see and evaluate their actions not in terms of the cultural code of the dominant ideology, but in terms of their experience having to do with the necessities of life. Parish elaborates how the Untouchables exhibit their pragmatic strategy to interpret and conform to caste rules with a twist that gives them a different meaning:

> Low caste actors ask us to do what they do — to reinterpret their conformity, to translate it into the idiom of necessity, the language of pragmatic survival strategies.... With Untouchables we may have to "translate" the meaning of their conformity to caste rules into the terms and concepts they themselves use to interpret it which give a different "spin" to things. We can only do this by paying very close attention to the fine texture of their communicative practices — and by not giving in to the temptation to ignore their inflections of the language of domination. It is easy to privilege the dominant ideology, to take it too literally, and grant it monopoly status as the foundation of cultural reality and worldview. Untouchables know and articulate it, but also inflect, question, and reinterpret it.[94]

There is an identification of the language of experience with the language of necessity for many Untouchables. The low caste actors seem to speak the language of purity and impurity on their acts; but they may be speaking the language of necessity.

5. Ascetics and the Dalit Critique

There is another set of Untouchable voices from Lucknow, the capital of Uttar Pradesh, where R.S. Khare [1984] did his fieldwork. He explored the cultural consciousness of three different *Chamars* (an urban Untouchable group) neighbourhoods, embodying different aspects of *Chamar* experience. One of the neighbourhoods is inhabited by somewhat well to do and well-placed *Chamars*: educated professionals, skilled workers, government employees, shopkeepers, etc. Labourers, leather workers, small vendors, etc. inhabit the second neighbourhood, which contrasts with the first. They have low payment; and they are not protected by the city government from the flooding of the open drain along their living area. They are a neglected group. They experience alienation and deprivation. Though many active reformers, radical ascetics, Buddhist households lived there, their helplessness and deprivation continued. The third neighbourhood lives on the outskirts of the city, like an urban hamlet, a village-like settlement where reform consciousness is muted. Among them, there are city workers who lead the community towards city prospects, life styles and social change. The rest, the majority, work as field labourers – a position rejected by the younger and urban oriented ones. Khare's interest lies on the meanings for the Chamars of the low caste ascetics found in all three neighbourhoods, and on how they see reform ideology as supported by and grown from the values and practices of low caste asceticism.

Khare introduces asceticism as the significant cultural form that is shared both by the Untouchables and the Brahmins, but sees its different meanings. He writes that the attempt by the untouchables to "liberate" the concept of asceticism from the distortion is done by distinguishing a "culture of the deprived" from the culture of the upper caste in thought and experience. Such an asceticism delivered from the distortion of the upper caste Hindus embodies the hopes and aspirations of the Untouchables. The ascetic symbolises in the minds of the Untouchables a "moving utopia," as they represent "a forceful moral critique of a caste ordered society," "subverting unjustified inequality and launching "alternative symbolisations" of the social world.[95]

Khare lists five central features of Indian asceticism:

1. Identification of the personal self and ultimate sacred self.
2. The ascetic is beyond the moral categories and controls of society: not immoral, but amoral,
3. Egalitarianism...
4. The ascetic achieves an "ultimate" spiritual state from which he can know and reveal the "roots of morality that upholds the length and breadth of the entire Indian tradition."...
5. The ascetic is a symbol of self, representing an aspect of the ideal self; and as such the ascetic is treated as "a moral image immanent in all humans." Untouchables and Brahmans alike told Khare that "the *yogi* and *bhogi* [the ascetic and enjoyer of life] reside in everyone." The self-image the ascetic embodies is supposed to be cultivated over the long term as self-control. (pp.24-25.-as summarised in Parish, 185)

According to Khare the first three of these features are traditionally recognised by the Hindu society as well, and so are not contested as others.

Politics of Asceticism and the Countercultural discourses

This concept of asceticism is used also by Brahman but differently. The Untouchables using this concept always try to gather argument and force for the establishment of equality and mutual recognition. Khare quotes an Untouchable intellectual and writes, Jigyasu, who brings out the characteristics of asceticism, to formulate distinct cultural propositions for Untouchables, comparing them with the Hindu scheme:

> Ascetics as gurus have always been very important to the Chamar. We have lived in their company in villages and cities for centuries. For the people whom the Hindus had systematically isolated and excluded, the Untouchable or low-caste ascetic was a guide, a doctor, a teacher, a benevolent companion, and a true friend. We, the Chamars, did not have ambivalence toward the ascetic. He was always more on our side than any Brahman. Even if we did not dislike Brahman, he did. A Brahman ascetic, on comparison, was congenial only out of his benevolence; if he did not care for us, there was nothing that we could do to change his mind, except try to win him by our genuine devotion to a Hindu deity. The common Chamar is still too much in awe of a Brahman ascetic, though it is unnecessary and out of ignorance. The awakened Chamar should suspect the Brahman ascetic especially these days. He should do so only if he put distance between himself and all things Brahmanical. The Chamars routinely bring their families into close contact with a sympathetic ascetic. Again, unlike the Hindu, they do not know ambivalence toward him. The Hindu householder fears the ascetic's wrath, but craves for his miraculous blessings. He is caught forever in his own doubts about the nature of the sacred. Actually, this is a trap Brahminic thought has produced and maintained. Spared of this the Untouchable ideally approaches the ascetics with full, unwavering faith. The householder interiorizes the ascetic. The Untouchable has little difficulty in doing so, for both the Untouchable and the ascetic receive little from society, the first under denial and the second under self-denial. But both the Chamars householder and the Untouchable ascetic impart critical lessons to each other: The Chamar reminds the ascetic of worldly reform and of restoring will within the oppressed. The ascetic reminds the Chamar of his true spiritual heritage and individual worth. (p. 26)

Jigyasu distinguishes the different kinds of ascetics. The best among them would be the ones who are not dominated by Brahminical premises, and the ones who symbolise hope in times of despair and those who remind and teach others about social justice based on spiritual equality. Khare believes ascetics who affirm Brahminical ideology and misinterpret *dharma,* and blind to social justice and its connection to the true spiritual order:

> Those (ascetics) still dominated by the Brahminic rites and viewpoints are counter productive; those unwilling to see a fundamental difference between the social justice of the caste system and of the spiritual order (*atmavadi dharma*) are of limited value. The ascetics of the spiritual order clearly see how the Hindu weaves a cobweb along castes, gods, Brahminic rites, *karma, maya* (illusion), and *samsara* (rebirth) that he begins to view social exclusion and injustice as a form of *dharma.* (p. 34)

Counter-culture and Ascetics

Khare also brings out the traits of true ascetics who are free and are capable of leading others to freedom bringing justice and well-being to all:

> The ascetic tradition of true persuasion, however, needs to be carefully rescued from the surrounding Brahminic forms and images. The mentality of this ascetic, who is most often not a Brahman, is best tested when he fights for the social justice denied to others. He does not believe in Hindu gods and their discriminatory rites... He is a true wanderer and true renouncer. He is free himself and makes others free. He is a mystic and a well-wisher of everybody. (p.34)

The contrast here is between the true ascetics on the one hand, who engage themselves in dialogue with others imparting critical lessons leading to emancipation, and that the caste Hindus ascetics who are depicted as possessed by illusions and are oppressors of the lower and the least on the other hand. The true ascetics seek to formulate an alternative cultural ideology for Untouchables. Khare strives to make the ascetic independent variable within the Indian spiritual and social order, and thinks that the ascetics could reveal and expose the evils around the caste system. To realise this awareness, the Untouchables' ideology must be supported by a culturally genuine value order. Jigyasu, the Untouchable thinker, portrays the ascetic as a key symbol capable of rescuing the mystifying distortions of the Hindu culture that have obscured the potential for emancipation and transformation embodied by the ascetic. The true ascetic who takes a critical stance will be one who is always engaging him in dialogue and reminds others of the critical values he strives for. People with such awareness and ideas can generate social action. Protesters turn into social activists, yielding a popular ethnographically evident social awareness.

Parish introduces Krishna Bahadur's story to bring in the close connection between the Untouchable and the ascetic.[96] Untouchable Cyamkhala approaches a renouncer and accepts him as his guru. The renouncer gives him a mantra and with this mantra the Untouchable can cause fruit to grow magically on trees. The Untouchable uses this power to feed his family. A Brahman approaches Cyamkhala and pleads him to teach the mantra that he can feed his large and poor family. The Untouchable teaches him with the condition: "I will teach you. And then you will have to respect me as a guru." Though the Brahman was in a dilemma, finally he agreed and said, "I will respect you as my guru," and bowed to the Untouchable in respect.

He goes forth and makes his living by selling fruits. One day he sells fruit to a functionary, a soldier, associated with the King's court. The Brahman was asked to take a post in the King's palace and provide the King with fruit, and he does so. One day when the King has to go out from his palace and he takes the Brahman with him to provide fruits to eat on the journey. During the journey, the King asks the Brahman who taught him the mantra. Brahman could not say Cyamakhala was his teacher as he was ashamed and lies – he says a respected person, a great man taught him. From that time onwards the Brahman was not able to produce any fruit as a consequence of his lie.

Here the Untouchable was true and generous while Brahman was deceptive and unfaithful. In his effort to maintain the caste difference, denying his teacher, he loses the power he has gained. Parish interprets Krishna's general theory of hierarchy:

> As the Brahman can fall, so can the untouchable "rise up." The key is knowledge not birth status. Knowledge is learned and can be held and wielded by ascetics, and by ritual leaders such as himself. His denial of status as birthright aligns Krishna with the critique of the Chamars – arguably, this idea is as "good to think" for low caste people as purity and impurity for high caste people... The high castes also align themselves with the ascetics and draw him into their construction of the world. The renouncer is a resource in an ideological struggle, a tug of war between opposing viewpoints. High caste concepts have hegemony... but alternate views make inroads; reformist thinkers like Jigyasu subject the dominant view to critique and suggest alternative ideologies, which over time are picked up by others, who extend or apply them.[97]

The Ascetic renouncer as a cultural symbol can be thought and read in many ways. It can also be seen with the ascetic-Brahmin alignment. Fuller (1992) in his effort to summarise Popular Hinduism, discusses the way Brahman and renouncer are assimilated to each other:

> A vital aspect of the relationship between Brahmans and renouncers is that the former, although they are mostly householders living in the world, have come to be partially assimilated with the latter, so that the "ideal Brahman" is or is like an ascetic renouncer....The ideological significance of the Brahman renouncer assimilation is indisputable. In

particular it means that the social and religious supremacy of Brahmans partly depends on their likeness to renouncers. Hence Brahmans can represent themselves as independent of inferiors, just like renouncers who ideally avoid all entangling ties with members of the society they have left, even though the Brahmans' purity is still partly preserved by the lower castes who carry out polluting tasks for them. Paradoxically, therefore, Brahman supremacy is a function of both their asymmetrical and complementary relationships with inferior castes, and their ideal detachment from such relationships.[98]

Parish compares Fuller's remarks with that of Jigyasu and Krishna:

This helps us see what is stake in Jigyasu's and Krishna's re-visioning of culture. By assimilating the renouncer to the Untouchable while rescuing the renouncer from the Brahman, a key basis of the social and religious supremacy of Brahmans is called into question. Jigyasu and Krishna might argue that Fuller has merely stated the Brahman's ideology, since they want to assert that the actual role of renouncer is to neutralise and subvert the Brahminical synthesis of a world in which the Brahman has supremacy... Fuller (1992), for example, does not mention the assimilation of untouchable and ascetic, the untouchable is seen in relation to the Brahman in terms of the purity complex and the caste society [1992:17], but not in relation to the ascetic renouncer. In fact, Fuller's remarks on the linking of Brahman and renouncer are found under the subtitle "Brahmans, Renouncers, and Kings." These three figures are presented, in Fuller and other academic discussions, as crucial figures of Hindu culture, and they certainly are; but so is the Untouchable, about which much less is said. Hinduism is virtually defined in terms of the figure of Brahman, renouncer, king – but not in terms of the Untouchable, who defines the Brahman's purity, but is otherwise often represented, if at all, as a marginal figure.[99]

Even the single dimension of untouchability that is analysed – symbolic impurity – is often treated rather one-dimensionally when in fact it is a multi-faceted reality.[100] Brahman, renouncer, king – they share an identity that virtually defines Hinduism – are not Untouchables: the king's power is opposed to the powerlessness of Untouchables; the Brahman's purity against the Untouchable's impurity (knowledge against ignorance); the renouncer's freedom against the Untouchable's subjugation to a social world of suffering.[101] Untouchable is the neglected lot in the studies of Hindu culture and society.

6. The Untouchable's Symbolic world

The cultural and religious sphere of the Untouchables play a great role in their emancipatory process without discounting the role of economic and political aspects. "Cultural and religious symbols house human communities and fund their collective action. In other words, the cultural and symbolic world-view of the Dalits is a meaning system that arises from the depth of their collective experience; it thus sustains, nurtures and directs their life in the world".[102] Stressing the need of symbols that represent structures, religious or otherwise, to be carefully analysed to bring out the exploitative nature in them, and the way the subalterns become agents in making symbols, Maria Arul Raja says:

> The awareness about the 'contradictory consciousness' of the subalterns warns us to be rather cautious in conceptually understanding reality as the infra-structure (wealth and power) above which the superstructure (culture and religion) would be built. In spite of the fact that religion can be an ideological construct hiding the exploitative nature of the structures, the agency of the subaltern people in religion-making cannot be ignored.[103]

Subalterns are instrumental in resisting hegemonic symbols, but they also create their own as symbols. "Religion posseses the capacity to function as a counter-symbolic factory whereby subaltern communities reject the hegemonic symbolic universe of the dominant communities and conjure up one of their own. The act of 'making' their own symbolic world-view in the face of severe domination becomes the basis of hope, not just for their resistance but, more importantly, for the working out of their own subjectivity."[104]

As the Dalits endeavour to articulate and possess their own historical consciousness they become capable of creating their own cultural and symbolic world. Sathianathan Clarke mentions the interaction of two tendencies adversely affecting the Dalits for reclaiming and reinterpreting their cultural symbols. The first is the dichotomising tendency which takes all phenomena as belonging to one of the two polarities: the dualism of good and evil, spirit and body, divine and demonic, spiritual and material, etc. The second tendency is trivialising Dalit cultural symbols by certain Marxists and materialists who in their bias disregard the culture of the masses as "sugary trash".[105] The resolute attempts to capture the self-affirmation and self-expression of the Dalit culture can be noticed in the contemporary Dalit scholarship, and the path to this lies in a "sympathetic and systematic ethnography: investigating the symbol system of the Dalits in order to discern their communal subjectivity."[106]

Subaltern solidarity is built upon the shared experience of powerlessness. The elite discourse on the reality of suffering is mostly based on the hair-splitting metaphysical analysis of *karma*, rebirth, fatalism, determinism or divine will. In this approach, the suffering caused by the heartless oppressive socio-cultural systems is placed on the victims. Maria Arul Raja asserts that the subalterns will have to come out from the passivity and fatalism with which they take upon themselves the responsibility of all the sufferings caused by the systemic historical injustices and suggests garnering all potentials by way of voluntary suffering that has the power to effect liberation, for which the subalterns have to make conscious attempts:

If voluntary suffering is an entry point of the individual into the sacred space of the deity, subaltern oppression could also be *consciously suffered* in view of giving birth to the new counter-cultural community revolting against subjugation. This serves not only as the start of a new community but also as the foundation for solidarity among all those struggling with concerted efforts towards liberation.... Subaltern suffering can be transformed into a spring-board that enables them to plunge into action. This action assumes their suffering is not as a transitory phase proper to contingent beings but a concrete historical reality blocking the possibility of realising their soteriological potential. In short, subaltern suffering and pain dehumanise them to the core, but it is a challenge to throw overboard the dominant forces causing them to suffer. That is to say that *suffering conscious* of being treated as subaltern is a *conscious revolt* against everything that causes suffering.[107]

The pressure one experiences in a stratified social system is great, and so life is not easy. The pressures political and economic realities exert on life generate a culture of dissimulation – a psycho-socio-cultural process of hiding knowledge from others and self. Psychologically it may bring some relief in the pressures of life. There is a tension in the process of understanding and the change envisaged. Parish brings the Untouchables into the picture and observes: "The way Untouchables are part of Hindu Tradition, but not part of it, and draw on it, but are not "at home" in it, stands as a case study of the tension between ideology and critique, structure and transformation."[108] Life is lived in contradiction, with multiple states of consciousness mediated often by conflicting values and cultural models organising a variety of activities and interactions.

Even though the dominant culture does not allow the Untouchables to find roots of and "a home" in the dynamic system of self-concepts they forge through multiple languages, it does not always succeed in controlling the Untouchables. They come out with a critique assembling and disassembling cultural schema to constitute new values, meanings, practices, perspectives, etc. The critique they forge is from the existing tradition – not from a foreign tradition – and so is a process of self-subversion. If they want to disseminate widely such counter-ideologies, critical discourses, etc., they have to be meaningful and capable of initiating a process of liberation, otherwise they may fall back to the dominant ways of thinking and practice.

CHAPTER VIII

COUNTER-CULTURAL PERSPECTIVES

George Soares-Prabhu states, "Poverty-Religiosity-Caste constitute India's *samsara,* its cycle of bondage".[109] These three factors – economic-political, cultural-religious, personal-social – are dialectically interrelated and influence mutually. Among these three factors, I believe, caste is the most significant one. Caste is at the centre of the socio-cultural world of India, especially when it is seen from the point of view of its relationality with poverty and religiosity. That is why we say that caste defines the typically Hindu (indeed Indian) worldview, and also determines the type of relationships that exist in Indian society that gives concrete expression both to India's religiosity and its poverty. It leads one to assert that India's religiosity is caste religiosity and India's poverty is caste poverty. Any countercultural and theological discourse in India has to be rooted in the socio-cultural and religio-cultural realities, determined by poverty, religion and caste and be in continuous dialogue with these threefold factors as they represent different aspects of the Indian reality as a whole. Now the question is: What kind of a contextual theology can take up the challenge?

It is commonly accepted that theology in Asia or India forms part of the quest for liberation *(moksha)*; knowledge is sought for the sake of and in self-realisation. George Pattery observes that "theology is not primarily an act of illuminating the mind as it is a committed listening to, deciphering, understanding and realising God's word.[110] Theological activities are a way of life belonging to an ultimate human attitude. A theologian sees reality as a whole. The different disciplines are not seen in watertight compartments as sociology, science, philosophy, theology, etc., but as contributing to a holistic perspective. The theology of liberation in Asia is understood as "our way of sensing and doing things as revealed in our people's struggle for spiritual and social emancipation".[111] Sathianathan Clarke asserts:

> I was convinced that the contextual core of liberation theology in India had to do with the emancipation of the Dalits. I was also convinced that Dalit theology ought to constantly and continuously reinterpret and re-image the Dalit community in the midst of insidious caste assertions of the dominating caste communities.[112]

When we search for an alternative culture or counterculture in the context of the caste cultural conflict which we see as the prominent factor in the present Indian reality, and in the general holistic perspective of doing theology in India we shall point out three options the theologian has to make, that is, the option for the poor - liberation, the option for the culture - inculturation and option for dialogue - interpretation. These options and countercultural perspectives are dynamically interrelated.

1. Option for the Poor - Liberation

In Christian theology "option for the poor (dalits)" is one of the most discussed and important issues. At the same time it is the most controversial issue. For the weak, voiceless, the victims and those who really opt and work for such underprivileged ones who are at the margin of subsistence, this option is basic to their lives and capable of bringing hope for a renewed humanity in an egalitarian world. Those who are in the other sector, who are wealthy, secure, powerful and successful in always finding ways to serve their interests, it is a threat that brings chaos by its revolutionary thrust, destructive of age old and cherished institutions. For many the "option for the poor" remains merely a slogan. In certain circumstances they may spiritualise and universalise the term "poor" in a very concrete and real sense by saying that 'we are all poor in the beneficence of God'. EATWOT gives guidelines to Christian living in a three-point formula: a Christian is a person who has made an irrevocable option *to follow* Jesus; this option necessarily coincides with the option *to be poor*; but the option to be poor becomes a true "following of Jesus" only to the extent that it is also an *option for the poor.*[113] The test of Christian discipleship or spirituality may be the coincidence of these three options.

If we take "option for the poor" seriously in the forming of the community there will be enormous implications. John Sobrino indicates some of them:

> They would include radically different priorities in the allocation of resources and personnel, an alternative decision making process privileging the voiceless and a training programme for aspirant leaders..... that emphasised actual participation in the struggle of the poor. It would, moreover, mean significantly modifying the accepted methods of faith reflection. Since the faith that seeks understanding in theology is a faith that impels us to take the side of the poor, making an option for the poor becomes a privileged interpretative standpoint from which further understand this faith.[114]

Option for the poor as a perspective means the choice one takes to love all in and through a partisan love for the oppressed. This option is a practical, existential reality, a way of living that codetermines one's manner of perceiving and understanding.[115] By "perspective" we mean "the practical rootedness that codetermines the manner in which an object is viewed, perceived and construed in one's way of thinking".[116] In a society divided between haves and have-nots, exploiters and exploited, the dominant and the dominated, one confronts the question whether he or she has to opt for the poor or not. The exploitation and domination takes place not only in the realms of economics and politics but also in the social, psychological, cultural and religious realms. Amaladoss points out how the domination and oppression enters into the whole system and the need to look from the optic of the poor:

The dominant world-view and value system legitimate the existing structures and favour the power of the dominant group, even if it proposes to them some reform to correct glaring injustices. Inequality will be seen as an inevitable part or consequence of the system. Only a look at the system from the point of view of the oppressed will bring to light the exploitative dimensions of the dominant cultural and social order and show what are the sort of changes that are required.[117]

Now the question is – who makes this option for the poor? All make this option — or at least all are called to do so — but all do not make it in the same way. In the Church circles those who are in the leadership roles assume a middle class identity and value system. And they justify the privatisation of property, spirituality, the Church and God. In this context O'Brien points to the need of a change and conversion in them, even a change in the stand they take, if they really opt for the poor:

> In this context, the option for the poor means giving priority to the standpoint and experience of the poor over their own. It means entering into a genuine dialogue and *koinonia* with the excluded and the voiceless and the process and content of revelation from their perspective. Those who are actually rich and powerful seem called to even more profound conversion. Their dialogue with the oppressed will be for themselves a process of liberation from the tyranny of possessions and possessiveness.[118]

The poor and the underprivileged too have to make an option for themselves by engaging themselves in a dialogue with the situations they are in. This will empower them to appreciate and trust themselves, their own experiences. We can expect such a positive outcome, a retrieval of the heart of the Gospel, if they have the experience of being listened to. The poor and the oppressed are already in a process of change and conversion: "For the poor too, a willingness to embark on this process involves conversion. At a profound level, it implies a readiness to be surprised by the joy of knowing that they are God's chosen ones. But then, they have the responsibility of living on this basis. In an ongoing way, it means liberating themselves from the patterns of immediate gratification, apathy, and a predisposition to blame and complain rather than to analyse and act."[119]

The poor own for themselves ample raw materials of suffering and oppression which are capable of effecting transformation of the structures of injustice, thus mediating the reign of God, but they lack the differentiated consciousness adequately formed theologians possess. The option for the poor involves a particular type of dialogue between the poor and the theologians. The positive results of liberation and transformation depends upon how these enrich themselves mutually. O'Brien sees this option for the poor as a matrix of four mutually interpreting dimensions, personal evangelical simplicity, existential solidarity with the poor, the employment of transformational socioanalytical models, and a self-critical presence in one's own institutional context.[120] We are called to interpret the meaning and exigencies of Christian faith viewing the socio-cultural reality from the stand point of the poor, identifying ourselves with their struggles. This gives theology a privileged interpretative perspective, which is always in dialogue with other perspectives. These theological conversations, according to O'Brien exercise a therapeutic function leading to conversion.[121] It does so because of the ability this perspective has to create conditions for other theologies to enter into dialogue with and discover their partial rootedness in, and relatedness to, structures of oppression, leading to a new methodological awareness for theology.

Human experience is a quite unknown territory for many theologians. Today we speak of a "new" theology resulting from a new methodology, a paradigm shift in theological thinking. K.C. Abraham describes this change:

> The change is described as a change from naturalistic/ substantialistic forms of thought to historical/personal categories. While the emphasis of the former is on the static continuities of human life, the later helps us to focus on the dynamic aspects of human experience and relationships.... In modern times there is a stronger emphasis on a relational dialogic kind of knowledge. Even empirical knowledge is challenged and deepened at every stage with new experience. The change of paradigms is also reflected in the way reality is perceived and interpreted. The classical model of discourse is characterised by dichotomies such as material *versus* spiritual, inner *versus* material, personal *versus* social and so on. Today the consensus is that a holistic view of reality is true to our experience.[122]

In the changed theological method, the focus is the dialectical reading together of the two poles, the pole of the Judeo-Christian tradition of faith experiences and the pole of our present day experiences in a specific cultural and historical matrix.[123] Theology as hermeneutics seeks critical understanding based on the socio-cultural analysis and challenges a culture that is de-humanising, paving the way for a counter-culture which is life-affirming, liberating and communitarian.

When we say liberation is central to theology, we mean that theology has the function to facilitate human and collective living under the Divine. It has to aim at living with a sense of justice and freedom in the economical, political, social, personal, cultural and religious realms. It is historical, inclusive and holistic. Santhinathan Clarke observes: "The emancipation of the Dalits cannot be achieved without a direct encounter and reconciliation with their history, which is inclusive of religion and culture... Liberation in a holistic sense includes finding the Dalit identity through encountering the various forms manifested in its particular cultural and religious representations."[124] To achieve the goal of liberation and freedom from all forms of oppression and dehumanisation it is important to have a closer understanding of the nature of evil operating in society. Although, the Marxist analysis showed itself as a useful tool in unmasking the nature and the mechanism of injustice and oppression in most societies, it was found inadequate to explain the function of Indian society with its specific element of the caste system. Indian Theological Association stated:

> In our search for effective tools, the value of the Marxist analysis must be given due recognition as it has made valuable contribution to the understanding of our situation in India. While acknowledging the specific merit of Marxist analysis, we feel the need for a holistic analysis incorporating all aspects of reality including the dimension of transcendence.[125]

A holistic approach is needed to enter into the Indian worldview which insists on the interrelatedness of everything and a cosmic wholeness, avoiding any sort of dichotomy. Felix Wilfred referring to the holistic Indian approach states:

> Employing the traditional resources of the people, which resonate with their present life and experience, roots the liberation praxis in culture and thereby makes it effective. The Indian praxis of liberation must go hand in hand with the holistic and integral vision of reality, characteristic of the traditional Indian culture and heritage. In this vision, the socio-political struggle for liberation is not simply a matter of the empirical order or of ethical concern. The Indian approach places the empirical and ethical concerns within a framework of a totality of reality, which comprises the divine, cosmic and human dimensions.[126]

Theologising in the Indian context has to take into account of the communal, critical, constructive, contextual and liberational aspects. Applying this to the Dalit situation Clarke writes:

> This particular constructive model is most suited to Dalits, even as it leads to the expansion of the scope of theology itself. First, it deliberately and substantively includes the collective religious world of the Dalits..... Second, it constructively refigures a framework that would lead to a

humane and collective way of living under God for the community, particularly inclusive of the people struggling against the multidimensional forces of hegemony. It does this by resurrecting the religion of the Dalits which we presume sustained and nourished them through centuries of oppression.[127]

The focus of liberation in theologising will lead the Dalits as a community to enter critically and constructively into their own cultural and religious symbols, submitting them to continuous reflection and practice. Such an approach gives more stress to praxis and enables them to recapture their identity and throw away the one that is thrusted upon them by the dominant castes.

Liberation has its roots in pathos, the people's experiences. A.P. Nirmal asserts this fact as he gives guidelines to a Dalit theology: "For a Dalit Theology Pain or Pathos is the beginning of knowledge. For the sufferer, more certain than any principle, more certain than any proposition, more certain than any thought and more certain than any action is his/her pain."[128]

There are political and ethical overtones in any kind of liberation process. The process has its roots in human culture and people in interpreting it. There is no neutral stand. For instance, the dominant caste has been using the "Hindu mode of absorption" representing a "culture of domination and oppression". Correspondingly we have also a "culture of protest" evolving a method of resistance. That does not always mean that the "weapons of the weak" are adequate to the violence of the strong, but they are powerful enough to keep alive a memory and a voice to work out an alternative ideology and identity. Rudolf Heredia observes:

> No dominant hegemony can be absolutely monolithic, for it cannot completely suppress every group conflict or contain all antagonistic interest. Hence the contradictions and cracks in the social systems will inevitably reflect the complex ways in which relationships of meaning are produced and fought

over. For in the complex dialectical tension between dominance and subordination the incorporation of such groups and interests will often be limited and selective, allowing scope for differing perceptions and an alternative consciousness.[129]

As a strategy of survival and political action the subalterns build up zones of resistance, which may sometimes seem marginal and non-political but will be powerful enough to inaugurate a "cultural revolt" with economic and political overtones. The recent political assertion by the subaltern groups, though with fractured verdicts, is in the direction of an alternative to the dominant caste politics. Dalits have their own option for their ideological orientations and liberation plans. For Ambedkar, Dalit liberation means the national goal of creating conditions for liberty, equality, justice and fraternity as enshrined in the Indian Constitution. In his *The Buddha and His Dhamma* he refers to this ideal frequently. What is urgently needed is a feasible subaltern praxis. Rudolf Heredia argues for a subaltern hermeneutics:

> Action follows vision! If our action is to be liberative for the subalterns, then our vision too must reflect their situation. Now reflection is always at least implicit in human action, or else it is not 'human action' but just the 'acts of humans'; and reflection must somehow be actualised and become real in action, or else it is mere speculation and less real for it. This calls for a radical praxis that can only keep its authenticity within a hermeneutic circle and only preserves its radical nature when it is premised on a subaltern hermeneutic.[130]

Subaltern praxis demands a prophetic mode of existence grounded on love. A. Thumma points out its characteristics:

> People in praxis love their folks, and so are ready to risk themselves for their well-being and the fullness of their lives. They exist in a mode of being-in-love; it entails being-with-others and being-for-others. It is also a prophetic mode of

being for their love takes the form of struggle and solidarity to destroy the unjust structures of domination and bondage, to build up the new world order based on the spiritual values of righteousness, equality and peace.[131]

In a society that is divided between rich and poor, powerful and powerless, exploiters and exploited, dominant and subaltern etc., Christian discipleship demands that we take the side of the poor. When people are placed poles apart, not only economically and politically but also socially, psychologically, culturally, religiously, etc., the role of the agents of liberation is to denounce the death-dealing forces on the one hand and announce the dawn of a new age and establishment of a new world order inspired by the divine. James H. Cone in his volume *God of the Oppressed* understood liberation as "not a theological concept but a liberating presence of God in the lives of the poor in their fight for dignity and worth. Liberation is not a human possession or object but a divine gift of freedom to those who struggle in faith against violence and oppression".[132] Liberation, the pressing need of India, is a matter of delivering the lives of the masses from death, destruction and inhumanity.

2. Option for the Culture – Inculturation

Religious traditions and cultures have been a major resource of the Asian peoples to situate themselves, to find their identity and ultimate meaning. Every generation is rooted in and nourished by its religious tradition, which is the bearer of the culture and spirit of the people. Today social and religious structures have become the arena of the conflict between the traditional value system and the challenges of modernity. There are also the conflicts between the macro and the micro, the dominant and the subaltern, etc. – the big and the powerful against the small and the weak, the former trying to control the later and the later refusing to be dominated by the former. At the level of culture there is also a trend to transform the world into a monocultural zone.

Though there are forces of division and fragmentation operative in the socio-cultural life, we also observe counter movements of unity and integration existing side by side. Felix Wilfred observes:

> In spite of many fragmentations characterising today's world, we also note, on the other hand, signs of hope. The human family is moving towards a unity, which was, perhaps, never before achieved in history. There is a deep aspiration to get out of situations of division and to reach integration. If fragmentation is self-destruction of humanity, the movement towards unity is the sign of its redemption..... The myth that the reality can be known by atomising it is giving way to holistic and integral approach that can unfold the web of relations connecting all parts of reality.[133]

The emerging movements of today such as the ecological movement and the feminist movement are signs of this orientation and approach to unity and integration and at the same time a protest against fragmentation. People today are realising the need for dialogue and are ready to recognise the importance of pluralism in all areas of life. Felix Wilfred continues:

> Centralisation of every kind – political, economic, religious - will be forced to loosen its grip. Decentralisation of power, wealth, ideology, etc., will begin to happen keeping alive, in spite of many signs of divisions and conflicts, the dream of the unity of humanity in diversity. Pluralism is going to be the strongest antidote against all domination, control and regimentation. Its language is dialogue and its attitude and praxis is participation. For pluralism is based on the recognition of the otherness of the other. The liberation of the oppressed and the quality of the human life will depend very much on the measure pluralism will be practiced in the decades ahead.[134]

In the midst of poverty and misery of the vast majority of our people, culture plays a key role in the emancipation process, in realising economic development and political empowerment, and more importantly, in awakening the selfhood of people as they become the agents and subjects of history. Referring the role and the dynamics the culture play in the reconstruction of the lives of the people Felix Wilfred says:

> The culture of a people expresses its spirit, its collective unconscious. Like the trees of the forest which preserve the soil from erosion, the cultural roots of a people give them strength and selfhood to withstand the oppression and exploitation of the powerful. It is the living embodiment of its experiences transmitted from generation to generation. It is the specific way of peoples' knowing, feeling and perceiving the reality and interacting with it.[135]

In our encounter with any culture there is the need to discern it well and to fully cooperate with the Creator in growing in it. In this process, denouncing certain cultural expressions on the plea that they have become instruments and signs of oppression, without taking into account the objective value of these expressions would be unwise.[136]

Centrality of Culture

Felix Wilfred shows that the centrality of the culture is manifested differently in West and East:

> The centrality of the culture manifests itself differently in the West and in the East. In the West it has begun to express itself as a quest for meaning and search for new symbols. It expresses itself also as virulent critique of the empirical rationality characterising the present mode of development, which is in many respects anti-human and devoid of humanising culture. In Asia and in the rest of the developing world, which were dominated by colonial powers, the centrality of culture can be seen in the affirmation of the identity of a people as a group or nation and in the search for cultural roots to undergird the present economic, social and political life. The cultural comes to the fore in our Asian societies also in the aspirations of the people to determine

for themselves, on the basis of their history, tradition and values, their own patterns of development and forms of self-government.[137]

All those who work for the creation of a better world by theological and pastoral action should be furnished with an adequate understanding of the cultural forces at work in society and so enter into the world of values, motivations and attitudes. My effort here, against the background of India's present cultural situation in general and the caste cultural situation in particular, is to point out that "the option for culture - inculturation" is an important countercultural perspective indispensable for theology that wants to be contextual.

Culture, Faith and Theology

The dialectics between theology and culture is of great importance in theologising in India, as theology is faith seeking understanding. Sebastian Painadath explains the theologising process clarifying different terms:

> Faith is a response to the Spirit of God transforming the human spirit. Theology is the perception of the word of God transforming human culture. Hermeneutics is the way of interpreting the symbols of faith in a contextualised theological pursuit. Such a pursuit is always conditioned by the cultural fabric of the people. Hermeneutics is therefore an exploration into the dynamic elements of a culture by interpreting the format of myth and language. There is no abstract faith, no neutral theology of global validity. Faith and theological reflection are always in correlation with the culture of a people.[138]

The interpretation of culture and tradition, a critical and creative process, is very much part of this theological activity. It is an option the gospel-community has to make in India in the theologising process, a challenge posed by the complex multicultural situation in India. Given the importance of the interpretation of cultures and traditions in fashioning a counterculture, Kappen calls this process a critical and creative involution:

> By involution I mean a return to our own culture, but not so much to its developed forms as to its primal sources. This is because the original insights of a culture often tend to become distorted in the course of history. But involution to one's own cultural roots must be critical and creative, and this both in regard to tradition and modernity. That is, while rejecting what is not humanising in traditional and capitalist cultures, we must be open to the positive elements of both.[139]

Critical questions should be raised about the credentials of any religion, culture or traditions in India, whether they respond positively and creatively to the challenges posed by the humanisation process. When Christians take part in this collective process of humanisation and integration in the socio-cultural milieu we call that inculturation. Dorr recalls that this process, as "the work for liberation, ultimately involves a *spiritual battle*, even though it is necessarily carried out in the economic, political and cultural level."[140] It demands solidarity and identification with the brokenness of the people and sharing their cup of sorrow; it means hoping with them for the dawn of a new day of love, truth, freedom and justice.[141] The struggle for the emancipation of the people and the transformation of society should aim at changes in the thought patterns, interests and values prevalent among the people. Simon Sebastian explains culture and argues that the Creation account in Genesis lays the foundation for a theological reflection on the nature of culture itself:

> If one understands culture in general as the prevalent thought-patterns and collective consciousness of a given society, or as the world-view that controls, shapes, animates, modifies and forms one's thought patterns and the collective consciousness, then the Creation account in the Bible is the world-view that informed the collective consciousness of Israel and was an expression of its culture.[142]

Human beings as co-creators relate with nature through their labour and culture. Culture is not simply the work place of God in continuing the work of creation, but as God collaborating with humans in the ongoing process of creation. This intimate relationship of God with the human community in and through culture explains the concepts of spirituality, faith, etc. Sebastian Painadath explains:

> Culture... articulates the world-view of a people. Spirituality keeps alive the orientation to the ultimate horizon of meaning in cultural perspectives. Spirituality is the ultimate source of creativity in the unfolding of a culture. Spirituality is the heartbeat of the myth of a culture. ....Spirituality gives rise to faith. The experience of being gripped by the divine Spirit evokes faith in the person or community. Faith is the surrender to the divine Spirit manifest in a particular instance.[143]

Faith is manifested in the belief systems and spirituality in the forms of religiosity. Symbols unfold, identify, assimilate, and interrelate diverse levels of reality. The specificity each symbol upholds is to be understood in the horizon of the self-revelation of the divine in history. And the revelation of God to the humans happens through the medium of language that roots itself and emerges from culture. The revelation of God in history is the event gathered up in words. The word that opens the core of the person and integrates the community is the symbol of reality. About the word that emerges out of a world-view and its relationality and function in culture and interpretation. Painadath writes: "Through the word, *natura* becomes *cultura*: the word creates culture and culture embodies words. The word is articulated through the specific dynamics of a culture and the culture nourishes the word. Hence the word has to be interpreted in the living context of a culture, and the culture has to be understood in relation to word."[144]

Raymond Panikkar explores the word, its vital relationship with the world and the universe of discourse: "Each word is a microcosm; it carries with it an entire universe, and when in freedom (when it is free) it reveals a whole world contained implicitly in a particular word. Words do not live in isolation; they are nurtured in a much larger universe of discourse."[145] The incarnate Word (Logos), God's self-communication, is understood as the theological foundation for inculturation. The incarnation of the Word is a "mystery [that] took place *in history:* in clearly defined circumstances of time and space, amidst a people with its own culture."[146]

Now the question is how can the Gospel community be the carrier of good news when a large majority feel that they are at the margins? How does the Gospel community enter into dialogue with different cultures, both dominant and subaltern, when the gospel has a special option for the poor? Questions should be raised about the credentials of any religion, culture or tradition, whether they respond positively and creatively to the challenges posed by the humanisation process, or they call to make this world a better place to live in freedom, justice and dignity. Taking inspiration from Jesus, the incarnate Word of God, the Church community has to appropriate and realise the core message of liberation by a similar process of incarnation and identification with the suffering humanity: this we call inculturation. It means solidarity and identification with the brokenness of the people and sharing the cup of sorrow. It means the immersion of baptism in the Dalitness of the oppressed in order to remove its victims and plant them in the realm of freedom, dignity and creative living.[147] Every religion has failed in more than one way in the challenge of humanisation, and contributed to the dehumanisation and enslavement of people, their subjugation and oppression.

The Gospel community has to respond to this realm of culture by obeying the Gospel command to opt for the poor and the underpevileged. In India many regional cultures, subcultures and subaltern cultures exist side by side with the dominant and powerful cultures.

Amaladoss asserts the need of the Gospel community to be countercultural:

> The people have to seek to live the meanings and values of the Gospel in their own culture. However, the Gospel should always be a challenging presence, never domesticated, but counter-cultural. The cultural embodiment of the Gospel however should not be such as to make it a ghetto. The Gospel-community is a community on mission and it should always be ready to challenge the wider culture, whatever be its relation to it.[148]

Any religious community that strives to be counter-cultural has to be at the service of the growth and blossoming of the human family and has to enter into the process of history to become part of the countercultural movement. This challenges religions and theologies to enter into a dialogue with the socio-cultural processes in participation and mutual enrichment.

3. Option for Dialogue – Interpretation

The picture of India we have is that of a country in sharp conflict: ethnic, cultural, ideological, etc. Some groups and political parties ideologically and politically favour liberal capitalism, some others represent more egalitarian ideologies and still others follow the legacy of Gandhi as the ideology more suited to India. They are all in conflict with each other. The fiercest conflict, however, is between Brahminic caste-ideology and the challenge represented by the marginal groups like the Dalits and the tribals.[149] In the light of these conflicts and the pluralities of cultures and traditions a theology that makes sense in India has to safeguard a dialogical character. Felix Wilfred explains:

> To theologise in India means to theologise within a great civilisation characterised by immense diversity; it means to do theology in the midst of contradictions and conflicts, and unprecedented challenges at all levels…Theology would make sense in India as service to life and it needs to be fostered through continuous dialogue. It is a way to bring the Good

News of Jesus Christ closer to the lives of the people through concrete engagement. The importance of the theological task stands in bold relief against a serious crisis threatening and engendering life. Moreover, we are in the midst of a serious conflict between the forces of life and the death-dealing powers of darkness. The dialogue indeed here is not something referring simply to intellectual discussion, rather relating to the realm of praxis.[150]

Theology, the faith-seeking understanding, should be consistent with the faith praxis which enters into every dimension of God's salvific action, including cultural, social, and historical. The dialogical inter-dependence of the literary-critical, the historical-critical and the social-scientific, is the ideal each offering and receiving correctives at each level. The truth is attained in a self-correcting, mutually enriching process of theological conversation.[151] Dialogue in theology is not simply a clarification of the knowledge of faith but a movement: "Dialogue is open-ended and it leads us into the depths of the mystery, to understand which we need to be in continuous journey with others. For, dialogue is not simply a means to achieve something. Every dialogue has mystery as its horizon. Thus, the path of theology is not one which leads from faith to clarity of knowledge, but rather a movement from faith to its realisation in life through dialogue.[152] As a methodology, dialogue in the pluralistic situation, is the heart of theology which is based on the conviction that God is in dialogue with humanity and the world. It is important to understand that the starting point is the present day experiences where God discloses Himself in history.

Culture, Language and Interpretation

Culture that mediates God's presence is in the language of its people. The self-communication through the word in language is appropriated through interpretation. Painadath explains: "Hermeneutics is the way of understanding reality by interpreting the language through which the perception of reality in a particular context is communicated to another context. The experience of reality is communicated through *the word*: through symbols and scriptures, myths and folklore, ordinances and orientations, etc. Language is a primary medium of this self-communication of the author, which can be a person or a community."[153] In hermeneutics, as it is done in theology, it is very important to understand the dynamics and role of language, culture etc. Language, the primary medium of communication, is very much connected with the events taking place. It crystalises and codifies the experiences of events into texts, which seek interpretation. Painadath goes on to explain:

> That through which a specific experience of reality is communicated may be called a **text**. The text evolves out of the experience of the author and hence the text is his/her progeny. It somehow embodies the spirit of the author. It is a living reality. As a living reality the text has to be approached and understood, respected and interpreted. Encounter with a text is encounter with the author in his/her context; however this encounter takes place in a new context which opens new possibilities of understanding in fresh horizons of perception.[154]

Hermeneutics is a re-reading based on a given concrete situation.[155] It is a participation in the creative process of the spirit, which demands a threefold dialogue:

> This creative exploration demands a threefold dialogue: (i) Dialogue between the reader and the author on the basis of the text. In this dialogue the original context of the author confronts the new context of the reader. There is a fusion of horizons taking place in this process. (ii) Dialogue among the readers, each interpreting the text in a specific context. The diverse perceptions of the readers interact in a critical and creative way so that the depth of the meaning is probed into and the relevance of the message is explored. Such a dialogue is the only way to safeguard the interpretation from manipulating the text by one or the other reader. (iii) Dialogue

between the reader and the heritage of interpretation. The one who interprets, especially in the case of interpreting texts of faith experience, is part of a community (space) and heir of a heritage (time).[156]

There is no definitive singular interpretation. Interpretation has to convey meaning and meaning may be different in changed situations, in different cultures and traditions and in different periods in history. Text and interpretation belong together and understanding is seen to be linguistic. Painadath explains: "Being that can be understood is language. Language is not a mere speaking box; it is neither purely objective nor subjective. Language is a relational reality. It binds subject with the object and communicates depth to depth...... there is no hermeneutics without language and no language without hermeneutics. Language and interpretation coalesce in hermeneutics."[157] Theologising in India has to be in the Indian language as the language is the living expression of the culture of a people, which constitutes the understanding process. But the liguisticality of understanding transcends the limits of any particular language and it explains the capacity of the language to say many things at one time and to have plurality of interpretations:

> It is the concrete use of the language in conversation that promotes the horizon of understanding, which thus emerges as transsubjective and dialogical. As dialogue, language is not the possession of the participant but the medium of understanding. Insight is possible in conversation because words, due to their relationality to the whole of being, have around them a "circle of the unexpressed', drawing the partners into the "infinity of the unsaid".[158]

God acts in history, and this action finds manifold expressions in culture as the Spirit recreates the face of the broken earth. The theologian or the interpreter, if he/she wants to be relevant and adequate to the actual situation, must discern the divine dynamics and take into account seriously the responsibility of the self to all reality. Theologising has to take place in this milieu of the living context of the people with all their existential struggles:

> People's struggles for justice and freedom are suffused with God's will to human wholeness. They are best seen as the historical embodiments or incarnations of God's word of human liberation and God's will to human completion. The struggles are theological events. Articulating the theology latent in them serves to understand in depth the nature of the struggle, to see its affinity to ultimate realities and meanings, to sustain the hope of God's Reign on Earth and to keep the combat human.[159]

At times we come to know that an insight has dawned in on us; at other times that our interpretations and theological discourses are distorted either as a justification of our own privileged status or as a reinforcement of our oppression. In a limited way we know that we have internalised structures of marginalisation either as oppressor or as oppressed. At the moment of insight we realise real changes are taking place in the very process of understanding. It is not simply the acquisition of more information or a mere clarification that is taking place between partners of dialogue with roughly equivalent perspectives. O'Brien says: "We experience, in short, that it [interpretation understood as dialogue between partners] is a therapeutic experience – whether structured or not – that involves a moment of vulnerability or liminality, during which we gain a precious insight into the psychological roots of our discourse and consequently its distortedness."[160]

We reach such insights not merely by rhetoric but by committed search and action. "With those who want to change, not just to interpret, the world, like Phule and Ambedkar, the truth they seek is not just the object of an intellectual quest, nor merely a pragmatic technique, but rather truth as a reality, a *satya,* authenticated by its humanist and liberative potential."[161] Self-reflection and critique in the process of enlightenment can change the attitude, which presupposes strategic action capable of dissolving distortions and manipulations. The integral and dialogical character of this process is basic to the way of doing theology and interpretation. We look for a privileged perspective for our theology and interpretation which views the socio-cultural reality from the standpoint of the marginalised in all realms of life. We evolve this perspective by entering into and dialoguing with other perspectives, which will contribute to a mutual correction and enrichment, creating conditions for the therapeutic function of the theological enterprise. This dialogal approach helps to discover in theology the partial rootedness in and relatedness to structures of oppression leading to a new methodological self-awareness capable of effecting counter-theologies and counter-ideologies. The dialogal approach aims at a conversion among the partners so as to bring about transformation and change in society.

CHAPTER IX

JESUS AND COUNTER-CULTURE

We say culture is in crisis when there are conflicting cultural trends with opposing value-systems adversely affecting human hearts and communities, social structures and religious associations. At different points of time we see prophetic individuals and groups keenly active to bring about cultural transformation in such crisis situations. They challenge the dehumanising and death-dealing aspects of culture and initiate countercultural processes for a new humanity and society. We have narrated a few [in the first chapter of this part] in the context of caste cultural conflict in India. Prophetic figures swiftly diagnose the malaise rooted in culture and expose and challenge the dominant elements that control and oppress the weak and keep up the status quo to protect their own interests. At the time when they identify and develop their insight, realisation sprouts in the consciousness of the subaltern groups that the prevailing oppression and dehumanisation is the handiwork of the masters. The result is an upsurge of mass discontent. "Such discontent seething beneath the surface will naturally seek an escape by rupturing the cultural integument imprisoning people's consciousness. The agents of this rupture are prophetic individuals and groups."[162]

Jesus, a counter-cultural prophet, with his discourses and interpretation was a challenge to the dehumanising and oppressive structures and principalities of his time. The counterculture that Jesus proposes is valid today in the Indian context of caste crisis in its different dimensions: economic, political, personal, social, cultural, religious. I approach this chapter "Jesus and Counter-culture" with the different caste cultural dimensions of the Indian scenario in mind, according to the pattern followed in this inquiry: "Jesus: the Prophet of a Counter-culture", "Jesus versus the Power and Prestige", "Counter-culture demands Active Faith", "Jesus' Vision of a Society of equals", "Towards a Counter-cultural Interpretation" and "A Prophetic Counter-cultural Movement." In the first part of the thesis the focus was the caste reality experienced in the Indian cultural scene — a way of experiencing the caste culture. In the second part I tried to analyse the caste culture in the six fold dimensions: economic, political, personal, social, cultural, religious. In the third part comes the final phase in theologising process, i.e., interpretation starting from experience and then analysis. In this final chapter the objective is to give an Indian Christian response focussing on the vision, teaching and life of Jesus.

1. Jesus: the Prophet of a Counter-culture

In his words and deeds Jesus strikes a countercultural note, which for the Christians in India who are also surrounded by the caste reality and its struggles, contains the elements for the Indian Christian vision of a new society. The questions posed in the following discussions are: Where does Jesus stand in the caste scene of India today? How is Jesus as prophet of counterculture reflected in the consciousness of the Indian people seeking emancipation in the caste cultural crisis? What is the relevance of Jesus in India's efforts to work for a culture that affirms genuine values?

At the time of Jesus the Jewish society was facing deep-seated socio-cultural crisis in all realms of life: economic, political, cultural religious etc.[163] Five centuries of political domination, first by the Persians, then by the Greeks, and lastly by the Romans, had left deep scars in the Jewish history, and led up to the profound crisis at the turn of our era, which among other things occasioned the Jesus movement.[164] Economic exploitation and political domination of the Palestinians was a feature of the Roman colonial rule at the time of Jesus. Nobody occupies another country with altruistic motives. From the large crowds of the beggars, the sick, the crippled, the lame and the 'possessed' we meet in the Gospels it is clear that the poor made up a large part of the population of Palestine at the time of Jesus, and that it was from among these poor sections of society that the Jesus movement drew its main support.[165]

Culturally also the Jewish society at the time of Jesus was dominated by the colonisers, and a section of the indigenous population, the priestly and lay nobility and the prosperous city population, welcomed the cultural invasion. This inevitably caused a cultural shock and a profound psychological trauma among the common people. Though some interiorised the colonisers' contempt for the 'native' customs and culture, some reacted aggressively by rejecting them and even uncritically idealised their own past. Some clung to the faith of their fathers and resisted the alien culture.

What was more crucial and affected more deeply the social and religious life of the people and community was the oppressive character of Judaism, in the way it was lived. Kappen gives some of the cultural forces and religious trends that cumulatively contributed to the cultural crisis at the time of Jesus:

> Jesus lived at a time when cult, law and apocalypticism had supplanted prophecy. This meant there was none to defend the cause of the poor and the oppressed. The priestly aristocracy allied itself with the lay nobility and lived affluently on the profits they made by exchanging the grace of God for money. In the absence of genuine prophecy, the apocalyptic movement came to the fore. Whereas the prophets had announced a future age of justice whose realisation depended on the free response of man, the apocalyptic seers viewed history as following a predetermined course: an intensification of misery in the present age followed by a new aeon of freedom and happiness. Though meant to console

the people in a period of intense tribulation, these visionary writings also served to legitimise the ills of society in so far as these were conceived of as inevitable and divinely ordained.[166]

The society at the time of Jesus was overgrown with legalism and casuistry, manifested in the circles of Pharisees and Scribes. Kappen observes, "Knowledge of the Law gained ascendancy over love. Underlying this development was a change in the class basis of the Jewish religion. Love can be practiced by all whereas knowledge is non-democratic... What was originally a religion of the common man thus became a religion of the elite that set itself apart – that is what the word *Pharisee* means – from the masses".[167]

If at all Jesus emerged as a prophet of counter-culture, it was out of his and of his community's experience of the brokenness, enslavement and subjugation that were rampant. Describing the personal experience of 'dalitness' and enslavement of Jesus, Thumma writes:

> Jesus the slave and servant of the people, embodied in himself dalitness in many ways and experienced the dalit pathos, degradation, ignominy and dehumanisation. Insulted with all sorts of bad names, outcast and rejected by his own people and the leaders, finally Jesus was subjected to a ruthless, shameful death of a slave and criminal, out the gate... Jesus becomes a slave accepting the condition of the lowliest, the least and the last in the society, lower than the weakest servant, an oppressed and exploited non-person, an outcaste, with no place to lay his head, nor a tomb when he was dead.[168]

Samuel Rayan describes the experience of Jesus' dalitness coming closer to that of an Indian Dalit, when he writes, "In our language we should say he refused to grasp at power, prestige and profit; he refused to side with the votaries of these. Instead he chooses to be a Dalit, a *Paraya,* and the lowest among the outcastes. And as he was wantonly insulted, harassed and killed by the landlord's hirelings."[169] Jesus was victimised for his poverty and powerlessness, which is clear from the insults, mockery and contempt he met with. Ample references we have in the gospels: "a glutton and drunkard and a friend of tax collectors and sinners"(Mt 11:18f), "a mad man" (Mk 3:22-30), "a Samaritan.... possessed by a devil" (Jn 8:48-52), "the carpenter's son" (Mk 6:3).

The Role of the Prophet of Hope

In our ambivalent human experience all people without exception experience pain, anxiety, injustice, inequality, etc. on the one hand, and love, beauty, harmony, peace etc. on the other. Instinctually we reject the former and embrace the latter. We naturally desire that good and beautiful experiences remain forever and nurse the hope that the desired fullness of being will one day be realised. All our efforts and actions are focussed at this realisation. Kappen visualises the quality of and the way to realise such a hope in a community:

> The more truly human we are, the more our individual horizons of hope tend to coincide with that of society as a whole. The concerns of all become our concern. Every blow dealt to neighbour is experienced as dealt to us. So, everything that gladdens the hearts of others will find an echo in us. It becomes impossible for us to seek our own happiness unconcerned about the happiness of others. The measure of our humanity, then, is the measure in which we find our well-being in the well-being of the community.[170]

The personal-social horizon of hope stands out as the test for the ultimate fullness of man. The ultimate goal of human striving is to reach the fullness of light and life and love, which we call the Divine. Kappen explains the dynamics of the realisation of this goal of life by every human in any culture or tradition and the result of positively or negatively cooperating towards this goal thus:

> To let oneself be taken hold of by the divine is to have one's instincts, drives, sensuousness, knowing and willing brought

to a point of concentration where one becomes capable of changing one's environment of persons and things. On the other hand, whoever blocks the invasion of the Divine suffers decentration and dissolution, and in the end succumbs to the forces of death. In the process he or she becomes a matrix of violence and aggression. Such violence takes a threefold form depending on whether it is directed against the body (economic), the will (political), or the mind (ideological). Contrastively, those who are divinely empowered promote life, freedom and creativity.[171]

Inevitably, at this point, there is an ushering forth of the divine taking hold of us in such a way that we are under its command, though we experience it as a human experience. It is to this human fullness we are hoping for, manifested at the same time as the divine fullness. Those who experience the intimacy with both divine and human are called prophets. Painadath draws out well the becoming of a prophet and his functions as the mediator between the human and the divine to proclaim the divine command of justice in all realms of life:

> The prophet is a person who feels the inner call to articulate God's Word in a concrete situation. The prophet is in a sense a mouthpiece of God and the spokesman of the community as well (*nabi*=the one called; *prophet*=the one who speaks before others). Prophets speak out of an intense experience of the demands of the Spirit "to pluck up and to break down, to destroy and to overthrow, to build and to plant"(Jer 1:10). With this radical sensitivity to the transforming presence of God they proclaim the divine command of justice in all realms of life. For prophets a religious symbol has meaning only in so far as it unfolds the divine depth of human relations.[172]

The prophets are specially called to articulate and bear witness to the ultimate dimension of hope revealed in the concrete historical situations and events. The analysis they make is not neutral but determined by the call they have received for an alternate vision. "This vision runs counter to the vision of the dominant groups in society. It is essentially a revolutionary vision which projects a free, equal, nonexploitative 'alternative community'.[173]

Jesus of Nazareth belongs to such group of prophets. He appeared in a critical period of Jewish history, was taken hold of by the Divine, and deciphered the signs of the times which led him to transform everything around him bringing wholeness. Kappen speaks about his transforming presence:

> In his presence the chaotic reverted to form, death ebbed away to make room for the influx of life. At his command the tempest subsided, the raging sea resumed its calm, withered bodies turned whole, the leper was cleansed, the blind regained sight, the recesses of the human spirit diffusing light and love. Power went out of him to heal not only individuals but also a sick society and a decaying religion.[174]

In an exceptional way he was taken hold of the horizon of hope for humanity as a community filled with love, justice, and freedom. When he said to his disciples, "Set your mind on God's Kingdom and his justice before everything else, and all the rest will come to you as well" (Mt 6:33), all his focus was the realisation of the fullness of man, which he meant as the Kingdom of God, a vision of the future of human-divine community of the end-time. "It is therefore in the light of Jesus' hope in the reign of God that we should understand his teaching, his controversies with adversaries, his practice of working cures and driving out demons, and above all, his tragic death on the cross."[175] The manifestation of power in Jesus was opposed even to the extend of removing him from the face of the earth by murdering him at the prime of his youth. The murderers were the powerful people of society who held on to the prevailing ideology of the dominant ones with an effort to keep the *status quo*.

Nature of the Counter-culture – the Kingdom of God

Jesus began his proclamation by saying that the Kingdom of God is at hand, repent and believe in the good news (Mk 1:15). Through his words and deeds he shows that the kingdom of God has already arrived but its fulfilment rests on the response people make. The newness of the kingdom Jesus preached depends upon the conversion people make to come out from the old ways that are enslaving and dehumanising to one that is leading to freedom, fellowship and justice. He considers himself to be a special messenger from God to bring good news to the poor, freedom to the captives and liberation to the oppressed (Lk 4:18). This good news of the reign of God that Jesus proclaims is the revelation of God's unconditional love towards us.

Soares Prabhu beautifully explains the newness of the kingdom and the demands the kingdom preached by Jesus makes on the people, urging to change mutual relationships and structures:

> It leads, that is, to *new liberating relationships* with God and with men (God is experienced as *abba*, the Father who loves us unconditionally, and men and women are experienced as brothers and sisters accepting each other in a fellowship of mutual concern), and to *new liberating structures* in society (the end of economic exploitation and political domination of one class by another). The kingdom thus calls for a change of hearts and change of structures. Both are necessary. A change of hearts without a change of structures, besides being suspect (for love must show itself in deeds - 1 Jn 3:17), will leave the present oppression unchanged. A change of structures without a change of hearts will lead to new oppressions, as the 'liberated' oppressed are driven by the as yet unexorcised demons of selfishness and greed that possess them to become oppressors in their turn. Only the two together can shape a world in which there will be neither oppressor nor oppressed, because men have learned, to live together without exploiting one another in fellowship and freedom.[176]

Unlike the expectation and hope of Israel centred around the re-establishment of the new Kingdom in history in the manner of David, with power, Jesus emphatically says that the Kingdom he is planning to establish is based on love and service. "There can be no genuine liberation through an exercise of power, for power does not really make us free, it merely creates new structures of unfreedom. The only truly liberating force in the world is love, and it is this that Jesus offers when he proclaims the coming of the Kingdom."[177] The unique teachings of Jesus like "The Kingdom of Heaven is within you" reminds the fact that in every individual person and in depressed classes there is a potential of God, a given power, or an inward centre which will make you to learn about yourself and gain the self-esteem and self-identity. Jesus was insisting on the need for every man and woman when he said, "You shall know the truth and the truth shall make you free", that God the Creator has assured every human being the experience of the Kingdom of heaven with the needed potential for the business of living in this world.

Counter-culture and Option for the Poor

The good news that Jesus brought to the poor and the oppressed was a prophecy which visualises a future event of blessings to the poor, the coming of God's kingdom. In the gospel passage which we call beatitudes contains this prophecy:

> Blessed are the poor
> because yours is the kingdom of God.
> Blessed are you who are hungry now
> because you shall be satisfied.
> Blessed are you who weep now
> because you shall laugh. (Lk 6: 20-21)

The main thrust of the beatitudes is the subversion of the old and the recreation of the new. "The subversive-constructive character of the Kingdom may be viewed from the different angles — man's relationship to the earth, to his fellowmen and to God."[178] The good news of the reign of God means first of all the abolition of man's estrangement from the earth, which is a future state of affairs when the poor will no longer be poor, the hungry would be satisfied and the oppressed would no longer be miserable. "Blessed are the meek, for they shall inherit the earth." The word 'meek' here also stands for the same class of people referred to as 'poor' in the first beatitude (Mt 5:5). Both words are translations of the same Hebrew word *anawim* which meant "those bent under the weight of oppression", those who have none to plead their cause, and therefore, look to God alone for liberation. (Is 61:1) Kappen writes, "What Jesus envisaged, therefore, is the overthrow of all economic systems in which an aggressive few deprive the helpless many of the earth (the means and fruits of production), and the creation of a new community in which the earth and its abundance will belong to all."[179]

The pursuit of wealth at the cost of others is diametrically opposite to the pursuit of the kingdom of God. We cannot love two masters, mammon and God. No compromise is possible, either love one and reject the other. The powerful and the dominant ideology favour wealth over God and his Kingdom, as wealth is seen as a concrete sign of divine favour and poverty was considered as to be a punishment for sin. Such an understanding suits very well the interests of the rich who can feel comfortable at being close to God and that they were not really exploiting the poor. But Jesus shattered such a complacent thinking by strongly advocating the incompatibility of the pursuit of mammon and the service of God (Mk 10:25). He went further by telling that the blessings of the new belong only to the poor. (Mt 5:3) Jesus, Kappen says, visualises the Kingdom that set a just economic order fulfilling the covenantal promise of God to his people as:

> He looked forward to the definitive vindication of the poor and the return of the land to the dispossessed so that these will not have "to build for others to inhabit, nor plant for others to eat" (Is 65:22; see also Ps 37:11). If so, the Kingdom of *Heaven* is nothing but our earth transformed into "a home of justice" (2 Pt. 3:13). It is the land flowing with milk and honey promised to "those who hunger and thirst for justice."[180]

Jesus' predilection for the poor is evident from his very first

Jesus and Counter-Culture

proclamation at Nazereth:

> The Spirit of the Lord is upon me
> because he has anointed me
> to preach the good news to the poor.
> He has sent me
> to proclaim release to the captives
> and the recovery of sight to the blind
> to set free those who are oppressed,
> to proclaim the Jubilee of the Lord.(Lk 4:18-19)

Jesus made it clear to his listeners that it is the sick that need a doctor (Mk 2:17). He was very compassionate to the helpless masses who were like sheep without a shepherd (Mt 9:36), which shows that he has come to seek and serve the least and the last (Lk 19:7-10). Soares-Prabhu identifies four elements in Jesus' closeness to the poor which spell out his compassion towards them:

> Jesus (1) identifies himself with the poor, in order (2) to show them an active and effective concern. Such a concern looks to (3) the ending of their 'social' poverty, while calling for (4) a 'spiritual' poverty that will set them and their rich exploiters free from 'mammon', the compulsive urge to possess. Together, these four elements spell out the 'compassion' of Jesus (Mt 9:36; Mk 6:34; 8:2) – that active, caring and passionate love which defines so sharply his life-style and sets a pattern for the life-style of his followers, because it is, ultimately, the 'life-style' as it were of God himself. "You must be compassionate, says Jesus, as your Father is compassionate" (Lk 6:36).[181]

Being born in a lower middle class artisan's family Jesus' parents could afford to present only a pair of doves in the temple during the presentation ceremony (Lk 2:24). "He consciously and freely chose to adopt the life-style of a poor wandering preacher and opted to live for, live with and live like the poor Dalits".[182] Jesus challenges the rich and the powerful to conversion, as they are blind, hard-heartedly distancing themselves from the Kingdom of

God promised to the poor by Jesus. As he blesses the poor he also pronounces harsh words towards the rich and powerful (Lk 6:24-26). "He sees his miracles as subverting the existing structures of oppression, dominated by Satan as the symbol of evil."[183] The Dalits who reread the Bible in the context of the struggle for liberation are there with many surprises. They see the struggles of Jesus were precisely against the practice of untouchability prevalent in his place and time. They discovered in Jesus as their God who died for their liberation. Jesus became a Dalit by choice. He chose to serve and not to be served. He reduced himself to a status of servant and slave. His incarnation serves as the critical principle for the liberation of the Dalits.

Jesus the new wine could not be contained in the prevailing economic system. Kappen explains the mode of economic system at Jesus' time and registers the suspicion about it contrasting it with the one that Jesus was envisioning in the new order:

> It was an economy in which a privileged few grew richer and richer at the expense of the many poor. At the root of it lays man's aggression against his neighbour. How could therefore the rich, whose hands were soaked with the blood of the innocent, belong to the new humanity, which God's coming was to usher in? How could those who worship the idol of wealth be at the same time worshipers of the true God? Hence Jesus' pointed criticism of the rich: "How hard it will be for those who have riches to enter the Kingdom of God? It is easier for a camel to go through the eye of the needle than for a rich man to enter the kingdom of God". It was an illusion for the rich to think that they can belong to the new humanity while remaining with in the economic order that made them rich.[184]

The rich young man in the story narrated by Mark carry the same burden as he clung to the economic system which violently deprived the many of their inheritance of the earth. (10:17-22)

This is an urgent call of Jesus to those who wish to enter into the socio-cultural order initiated by him, it is necessary to break with the economy of having and enter into an economy of giving.[185] To say that Jesus means here a reversal of values is misleading, if not incorrect. Kappen explains:

> He did not set more value on poverty than on wealth taken abstractly. Was it the case, the reign of God would be characterised by indigence. No, he spoke of the future as one of abundance, material as well as spiritual. Nor did he mean that the exploited of his day would be exploiters in the age to come and vice versa. That would only have amounted to a reversal of roles, not to the definitive transcending of all exploitation. If he opted for the poor, it was because they were the exploited and, as such, were open to the future God had in store for them, whereas the rich tended to hold fast to the conditions which made and maintained them rich, whereby shutting out the prospect of a radically new order of things.[186]

The poor and the oppressed of India see Jesus and his suffering as the symbol of all those groups and communities who are oppressed and subjugated by the dominant groups. In this, Felix Wilfred endorses that "there is an understanding of Jesus as a *corporate personality*, reflecting the reality of and being in solidarity with the marginal groups of India. In this context, the Biblical interpretation of Jesus as the suffering servant has found much appeal among the Dalits."[187] The long history of resistance and protest against caste-oppression and inequality that the poor and marginalised groups have undertaken enables them to understand the passion and the cross of Jesus in a prophetic point of view. To understand this prophetic dimension of the interpretation of Jesus Christ by the Dalits of India one has to place it against the background of the strong confrontation of the lower and backward castes and classes against the continuing political, cultural and religious hegemony of the Brahminic and other upper castes and classes.[188] In Jesus' praxis, his option for the Dalits and his solidarity with them, the victims and the outcastes was evident.

2. Jesus versus Power and Prestige

In Jesus' time and society money was given the second important value: the prominent value was *prestige* (*izzat* in North Indian languages). "In the oriental world to this day prestige is more important than any other factor and people will commit suicide rather than forfeit it."[189] In the society that was structured, everybody had a particular place in the social ladder. A. Nolan observes, "Nothing at all was ever said or done without taking the status or rank of the persons concerned into account. An insult from someone superior to you would be accepted, even expected! An insult from an equal would be so humiliating as to make life impossible. An insult from an inferior would simply not be tolerated. A constant recognition of status was essential. The people lived off the honour and respect which others gave them."[190] The position, rank, prestige etc. can be assessed by the way you dress and are addressed, though its roots are found in the ancestry, wealth, authority, education and virtue. Even in social and religious realms of life the consideration of status and prestige was very much there. The people who had no status at all, like lunatics, neurotics, the blind, the lame, the deaf, the maimed and minors, were totally excluded.

Jesus contradicted all these norms of honouring and positioning people differently and considered them as part of the fundamental structures of evil existing in society and world at large. He dared to hope for a Kingdom in which such distinctions would have no meaning.[191] We observe this bold attitude of Jesus against power and prestige-hungry people in quite many passages in the Gospels. 'Blessed are you when people hate you, drive you out, abuse you, denounce your name as criminal…'(Lk 6:22). 'Woe to you when the world speaks well of you..' (Lk 6:26). 'Everything they do is done to attract attention, like wearing broader phylacteries, and longer tassels, like wanting to take the place of honour at banquets and the front seats in the synagogues, being greeted obsequiously in the market squares and having people call them Rabbi' (Mt 23:5-7). In the Kingdom envisaged by Jesus those who are very concerned about the prestige and power are automatically out as they cannot be in tune with the Kingdom values. Jesus points out clearly in what the real greatness consists:

> The disciples came to Jesus and said, 'Who is the greatest in the Kingdom of heaven?' So he called a little child to him and set the child in front of them. Then he said, 'I tell you solemnly; unless you change and become like little children you will never enter the Kingdom of heaven. And so, the one who makes himself as little as this little child is the greatest in the Kingdom of heaven.' (Mt 18:1-4)

The little child, the image of the Kingdom, the live parable of 'littleness' as against greatness and power, is a symbol of those who have the lowest place in the society, the poor and the oppressed, the beggars, the prostitutes and tax-collectors – the people whom Jesus called little ones or the least.[192]

In a power hungry world Jesus lacked any position, power or prestige. Soares-Prabhu observes, "Jesus had no religious prestige: he was not a priest born into a priestly family. He enjoyed no intellectual status: he was not a recognised theologian who had been trained in a scribal school (Jn 7:15). He commanded no political power. He did not enjoy privileges of wealth. Yet he taught with authority in word and deed."[193] Jesus offers an alternative way of exercising authority. Amaladoss explains:

> The very idea of the Kingdom of God is the assertion that God alone is the ruler and every human authority is derived from and is accountable to God. Every person is free and responsible for himself/herself and answerable only to God. Jesus often criticises the religious and political authorities of his day for not being responsive to the needs of the people. He himself gives an example of authority as service: in becoming human he empties himself and becomes a servant. He washes the feet of his disciples as a concrete illustration of a new relationship between power and

service.[194]

The use and exercise of power must legitimise itself by its care for the poor and the oppressed. Jesus exhorts his disciples to become like children and enjoy the freedom they have in life. The Kingdom of God, which Jesus preached and pointed out as the true nature of the new humanity, consists of a life lived in human solidarity, sharing, service and freedom. Kappen points out the demands of the Gospel ideal of living out the new humanity that Jesus has put forward for his disciples:

> Common possession of the earth and its plenty is at once the result of, and the condition for, the reconciliation of man to man. God's reign will mark the end of all class domination and abolish the rule of private interest and competition. Not the market where the commodities are bought and sold, but the home where everything assumes the form of a gift, is the true symbol of the new humanity. With its coming, things, be they product of labour or not, will become the bond between man and man instead of being instruments for the exploitation of man by man. Similarly the authority and power will give way to service as the true measure of human greatness.(Mk 10:42-44).[195]

The teaching and the practice of Jesus were always posing a challenge to the culture of domination in political life prevalent in his time, be it in Herod, in the Sanhedrin or in Rome, or among the Zealots. Kappen refers to the ideology and the strategy of the Zealots whose activities were centred on Galilee, "The Zealots were determined to throw out the Romans by force and restore the kingly rule of David and Solomon. They looked forward to the coming of a political Messiah who would help achieve their goal. Ruthlessly crushed by the Romans more than once, they bided their time for decisive action, but meanwhile resorted to sporadic acts of violence in guerrilla style."[196] In the temptation of Jesus in the desert (Mt 4:8-10) Jesus made a definitive option against political Messianism. There are ample references in the Gospel that the crowd on seeing the miracles Jesus did, nursed the hope that he will soon proclaim himself as the political Messiah they were looking for. The option of Jesus against the political Messianism becomes clearer in the agony he underwent in the garden of Olives:

> It looks as though the ideological rift between himself, on the one hand, and the disciples and the crowd, on the other, assumed on the eve of his death the form of a chasm in his own soul between what he willed (the thoughts of men) and what God willed (the thoughts of God): 'Abba, Father, all things are possible to thee; remove this cup from me; yet not *what I will*, but *what thou wilt*' (Mk 14:36). The agony ends with his final acceptance of the thoughts and the purposes of God as opposed to those of men.[197]

Jesus was opposed to the kind of power structure in the political and religious spheres the Sanhedrin was wielding with its headquarters in the temple of Jerusalem. Kappen gives some of the reasons for Jesus to hold such a stand:

> First, his radical reinterpretation of the Law, his rejection of the distinction between the sacred and the profane, his re-affirmation of the primacy of love over cult, and his prediction of the destruction of the temple, undermined the authority of the priesthood. Second, in chasing away the vendors and the changers of money from the temple premises he challenged the economic infrastructure of the political power of the Sanhedrin. Third, the universal character of the new humanity he preached contradicted the nationalist particularism of Jewish political power, much as its guardians rejected the hopes and the strategy of the Zealots. Last, the priesthood had a vested interest in maintaining the status quo since they were ruling by the favour of Rome.[198]

Jesus could not accept a system which allowed the domination of a privileged few in the distribution of power, a domination of man by man. He taught his disciples that you should not follow the existing system where the rulers lorded it over their subjects and made the weight of their authority felt on them (Mk 10:42-44). He asked his disciples to renounce radically all exercise of power as he said, "Whoever would be great among you must be your servant, and whoever would be first among you must be the slave of all". Jesus is pointing towards "a social order where all are slaves to one another, and none is master over others. Rather, each man will be master and slave in one: slave, because he recognises each member of the community as an absolute value, not a mere means to his personal ends; master, because he, in turn, is recognised by all as an absolute value. In this sense, the future community is the dialectical supersession of mastery and slavery, a supersession, which preserves on a higher level the truth of both, namely, being-for-oneself (mastery) and being-for-others (slavery)."[199] In the new humanity Jesus favours the least and powerless as in it there will be neither rulers nor ruled. Jesus through his dissent sets into motion the resistive forces which challenge the socio-cultural structures that maintain the unjust division between the dominant and the subaltern. Jesus affirms the human identity of the subaltern on the one hand and empowers them in their own way against the discriminations and oppressions.

3. Counter-culture Demands Active Faith

Jesus was deeply moved by compassion for the poor and the oppressed, and so his focus was for the total liberation of humans (which he understood as the Kingdom). But this Kingdom that he thought to be imminent would be impossible without his belief in God. The realisation of the extraordinary high values like fraternity, dignity, equality, freedom, justice, etc., that are supposed to reign supreme in this Kingdom, might be thought as a difficult task, but could be appreciated to take place as a *miracle*. Though it is an impossible task, an utopia for humans, it is possible for God. Jesus hoped for a miracle. He might have thought of the Kingdom to be built like a building or a city. Such a Kingdom cannot be built but can only come. Nolan elaborates:

> Even the most powerful, most influential and most benign

leaders would not be able to establish a society like this. Worldly power, the power which forces its will upon others, even when applied ever so gently, could only produce something different from the total liberation and freedom that Jesus had in mind. People can be liberated from this or that form of domination but nobody can force a man to be free. All we can build are the conditions that will enable a man to be free if he so chooses. The kingdom itself cannot be achieved; it must be received – as a gift.[200]

There is a power that can work miracles, the supreme power that is behind all the powers at work in man and nature, the depth dimension of the world we live in. For Jesus the almighty power that achieves the impossible is called faith. Faith releases the power of God within us to enable us to receive the Kingdom as a gift. Those who have strong faith received the power of God, as we see in the miracles of Jesus in curing the sick, sinners released from their sins, etc. Kappen explains the dynamics of faith [faith understood as the openness to the divine] as the outpouring of the Divine through gifts to the humans even in the ordinary existence:

> The Divine presents itself to us either as a gift or as a challenge. As a gift in all experiences of beauty, love and joy where our inmost being reaches out to its highest possibilities. Here we are on the borderland where the human impinges on the Divine. We are taken hold of by the Divine in such wise that we are no longer our own masters but bonded to it in body and soul. This is no esoteric experience accessible only to the initiated few, but something that forms part of the very fabric of our day to day human existence.[201]

Faith is a radical commitment to life that admits no half-measures or compromise. No one can serve two masters: either the Kingdom of God and its values of basic orientations to life, or the anti-God. Faith is a decision for the Kingdom as the destiny of mankind. "Faith derives its power from the truth of what is believed and hoped for...If the Kingdom of God as preached by Jesus is true to life, if it is the truth about man and his needs, if it is the only thing that can bring mankind to fulfilment and satisfaction, then faith in this kind of Kingdom can change the world and achieve the impossible. The power of faith is the power of truth."[202]

Faith also is a *task* besides being gift. "The Kingdom in which Jesus wanted his contemporaries to believe was a kingdom of love and service, a Kingdom of human brotherhood in which every man is loved and respected because he is a man. Nobody can believe in and hope for such a kingdom unless he has learned to be moved with compassion for his fellow-man".[203] Man responds to God in the gift of faith with a prophetic action against hate, violence, injustice, exploitation and every form of human bondage. Kappen writes about the tension involved in the gift and task, contemplation and prophetic action, while one opens oneself to the Divine in faith in the realisation of the future:

> It [faith] compels us to make an option against the forces of death and dissolution at work in us and in society at large. Whoever hearkens to the challenge is bound to live in creative tension between the fracturedness of the human existence here and now and the hoped for plenitude of the future. If the Divine as gift calls for wonder, thankfulness, surrender, adoration and celebration, the Divine as challenge calls for hope, and for prophetic action. Faith as openness to the Divine involves a wide spectrum of human responses ranging from contemplation to creative-transformative action.[204]

In Jesus we can see the coming together of contemplative mystical insights and the prophetic-transformative-action, which resulted in his crucifixion, as he was instrumental in shaking the socio-economic and religio-cultural establishment of Jerusalem to its foundations and exposing its rootedness in the domination and enslavement of humans. Painadath mentions about the unity and the dialectics between mysticism and prophecy, "The mystical perspective evolves out of a unitive awareness of the divine immanence in the 'cave of the heart', while the prophetic approach emerges out of an encounter with the divine Lord in the struggles of history. **Ultimately every genuine mystic is a prophet and every true prophet is a mystic**".[205]

The greatness and relevance of Jesus lies precisely, "in his ability to hold together in an intimate and indissoluble unity man's God-experience and his Man-concern. He is in fact the living embodiment of their oneness... The divine, that is, has identified itself with the human. Humanity has become the locus of our encounter with God and our God-experience is mediated to us no longer through mystical contemplation but in interhuman concern".[206] The teachings of Jesus in the gospels are so strongly man - and world - affirming. "The gospel ideal is not the wholly unrelated man (the *sanyasin*) seeking self-realisation in absolute aloneness, but the radically committed 'apostle' spending himself and being spent (2 Cor 12:15) in the unstinted service of a freely accepted 'slavery' towards his brothers (Gal 5: 13-14). And the gospel way is not the way of Gnostic illumination (*jnana marga*) nor the way of cultic ritual (*karma marga*), nor even the way of mystical devotion (*bhakti marga*). It is rather the way of concern (*agape*)."[207] The liberation Jesus envisages is one that liberates the whole person in community. That is to say one has to abandon all things that makes one to cling on to oneself [selfishness, the opposite of love, is the root of sin], which we call sin.[208] Liberation of the community demands the liberation from all social sins, due to *papa* (sin), or *samsara* (bondage to the cycle of existence), or *avidya* (ignorance), in the form of unjust structures.

Jesus' love and freedom

Jesus, the mystic and the prophet, visualised the true liberation of humanity, which means to create a milieu for all to live in solidarity, freedom and justice taking up the cause of man entering into every sphere of life – economic, political, personal, social, cultural, religious etc. The quest for liberation is the test of faith, and the only truly liberating force in the world is love. Jesus proclaimed that the kingdom of God rests on the people's capacity to love and he traced the source of that proclamation in his own experience of God's unconditional love, God as *abba* – loving parent. This experience of Jesus, God as *abba,* loving parent, frees him from all inner conditioning, compulsions and fears.

The love commandment of Jesus (Mt 24:34-40) as taught by him does not ask us to love God and neighbour as if they were two distinct objects to our love. Rather it reads: "You shall love the Lord your God with all your heart, with all your soul, and with all your mind, this means, you shall love your neighbour as yourself." That is, in concrete, love God means to love the neighbour; and this is the 'great commandment' that Jesus gives which founds and includes all others. There is a significant question to ask: who is my neighbour? Soares-Prabhu explains, "In defining 'neighbour' Jesus allows no distinctions of caste, race, gender or class (Lk 10:30-37). For the love with which we love neighbour is not a human disposition (determined by human prejudices or preference) but it is the reflex of the experience of God's love for us. To the extend we experience God's love, we love neighbour the way that God loves us. But God loves us unconditionally. His love is not a response to our goodness…God's love for us can make no conditions and put no limits. It reaches out to the unrewarding, undeserving, even those hostile to us (Lk 6:32-36)."[209]

Jesus produced his manifesto of freedom when he, filled with the power of the Spirit, went up to the synagogue and read the passage which happened to be from Isaiah: "The spirit of the Lord is upon me; he has sent me to announce the good news to the poor, to proclaim release for prisoners and recovery of sight for the blind; to let the broken victims go free, to proclaim the year of the Lord's favour."(Is 61:1-2, Lk 4:18-19) The healing touch of Jesus made the victims to commune with nature, with humans and with God. The measure of such communion is in fact the measure of one's humanity. We marvel at Jesus' freedom, by which he experienced God as love in the neighbour. As he was not possessed by the demons of greed and pride he could say with authority: "The Son of Man has nowhere to lay his head" (Lk 9:15); "The Son of Man has come not to be served but to serve and to lay down his life as a ransom for many"(Mk 10:45). Jesus' message of good news to the poor is basically the same as in the Sermon on the Mount, where the stress is on God's intervention in history to set free those who are oppressed, weighed down under the yoke of exploitation, with none to defend their cause.

The revealed God, however, is the God who liberates the oppressed ones and who has sent Jesus as the messiah of the poor and the sinners, a God of justice who has a bias for the poor and the oppressed precisely because His beloved Son Jesus Christ was oppressed and a victim. Jesus is then the revelation of God's covenant with the poor. We can really witness to the specific role of Jesus Christ in history only in solidarity with the victims.

The heart of Dalit experiences is their pathos or suffering. The sufferer knows God in and through the pathos. God participates in the human pain, as is characterised in the New Testament as the passion of Jesus symbolised in his crucifiction. God's people are saved through the redemptive suffering of God in Jesus Christ who as the chosen servant of God will bring justice to the nations (Mt. 12: 18-21).

4. Jesus' Vision of a Society of Equals

Though Jesus was not aware of the structural origins of the evils of the society, as we are aware today, he was committed to the structural changes in society and to justice, which is amply clear from his vision of a new society implied in his proclamation of the Kingdom of God.

Jesus a Friend of Outcastes and Sinners

The people with whom Jesus wanted to have company and turned his attention to are called in different names: the poor, the crippled, the lepers, the hungry, the miserable, the blind, the lame, sinners, prostitutes, tax-collectors, demoniacs, the persecuted, the downtrodden, the captives, all who labour and overburdened, the rabble who know nothing of the law, the least, the last, the crowds, the little ones, and the babes or the lost sheep of Israel. Jesus spent most of his time with them. They include many of his disciples and a good number of these disciples came from such groups. Jesus was energised and empowered by their presence and the life shared with them, "as a knife that is sharpened in fire, to revolt against the oppressive system, in solidarity with his fellow Dalits, and liberate them in order to lead them to the counter-culture and new community of the Kingdom of God."[210] Rayan observes, "Dalitness need not mean resignation to unfreedom, or the loss of the heart's nobility. It rather sharpens the critical spirit, ferments the thrust for freedom, and energises the community for the struggle."[211] The solidarity of Jesus with the Dalits and outcastes is symbolised as the baptism of immersion "in the Dalitness of the oppressed in order to remove its victims and plant them in the realm of freedom, dignity and creative living."[212]

The solidarity of Jesus with the poor and the outcastes is symbolised in the incarnation of Jesus Christ: "The word was made flesh, and dwelt among us". Flesh stands for humankind, for all forms of life, in its transience and fragility. Flesh also stands for solidarity and relatedness, as Soares-Prabhu explains:

> Man and wife become one flesh (Gen 2:24); members of the family are of same "flesh and blood" (Gen 37:27); the poor and the needy of our people are our own flesh (Is 58:7). Flesh stands for the solidarity of humankind, for the fact that humankind is not a collection of isolated individuals, but an organic whole in which what happens to one happens to all...Humankind has now become the proper locus of our encounter with God. We meet God in neighbour; we love God by loving neighbour.[213]

The incarnation and its mystery must be understood as a call to follow Jesus in his solidarity with humanity, which is concretely expressed in his identification with the outcastes and the poor.

Table fellowship: symbol of Cultural Revolution

A person's greatness could be understood and graded in the measure he/she is capable of tuning himself/herself to whatever is true, beautiful and wholesome in the milieu he/she is in. As Kappen observes, "the more refined his sensibility the more intense is the revulsion he feels against all that mars the beauty of living: unlove, hatred, injustice, aggression and social fragmentation. He experiences every blow dealt to the least of his kind as dealt to himself. The agony he feels inevitably becomes word, protest and contestation. He thus becomes the subverter of the status quo, thereby inviting reprisal from the guardians of the law and order".[214] In Jesus of Nazareth we have such a person who is fully tuned to the revelation of beauty, goodness and love as well as sensitive to every mutilation and fragmentation of human beings. A clear example of this sensitivity of Jesus to the social wholeness is his table fellowship where he has shown courage to protest against the social mentality of purity-pollution existing in his time.

Marcus J. Borg in his study on Jesus shows that his table fellowship with tax collectors and sinners as "one of the most conspicuous and controversial aspects of the renewal movement founded by him".[215] To understand the significance of the table-fellowship of Jesus it is important to know the prevailing social conditions. Kappen gives some of the details of the social practices, relations and their implications:

> Gone were the days of tribal unity when social relations among the Israelites were founded on kinship and common property. Society had become fragmented under the system of private property, money economy, and state power. No less sharp was the division brought about by the theory and the practice of ritual purity. Pure were those who scrupulously observed every detail of the written and oral law; impure those who did not. Impurity was attached to various categories of people such as those engaged in unclean professions (shepherds,

barbers, tanners, tailors, tax-gatherers, etc.), the illegitimately born, and above all, the gentiles. Contact with them was shunned by the respectable classes; much more so sitting at the table with them.[216]

Jesus protested not only orally against the state of affairs concerning the question of purity and pollution but also he maintained a counter-practice by sitting at table with the tax-gatherers and sinners against the prevailing taboos (Mk 2:15f; Mt 9:10f). Jesus dined with the social and religious outcastes, for which he had to face sharp and sustained criticism. The meal-fellowship of Jesus, Kappen says: "is not just one among the many gracious deeds he performed. In a way it sums up his entire mission. In it are telescoped many dimensions of meaning, which need unravelling."[217] "The table fellowship of Jesus is more than a form of pastoral care. It is the expression of a radically new (and therefore thoroughly disturbing) theological vision, rooted in a new experience of God, and calling for a new kind of society."[218] About the revolutionary impact of table-fellowship on the social life Nolan writes:

> It would be impossible to overestimate the impact these meals must have had upon the poor and sinners. By accepting them as friends and equals Jesus had taken away their shame, humiliation and guilt. By showing them that they mattered to him as people he gave them a sense of dignity and released them from their captivity. The physical contact which he must have had with them when reclining at the table (compare Jn 13:25) and which he obviously never dreamed of disallowing (Lk 7:38-39) must have made them feel clean and acceptable.[219]

Jesus' table fellowship with the outcaste was a threat to all those who wielded power and position, even for the religious elite, as its revolutionary message was powerful enough to shake the foundations of the security the socio-cultural system was providing for the high caste and elite groups. It is true that Jesus ate and drank with the tax-collectors and gentiles and showed

Jesus and Counter-Culture

intimacy and compassion under the shadow of cross and he convincingly demonstrated that God's love and his kingdom are not conditional, that the powerful ones and the elite could not monopolise God. Without exception God reaches out to all and all can capture it by the practice of the love commandment.

5. Towards A Counter-cultural Interpretation

The prime focus of Jesus mission on earth was to gather all people together and bring them to God the Father. This mission of gathering human fragments prompted him to this kind practice, table fellowship forming community of equals linked together in the bonds of love. "Whoever does the will of my Father is my brother, my sister, my mother."[Mk 3:35] "Any meal shared expresses as well as creates community; it is a meeting of people in intimacy and friendship, a celebration of the togetherness of the living. What distinguishes the meal fellowship of Jesus from the usual family meal was its new basis. The latter had for its basis kinship; the former, the praxis of love".[220] For placing love as the central and unifying principle in the formation of a community of equals Jesus might have strongly repudiated any movement from the part of the people which tried to base their identity upon the loyalties and prejudices of race, nationality, language, culture, class, ancestry, family, generation, political party and religious denomination. Soares-Prabhu clarifies the stand of Jesus and the basis of his spirituality interpreting the table fellowship against the exclusive approach of the Pharisees:

> Against the background of these exclusive meals of the Pharisaic associations (*chaburim*) or the Essene community (*hayyachad*) at which 'members only', that is, only those who satisfied the rigorous conditions for membership in the group, were welcome, the table fellowship of Jesus with 'tax collectors and sinners', the religious and the social outcasts of his time, stands out as a powerful challenge. It challenges the Pharisaic and the Essene ideal of Israel as a holy community, whose holiness is to be maintained by preserving

a state of complete separation from all that is ritually unclean. It implies instead a radically new understanding of holiness, of community and of God... True holiness is no longer defined by a 'separation' from the world, which would reflect the 'otherness' of God; but by the 'mercy', which imitates God's utterly unconditional love. Religion is no longer a matter of ritual purity or cultic competence but of interhuman compassion.[221]

Kappen finds that the new basis of love for the practices like table fellowship of Jesus can pave the way for a counterculture: "In the new dispensation everyone will be brother, sister and mother to everyone else. In other words, man's relations with his neighbour will retain the intimacy and warmth of family ties while, at the same time, superseding their exclusiveness. Seen in this perspective, Jesus' eating and drinking with the marginalised was radical social praxis, aimed at creating a counter-community and a counter-culture."[222] Here in the table fellowship, Jesus brings in a change in the attitude of the existing economic relationship of buying and selling to an economy of giving. Kappen clarifies: "The meals he shared contain the seed of a new economy. Here the products of labour – food and drink – are not commodities but gifts. What is given in freedom mediates the mutual love of the giver and the recipient. As such it binds the many into one, into one community...Thus he dissociated himself from the economy of buying and selling, and inaugurated an economy of giving in which the product of work once again becomes the bond between the humans."[223]

The Pure versus the Impure

The question of purity and impurity is central to all religions. Kappen explores the question finding the distinction between the pure and the impure and its origin in the world outlook of 'primitive' men in their struggle to fashion the tools for controlling the forces that environed them; where it was crucial for them to discern the life-giving and the death-dealing aspects

Jesus and Counter-Culture

so that they could foster one and ward off the other.[224] Here we see the pure that is contributing to life, distinct from the impure, whatever is detrimental to it. Applying this principle the sages sort out the list of things pure and impure and frame rules of conduct for the ordinary people; eventually applying the principle to persons, groups, professions etc. "The pure was identified with the Divine and the impure with demoniac. What was originally a magico-mythical conception was thus overlaid with the religious meaning. This served to further intensify the contrast between the pure and the impure."[225] Starting from God, the most pure and sacred, everything is placed in the hierarchical order. Kappen elaborates how the hierarchical system of purity and impurity crept into the Jewish society and became an instrument of domination:

> Among the Jews this conception (hierarchical rendering of purity-impurity) found spatial expression in the belief that the temple, especially the Holy of Holies, was the centre of the sacred universe. The farther removed was any space from the temple, the less sacred it was. Society too, was structured after the pattern of a descending gradation of purity. Priests formed the apex, set apart as they were to mediate life divine and to deal with sacred things like the altar, sacrifice and worship. Lower came the laity, who, in turn, were classified in terms of descending degrees of purity in respect to origin, profession, food habits, and the like. This suited admirably the interests of the priestly class who, with their knowledge of the pure and the impure and with their control over the means of cultic purification, could henceforth exercise domination over the entire population. As far as the Hebrews were concerned, though the notion of pollution originated in very ancient days, it was the priestly class that elaborated it into a system.[226]

The whole system of laws of purity and their observance mattered much to the Pharisees and the Scribes, but it was not a matter of concern for the ordinary people. The notion of ritual purity, Kappen says, "is essentially amoral, in so far as purity or impurity is conceived as an objective quality inhering in things, actions and situations, irrespective of the free decision of the individuals. It becomes also *immoral* when human beings, too, are classified as pure and impure. For it leads to the fragmentation of the community and to the domination of some by others."[227] Such an understanding of purity and impurity has nothing to do with religion, as it is not connected any way with man's relationship with the transcendent ground and goal of being.

According to Soares-Prabhu there is a marked change in the relationship with God in the NT from that of postexilic Judaism, a change from God distinct from the profane world to God who reaches out to people in communion, when one dares to practice what Jesus did in the table fellowship, paving way to a new social order:

> Such a radical redrawing of the map of his social world is possible to Jesus, because he can draw on a radically new experience of God. God is not experienced by him primarily as 'holy' (the source of numinous power, the 'wholly other') sharply separated from the profane world, and demanding that his people become a 'holy' people, separated from other peoples by sharply defined purity lines, such as those elaborated in postexilic Judaism. Rather Jesus experiences God as 'merciful', a God who reaches out in forgiveness and love to all people, across all the lines of separation that we like to draw (Jew/Gentile; righteous/sinners; clean caste/dalit), and who summons his people to a similar compassion, that is, to an effective love that will reach out beyond the bonds of kinship, clan and race to the outsider, the undeserving, the enemy (Lk 6:32-36).[228]

In the controversy with the Scribes and Pharisees Jesus illustrates well his attitude with regard to the laws of pollution (Mk 7:1-23). He declares that all food are clean (Mk 7:19) and he justifies his disciples for eating food with unwashed hands saying, "There is nothing outside a man which by going into him can defile him; but the things which come out of man are what defile him"(Mk 7:15). "Evil desires, harmful intentions, discriminating biases and contempt for one another pollute a person. Hence, such malicious Pharisees and Brahmins are in fact polluted and not the tax collectors, sinners and Dalits.[229] Jesus quotes Isaiah to remind his opponents, "This people honour me with their lips, but their heart is far from me." Kappen interpreting the passage touches the root of the problem saying that it is not the periphery that makes us free but the centre, the heart, the seat of wisdom and love:

> The rules of purity touch only the periphery of human existence inasmuch as it is a moment in the cosmic process of life and death, birth and dissolution. In order to effect a rupture in the cosmic membrane and achieve a breakthrough into the true realm of freedom, one has to shift one's attention from the periphery to the centre. And that centre is the heart, the deepest core of each person where loving, knowing, willing and feeling have their common root. The heart is the seat of love and of the knowledge born of love. It is the point of irradiation from which humans reach out to communion with God and the humankind. It is through the heart that they hear every word God utters.[230]

Jesus took the radical stand that the source of all defilement is unlove and injustice. That is why the teaching and practice of Jesus based on the command to seek justice and love was capable of subverting the value system of his day based on the laws of purity made by man, and what he initiated was not less than a counterculture. "Jesus' cultural revolution transformed the dominated outcastes and untouchables and created a counter-culture that would be built not on hierarchy, inequality and competition but on cooperation, equality, fraternity, and liberty of all sections of the society."[231]

6. A Prophetic Countercultural Movement

There will be always a community as the medium and milieu for a counterculture to emerge. Jesus formed a community of his disciples around him to be sent out and preach with the same faith, hope, commitment and destiny of their master, Jesus himself. Just like the master, the disciples were supposed to sever all the ties with the dominant enslaving and dehumanising culture (which has its roots in personal and social sins) and promote a counterculture and community of freedom, fellowship and justice. Soares-Prabhu summarises the characteristics of the counterculture (kingdom of God), which Jesus was envisioning:

> When the revelation of God's love (the Kingdom) meets its appropriate response in man's trusting acceptance of this love (repentance), there begins a mighty movement of personal and societal liberation which sweeps through human history. The movement brings freedom inasmuch as it liberates each individual from inadequacies and obsessions that shackle him. It fosters fellowship, because it empowers free individuals to exercise their concern for each other in a genuine community. And it leads on to justice, because it impels every true community to adopt the just societal structures, which alone make freedom and fellowship possible.[232]

The post-Easter community came out of the launching of the Jesus movement in a big way. It had the traits of the counterculture envisioned by Jesus. According to the Acts, the early believers held everything in common, to be distributed to each according to his need. (Acts 4:32-35) Soares-Prabhu describes them as "a radically free community, which could respond to the economic plight of the poor by 'sharing'; face cultural threat by abandoning defensive encystment to cultural pluralism; overcome the 'will to power' through an unlimited readiness to serve; and confront the towering inequalities of a racist, sexist and slavish society by affirming the radical equality of all human beings. The movement was extraordinarily radical."[233]

As a countercultural movement the early Christian community was essentially prophetic, as it was centred upon the reign of God to come. It was rather based on a broad vision presented by Jesus and not a blueprint valid for all times. And so, it is the task of every generation to march forward to the unknown destiny, with Jesus as their head, translating Jesus' theological vision in sociological categories. Soares-Prabhu explains it again:

> The vision of Jesus summons us, then, to a ceaseless struggle against the demonic structures of unfreedom (psychological and sociological) erected by mammon; and to a ceaseless creativity that will produce in every age new blueprints for a society ever more consonant with the Gospel vision of man. Lying on horizons of human history and yet part of it, offered to us as a gift yet confronting us as a challenge, Jesus' vision of a new society stands before us as an unfinished task, summoning us to a permanent revolution.[234]

It is true that the prophetic-subversive thrust the early believers had in the beginning received from Jesus was not kept all through, but it was as a prophetic movement there in broad features up to the close of the first century. At the close of the third century, the Christian communities were coming to terms with the world and the movement was loosing its countercultural character. What originally was a movement of the disinherited classes drifted into a religion of the *status quo*. It is this Church, deeply entrenched in the values of the dominant classes, that was transplanted in India. Can the Church as a movement become prophetic, recapturing the values of Jesus once again? Kappen says, "For that to happen, she must be prepared to dismantle her cultic-legal-hierarchical apparatus, give up her secular institutions, end her dependence on foreign money, and throw overboard her theology of legitimation and spirituality of resignation... However, the conditions favourable to such a radical conversion may emerge if a cataclysmic social revolution were to overtake the whole of Indian society, which would, more or less violently, dispossess the Church of her property, money and institutions".[235] There is a sign of hope in the emergence of radical Christian groups who are bearers of the values of Jesus, of love, justice and freedom, who find no difficulty to join hand with all like minded people of different religious persuasions, to the creation of a more human social order.

NOTES

PART THREE

1. K. P. Rao, *Caste and Alternative Culture*, Madras: GLTC & RI, 1995, 86.
2. *Samatta Nikaya* 5:421 ff.
3. Aloysius Pieris, *An Asian Theology of Liberation*, Maryknoll: Orbis, 1988, 75.
4. *ibid.*
5. *ibid,* 76-77.
6. S. Kappen, *Cultural Revolution*, Bombay: BILD, 1983, 39.
7. *Dhammapada*, 1:5, *Sources*, 122.
8. R. Siriwardhena, *Equality and the Religious Traditions of Asia*, London: Frances Printers, 1987, 59-60.
9. *Ibid,* 60.
10. Piadassi Thera, *The Virgin's Eye*, Colombo: Buddhist Pub. Society, 1980, 33-52. Quoted by R. S. Vardena, *Equality and the Religious...*, 61.
11. Cf. Romila Thapar, *A History of India*, Vol. 1, London: Penguin Books, 1990, 306.
12. *Bhagavata Purana*, 337-362. Cf. S. Kappen, *Jesus an Cultural* ..., 43.
13. K. P. Rao, *Caste and Alternative* ..., 106.
14. Stan Lourdesamy, *Religion as a Social Protest*, Culcutta: Multibook Agency, 1993, 54.
15. Kosambi, *Myth and Reality*, Bombay: Popular Prakashan, 1962, 32. Cf. in Kappen's *Jesus and Cultural Revolution*, 43.
16. K. P. Rao, *Caste and Alternative....*, 107-108.
17. *Ibid*, 109.
18. S. Kappen, "Materialistic Conception of History and the Religious Tradition", *Negations*, 8 (Oct-Dec 1983), 7.
19. J. R. Kamble, *The Depressed....* ,53.

[20] John D Mello, "Mahatma Phule and Reinterpretation of Culture", *Jeevadhara*, Vol XXII, No. 127, Jan 1992, 51.
[21] *Ibid*, 52.
[22] Rosalind O' Hanlon, *Caste, Conflict and Ideology*, Bombay: Orient and Longman, 1985, 142.
[23] Jotirao Phule, Slavery in D. Keer and S. G. Malshe (eds), *The Collected Works of Mahatma Phule*, Bombay: Maharashtra Society for Literature and Culture, 1969 (Marathi), 91. Cf. John D Mellow, "Mahatma Phule and ...", 52.
[24] John D Mello, "Mahatma Phule and...", 52.
[25] Rosalind O' Hanlon, *Caste, Conflict....*, 158.
[26] K. P. Rao, *Caste and...*, 198.
[27] M. Amaladoss, "Periyar and Liberation in Tamilnadu" in *Towards an Indian Theology of Liberation*, (ed) Puthanngady, P., Bangalore:*ITA&NBCLC*, 1986, 184.
[28] K. P. Bhagat, "Dr. B. R. Ambedkar: The Modern Messiah of India", *NCCR*, Vol. CXV, No. 8, 1995, 705-706.
[29] M. Amaladoss, *A Call to* ..., 61.
[30] K. P. Bhagat, "Dr B. R. Ambedkar...", 706.
[31] B. R. Ambedkar, *Ranada, Gandhi and Jinnah*, 36. C.f K. P. Bhagat, "Dr. B. R. Ambedkar: The..., 706.
[32] Gail Omvedt, *Dalits and the Democratic Revolution*, New Delhi: Sage Publications, 1994, 223-224.
[33] B. R. Ambedkar, *States and Minorities*, Bombay: Thacker & Co. Ltd, 1947, 33.
[34] K. P. Bhagat, "B. R. Ambedkar: the ..", 708.
[35] Paradkar, "The Religious Quest of Ambedkar", 47. Cf. A. R. Thumma in *Dalit Liberation Theology*, Delhi: ISPCK, 2000, 35.
[36] Keer Dhananjay, *Dr. Ambedkar: Life and Mission*, Bombay: Popular Prakasan, (1954) 1991, 490.
[37] Ravinder Kumar, "Gandhi, Ambedkar and Dalits", *The Hindu*, May 23, 1994, 10.
[38] E. Zelliot, *From Untouchable to Dalit. Essays on Ambedkar movement*, New Delhi: Manohar, 1992, 153.

39 M. K. Gandhi, *Young India*, 1921. Cf. J. R. Kamble, *The Depressed Classes in India*, New Delhi: ICSSR, 1979, 181.
40 J. Maliekal, *Caste in India*...,50.
41 I. Jesudasan, *A Ghandhian Theory of Liberation*, Maryknoll: Orbis Books, 1984, 78-79.
42 M. K. Gandhi, *An Interpretation*, London: 1948, 77. Cf. by J. R. Kamble, *The Depressed*..., 181.
43 I. Jesudasan, *A Gandhian*...,78.
44 M. K. Gandhi, *An Interpretation*, Cf. J. R Kamble, *The Deppressed*..., 190.
45 Ravinder Kumar, *The Hindu*, May 23, 1994, 10.
46 *The Janata Weekly*, Bombay, 22 April, 1950. Cf. J. R. Kamble, *The Depressed*.., 191
47 Gail Omvedt, "Peasants, Dalits and Women: Democracy and India's New Social Movements", in M. Mohanti *et al* (eds), *People's Rights, Social Movements and the State in the Third World*, New Delhi: Sage Publications, 1998, 223-241.
48 Gail Omvedt, in K. L. Sharma, *Caste and Class* ..., 162.
49 V. Kumar, "Deconstruction and Reconstruction of Dalits in U. P.", in A. Pinto (ed.) *Dalits: Assertion for Identity*, New Delhi: ISI, 1999, 49.
50 V. Kumar, "Deconstruction..., 56.
51 K. L. Sharma, *Caste and Class*...., 156-157.
52 Bharti Kanval, *Kanshi ram ke Do Chere* (Hindi), Raipur: Bodisattwa Prakashan, 1996, 16. Cf. V. Kumar, "Deconstruction..., 61.
53 Gail Omvedt, "Peasants, dalits...., 163.
54 Bharti Kanval, Kanshi Ram ke..., 16.
55 Gail Omvedt, "Peasants, Dalits..., 164.
56 Sudha Pai, "The BSP in Uttar Pradesh", in *Seminar*, 471, Nov. 1988, 39.
57 Marya, C. L. et al, *BSP Supremo Kanshiram Press ke Samne* (Hindi), Allahabad: Kushwahu Publishers, 1996. Cf. Sudha Pai, "The BSP in..., 39.
58 *Ibid*.

[59] R. Kothari, "Dillemmas of Social Justice" in Ghanshyam Shah (ed.), *Social Justice: a Dialogue*, New Delhi: Rawat Pub., 1996, 133.
[60] "Verdict 2002: Changing Sociology of Politics in UP", *Hindustan Times*, New Delhi (ed.), Feb 28, 2002, 11.
[61] Vicziany Marika and Oliver Mendelson, *The Untouchable Subordination: Poverty and the State in Modern India*, New Delhi: Cambridge University Press, 1998, 228.
[62] V. Kumar, "Deconstruction..., 70.
[63] Sudha Pai, "The BSP in ..., 42.
[64] A. Maria Arul Raja, "Living through Conflicts: The Spirit of Subaltern Resurgence", *Vidyajyoti*, 65(2001), 465.
[65] *Ibid*, 465-466.
[66] A. R. Thumma, *Springs from the Subalterns*, Delhi: ISPCK, 1999, X.
[67] Cf. F. Frantz, *Black Skin, White Masks*, New York: Grove Press, 1967. Cf. S. M. Parish, *Hierarchy and* ..., 172.
[68] A. R. Thumma, *Springs from*..., 10.
[69] R. S. Khare, *The Untouchables as Himself: Ideology, Identity and Pragmatism among the Lucknow Chamars*, Cambridge : Cambridge University Press, 1984, X.
[70] *ibid.*
[71] *ibid.*
[72] S. M. Parish, *Hierarchy and* ..., 172.
[73] *Ibid*, 173.
[74] A. R. Thumma, *Springs from*...,18.
[75] S. M. Parish, *Hierarchy and*..., 173.
[76] *Ibid*, 174.
[77] Owen Lynch, *The Politics of Untouchability*, New York: Columbia University Press, 1969. Cf. *The Hierarchy and* ..., 175.
[78] *Ibid.*
[79] *ibid.*
[80] *ibid*, 176-177.
[81] A. Maria Arul Raja, "Living through ..., 471.

82 Sathianathan Clarke, "Subaltern Culture as Resource for People's Liberation: A Critical Inquiry into Dalit Culture Theory", *Religion and Society*, Vol 144, No. 4, 1997, 93.
83 S. M. Parish, *Hierarchy and...* 178.
84 James Freeman, *Untouchable: An Indian Life History*, Stanford: Stanford University Press, 1979, 35.
85 *ibid*, 50.
86 *Ibid*, 52.
87 *Ibid*, 3.
88 *Ibid*, 378.
89 S. M. Parish, *Hierarchy and...*, 180.
90 *Ibid*.
91 R. B. Joshi (ed.), Untouchable! Voices of the Dalit Liberation Movement, London: Zed Books, 1986, 99. Cf. Parish, *Hierarchy...*, 181.
92 James Freeman, *Untouchable: An Indian...*, 220.
93 S. M. Parish, *Hierarchy and...*, 182.
94 *Ibid*.
95 R. S Khare, *The Untouchable....*, 23-34.
96 S. M. Parish, *Hierarchy...*, 127-134.
97 *Ibid*, 187-188.
98 C. J. Fuller, *The Camphor Flame: Popular Hinduism and Society in India*, Princeton, NJ: Princeton University Press, 1992, 18, Cf. Parish, 188.
99 S. M. Parish, *Hierarchy...*, 188-189.
100 I. R. Levy, *Mesocosm: Hinduism and the Organisation of a Traditional Newar City in Nepal*, Berkeley: University of California Press, 1990. Cf. Parish, *The Hierarchy..*, 189.
101 *Ibid*.
102 Sathianathan Clarke, "Subaltern Culture ...,88-89.
103 A. Maria Arul Raja, "Living Through...", 471.
104 Sathianathan larke, *Dalits and ...*, 126.
105 Sathianathan Clarke, "Subaltern Culture...", 89-90.
106 *Ibid*, 94.

107 A. Maria Arul Raja, "Living through..., 474.
108 S. M. Parish, The Hierarchy...,194.
109 Soares-Prabhu, "Indian Church Challenged by Poverty and Caste" in Isaac Padinjarekutu (ed), *Biblical Themes for a Contextual Theology Today*, Pune: JDV, 1999, 143.
110 George Pattery, "Inculturation And/Or Liberation", *EAPR*, 30(1993) 3&4, 317.
111 *Ibid*, 317-318.
112 Sathianathan Clarke, "Subaltern Culture..., 85.
113 Aloysius Pieris, *An Asian Theology of Liberation*, Edinburgh: T & T Clark, 1988, 15.
114 Quoted in John O'Brien, *Theology and the Option for the Poor*, Minnesota: The Liturgical Press, 1992, 9.
115 *Ibid*, 10.
116 *Ibid*, 11.
117 M. Amaladoss, *Beyond Inculturation*, Dehi: ISPCK, 1998. 70.
118 John O'Brien, *Theology and the Option...*, 9.
119 *Ibid*.
120 *ibid*, 10.
121 *Ibid*, 143.
122 K. C. Abraham, *Two Essays: Paradigm Shift in Theological Thinking*, Bangalore: BTESSC, (n.d.), 3-4.
123 De Mesa, Jose M., & Wostyn Lode L., *Doing Theology*, Philippines: Claretian Publications, 1990, 17 ff.
124 Sathianathan Clarke, *Dalits and Christianity*, 46.
125 Kuncheria Pathil, *Socio-cultural Analysis in Theologising*, Bangalore: ITA, 1987, 8.
126 Felix Wilfred, *Leave the Temple: Indian Path to Human Liberation*, New York: Orbis Books, 1992, 5.
127 Sathianathan Clarke, *Dalits and Christianity*, ...47.
128 A. P. Nirmal, "Doing Theology from a Dalit Perspective" in A Reader in Dalit Theology, Madras: Gurukul, 1991, 141.
129 Rudolf Heredia, "Subaltern Interrogations of Hindu Nationalism", *Vidyajyoti*, 66 (2002), 916.

130 *Ibid*, 321.
131 A. R. Thumma, *Wisdom of the Weak: Foundations of People's Theology*, Delhi: ISPCK, 2000, 107.
132 James H. Cone, *God of the Oppressed*, Maryknoll, Orbis Books, 1997, XIII, 138. Quoted by J.B.C. Webster, Religion and the Dalit Liberation, Delhi: Manohar, 1999, 113.
133 Felix Wilfred, "On the Threshold of the 1990's: Emerging Trends and Socio-cultural Processes at the Turn of the Century", *Jeevadhara*, XX(115), 1990, 61-62.
134 *Ibid*, 63.
135 *Ibid*, 66.
136 P. Puthanangady, "Which Culture for Inculturation: The Dominant or the Popular", *EAPR*, 30(1993), 306.
137 Felix Wilfred, "On the Threshold...", 66-67.
138 Sebastian Painadath, "Hermeneutics in Indian Theology", *Vidyajyoti*, Vol 62, No. 5, 1998, 303.
139 Sebastian Kappen, *Tradition Modernity Counterculture*, Bangalore: Visthar, 1994, 50.
140 Donal Dorr, *Mission in Today's World*, New York: Orbis Books, 2000, 93.
141 Felix Wilfred, *Sunset in the East*, Madras, University of Madras, 1991, vii.
142 Simon Sebastian, "Inculturation as a Dialogue with the Poor", *Vidyajyoti*, Vol. 65, No. 6, 2001, 418.
143 Sebastian Painadath, "Hermeneutics in...", 306.
144 *Ibid*, 307.
145 Raymond Panikkar, "The Power of Words" in Francis D'Sa (ed.), *The Dharma of Jesus*, Pune: Institute of Study of Religion, 1997, 411.
146 John Paul II, *Ecclesia in Africa: Post Synodal Apostolic Exhortation of Holy Father*, Nairobi: Pauline, 1995, 45.
147 S. Rayan, "The Challenge of the Dalit Issue: Some Theological Perspecives" in *Dalits and Women:Quest for Humanity*, Devasahayam, V.(ed), Chennai: Gurukul, 1992, 129.
148 M. Amaladoss, *Beyond...*, 71.

149 Felix Wilfred, *On the Banks of Ganges*, Delhi: ISPCK, 2002, 3.
150 *Ibid*, 4-5.
151 John O'Brien, *Theology and the Option*..., 56.
152 Felix Wilfred, *On the Banks*..., 9.
153 Sebastian Painadath, "Hermeneutics in Indian..., 309.
154 *Ibid,*.
155 John Sobrino, *Christology at the Crossroads*, London: SCM Press, 1978, 397.
156 *Ibid*, 310-311.
157 *Ibid*, 312.
158 John O'Brien, *Theology and the Option*..., 139.
159 Samuel Rayan, "People's Theology", *Jeevadhara*, 22 (1992), 202.
160 John O'Brien, *Theology and the Option*...., 136.
161 Rudolf Heredia, "Subaltern Interrogations ..., 321.
162 Sebastian Kappen, *Jesus and Culture*, Delhi: ISPCK, 2002, 5.
163 Gerd Theissen, *The First Followers of Jesus: The Sociology of Early Palestinian Christianity*, London: SCM Press, 1978, 97.
164 George Soares-Prabhu, "Radical Beginnings: The Jesus Community as the Architype of the Church", in Francis X. D'Sa (ed.), *Theology of Liberation: An Indian Biblical Perspective, Collected Work of George Soares-Prabhu S. J.,Vol. 4*, Pune: JDV,2001,138.
165 *Ibid*, 139.
166 Sebastian Kappen, *Jesus and Culture*, 10.
167 *Ibid.*
168 A. R. Thumma, *Springs from the Subaltern: Patterns and Perspectives in People's Theology*, Delhi: ISPCK, 1999, 4.
169 Samuel Rayan, "Outside the Gate, Sharing the insult", *Jeevadhara*, 11, 63(1981), 222.
170 Sebastian Kappen, *Jesus and Society*, Delhi: ISPCK, 2002, 3.
171 *Ibid*, 106.
172 Sebastian Painadath, "Spiritual Dynamics of Dialogue", *Vidyajyoti*, Vol 60, No 12, 1996, 820.

173 George Soares-Prabhu, "Socio-cultural Analysis in Prophetic Theologising: A Biblical Paradigm", in *Collected Works of George Soares-Prabhu S. J., Vol. 2*, Pune: JDV, 1999, 66.
174 Sebastian Kappen, *Jesus and Society*, 106.
175 *Ibid*,8.
176 George Soares-Prabhu, "The Kingdom of God: Jesus' Vision of a New society", *Theology of Liberation...Collected Writings..., Vol. 4*, 242-243.
177 *Ibid*, 236.
178 Sebastian Kappen, *Jesus and Society*,..., 7.
179 *Ibid*.
180 *ibid*.
181 George Soares-Prabhu, "Jesus and the Poor", *Theology of..., Collected Writings..., Vol. 4*, 176-177.
182 A. R. Thumma, *Springs from the Subaltern...*, 14.
183 M. Amaladoss, *A Call to....*, 109.
184 Sebastian Kappen, *Jesus and Society*, 156.
185 *Ibid*, 157.
186 Sebastian Kappen, *Jesus and Culture*, 13.
187 Felix Wilfred, *On the Banks of...*, 156.
188 *Ibid*.
189 J. D. M. Derrett, *Jesus' Audience: The Social and Psychological Environment in which He Worked*, London: 1973, 40. Cf. A. Nolan, *Jesus Before Christianity*, Phillipines: Claretian Publications, 1988, 54.
190 *ibid*.
191 *ibid*.
192 *ibid*, 56-57.
193 George Soares-Prabhu, "The Jesus of Faith: A Christological Contribution to an third World Spirituality", *Theology of liberation.., Collected Writings..., Vol. 4*, 284.
194 M. Amaladoss, "A Christian Vision of a New Society", *JPJRS*, 2/1, 1999, 115-116.
195 Sebastian Kappen, *Jesus and Society*, 7-8.
196 *Ibid*, 162.

197 Ibid, 164.
198 Ibid.
199 Sebastian Kappen, *Jesus and Culture*, 14.
200 Albert Nolan, *Jesus...*, 82.
201 Sebastian Kappen, *Jesus and Culture*, 129.
202 Albert Nolan, *Jesus Before....*, 84.
203 Ibid.
204 Sebastian Kappen, *Jesus and Culture*, 129.
205 Sebastian Painadath, "Spiritual Dynamics...", 821.
206 George Soares-Prabhu, "Jesus Chrict Amid the Religions and Ideologies of India Today", *Collected Writings of George Soares-Prabhu S. J., Vol. 1, Biblical Themes*...,198.
207 Ibid, 198-199.
208 George Soares-Prabhu, "The Man Born Blind: Understanding a Johannine Sign in India Today", in *A Biblical Theology for India, Collected Writings..., Vol. II*, Pune: JDV, 1999, 196.
209 George Soares-Prabhu, "The Jesus of Faith...., *Theology of Liberation......, Collected Writings* ..., Vol IV, JDV, 2001, 286.
210 A. R. Thumma, *Springs from* ..., 12.
211 Samuel Rayan, "The Challenge of the Dalit Issue: Some Theological Perspectives", in V. Devasahayam (ed.), *Dalits and Women, Quest for Humanity*, Chennai: Gurukul, 1992, 129.
212 Ibid, 121.
213 George Soares-Prabhu, "The Jesus of Faith...", 289.
214 Sebastian Kappen, *Jesus ans Society*, 83.
215 Marcus J. Borg, *Conflict, Holiness and Politics in the teaching of Jesus*, New York: Million, 1984. Quoted by George Soares-Prabhu, *Biblical Themes....*, 223.
216 Sebastian Kappen, *Jesus and Society*, 84.
217 Ibid, 85.
218 George Soares-Prabhu, *Biblical Themes...*, 226.
219 Albert Nolan, *Jesus Before...*, 39.
220 Sebastian Kappen, *Jesus and Society*, 85.

[221] George Soares-Prabhu, "The Table Fellowship of Jesus: Its Significance for Dalit Christians in India Today", *Collected Writings of George Soares-Prabhu, Vol. I, Biblical Themes...*, 228-229.
[222] Sebastian Kappen, *Jesus and Society*, 85.
[223] *Ibid*, 86.
[224] Sebastian Kappen, *Jesus and Culture*, 17.
[225] *Ibid*, 18.
[226] *Ibid.*
[227] *ibid*, 19.
[228] George Soares-Prabhu, "Table Fellowship of Jesus..", *Collected Writings....,Vol. 1*, 232-233.
[229] A. R. Thumma, *Springs from...*, 17.
[230] Sebastian Kappen, *Jesus and Culture*, 20.
[231] A. R. Thumma, *Springs From...*,23.
[232] George Soares-Prabhu, "The Kingdom of God: Jesus' Vision of a New Society", *Collected Writings..., Vol. 4,Theology of...*, 238-239.
[233] George Soares-Prabhu, "Radical Begennings..., *Collected Writings...Vol. 4*, 148.
[234] George SoaresPrabhu, "The Kingdom of God.., *Collected Writings..., Vol. 4*, 244.
[235] Sebastian Kappen, Jesus and Society, 131.

CONCLUSION

The caste cultural conflict is a contextual question, and is the most significant issue in the socio-cultural reality of India, with its rampant poverty and pluriform religiosity that affect the lives of the people individually and in society. It requires from the believer a change in the approach to theology and interpretation, from traditional-dogmatic to contextual-experiential, a change which is urgent for any kind of relevant theology that seeks the total liberation of people in society in the different dimensions of life: economic, political, psychological, social, cultural and religious. Theology, faith seeking understanding, should be consistent with a faith praxis which enters into every dimension of God's salvific action, including the cultural, social and historical. This study has sought to offer the kind of cultural hermeneutics that follows the scheme experience-analysis-interpretation, as found in the three parts of the thesis.

This research has been concerned with the caste and the problems associated with caste life in Indian society, focusing on the conflicts in the encounter between the dominant caste culture and the Dalit culture. The alarming socio-cultural realities like untouchability and the oppression and the subjugation that we see in the Indian society are expressions of the crisis we see in the caste cultural system. Though laws and democracy abolish untouchability, it is still practiced in India. The traditional hierarchical caste ideology has a decisive role in our cultural systems.

Culture is for the people, for their well-being. We say that a culture is in crisis when there are conflictual cultural trends with opposing value-systems affecting adversely human hearts and communities, social structures and religious associations. At different points of time we see prophetic individuals and groups keenly active to bring about cultural transformation in such crisis situations. Culture demands introspection, discernment and an interpretation that promotes and liberates the self and society. People on the one hand to create and recreate culture in order to preserve and enhance life in the world, and to make it more human; and on the other hand to challenge and destroy all elements that are dehumanising and death-dealing. This is an ongoing process in which the day-to-day experiences of people interact with culture, creating, modifying, preserving and changing it because they become more sensitive to the justice issues affecting other lives and cultures which are considered as equal partners.

There is always the tendency or the risk that discourses and interpretations detach culture from their lived worlds and turn the self, life and action into an arid and one-dimensional cosmos. Culture then becomes dominant and oppressive, erasing the "others". In such cases movements supported and guided by theological and hermeneutic discourses motivate and create countercultures capable of taking the path to liberation, freedom and justice.

My attempt in this research into the Indian cultural caste situation has been to make a contribution to the struggle of the oppressed by isolating, and challenging, all elements of domination and subjugation and pinpointing and clarifying some of theological perspectives for an alternative counterculture that can hold together all men and women in freedom, equality and justice. By this I wish to participate in the process of liberation of the marginalised and oppressed subaltern groups, especially the Dalits, seen as the main victims of the traditional Indian culture.

The thesis was conceived in three parts. Part I, with the title "A brief Survey of Caste Cultural Reality of India", tries to get a glimpse to the caste cultural life lived by the Indians entering into its historical rendering and contemporary experience in a brief manner. As mentioned above the study with its conceptual framework of cultural hermeneutics follows a scheme of experience-analysis-interpretation. I study caste and culture not as a researcher in anthropology or sociology, but as a theologian with the aim of arriving at a theological discourse analysing and critiquing culture to discover the countercultural perspectives and trends that contribute to the transformation and change of the life of society from the death-dealing aspects of caste culture. In the hermeneutical scheme, first comes the 'experience', as it is the starting point of any theological enterprise. I had to place myself in the varied experience of the caste culture I have inherited and acquired as an Indian from the encounter with others whom I meet in the day-to-day life. Thus, besides personal interviews and visits of different places, I tried to explore the writings of some of the relevant authors mentioned in the bibliography who articulate reflective views on caste out of the experience they had by living in the midst of the struggles and conflicts that surround it.

Part I surveyed the reality of caste and culture in three chapters. The first chapter unfolded the experience of caste in myth and history enabling us to have a general picture of it. The discussion focused on the encounter between the dominant caste culture and Dalit culture, the interaction between castes, the challenge of religions and religious leaders against the caste domination and caste rigidities, the mobility in the caste system, etc. From the general picture of caste in history I have introduced in chapter two the contemporary experience so as to clarify and project the problematic. The focus here is the discontents and sufferings of the people arising from the way the caste is lived and the pressures it exerts on their lives. The experience of caste oppression as expressed in the writings of the victims, especially their songs and poems, graphically picture the indignity and the helplessness they feel. In the second chapter the discussion about

Christianity and Dalits, the impact of modernity, modern transformation of caste, caste and class, etc., complete the contemporary picture.

The caste system in India was analysed and understood in the framework of culture with its different dimensions. The third chapter of Part I, offered a framework for a discussion on the cultural dynamics. The underlying feature of the research undertaken has been a cultural *hermeneusis* that analyses caste by pointing out the theological and countercultural perspectives demanded by theological and pastoral concerns.

There have been numerous analyses on caste system in India and in the West. Many analyses and interpretations are found to be one-dimensional and fail to give true 'being' or value to individuals – for example, the image given to Hindu as *Homo Hierarchicus* by Louis Dumont (1980). In Part II an integral analysis of the caste culture was attempted in two chapters. In the first chapter the relevant part of Parish's description and analysis of the famous 'Chariot pulling' in the spring festival in a Hindu city, Bhaktapur, Nepal, was introduced. He analysed the caste culture and cultural dynamics, focussing on the cultural psychology of moral life through some of the caste actors. Parish's analysis and interpretation was found relevant as, unlike many others, he stressed that caste culture is to be approached integrally and showed that men and women in the caste cultural context are asserting and resisting hierarchy as the central social, cultural and personal reality.

There in chapter five we entered into the second phase of the thesis, the analysis of caste culture, in the scheme of experience-analysis-interpretation. We made use of the scheme Amaladoss introduced, a grid of six elements: economics, politics, individual person, society, culture and religion, which interact with each other integrally in a dialectical framework of symbolic or meaning and ideological structures. In freedom and fellowship with others a person can creatively interpret cultural and religious tradition and transform the social, including economic and political structures. The economic disparity that has its root in the caste norms concerning occupation and the production and distribution of material goods, plays a great role in the discontentment of the caste cultural life. The political power is exercised not on behalf of the community at large and in defence of the poor and the weak, but to defend individual and collective selfishness and to dominate and exploit others. The democratic sense of community participation is not considered a value.

The social disharmony found in the caste cultural life on account of inequalities and social oppressions has its main root in the socio-cultural and religious principle of purity and pollution maintained by the dominant castes in Hindu society. Such dehumanising and conflicting situation makes the lower castes, the victims, think differently and come out with levelling discourses. The inabilities imposed by the inequalities tend to be cumulative. The economically poor Dalits tend to be politically poor. However, though hierarchy is dominant, there are voices evoking a sense of equality and justice, heard in the struggle to shape a culture that is more humane, seeking the fullness of personhood. Dissent exists. A process of re-imagining occurs, often private, sometimes public.

Important as the concept of hierarchy is, it co-exists with the concept of equality, solidarity and justice. People invoke multiple models in cultural life and in moral discourse. Cultural subjectivities are not fixed and encompassed in a single ideology but move fluidly in the mutually entangled webs of meaning that are ideology and critique. The many symbols of the caste culture in the religious realm like purity, diet, dirt, sexuality, religious power, etc. are perceived and practiced by different actors differently. While the low caste actors react to the dominant ways and practices out of their existential pragmatic necessities, the high caste actors use the support of the religious ideas like *dharma* and *karma* to make hierarchy seem natural and necessary. "Equality" as an ideal would demand from the householder to distribute wealth, prestige, and freedom of action, which is something that cannot happen in his life. Equality is an ethical goal can take place only in the world of the renouncer. This means that equality as principle of subversion of hierarchy or as abolition of differences is a theoretical spiritual possibility.

Analysis of caste culture should take one to its roots and dynamics and to its external expressions, bringing into focus the life and consciousness of its different actors. Correcting the one-dimensional approach to caste culture one has to emphasise the dialectic approach by pointing out the politics of consciousness in the caste cultural conflict. Any critique on the caste culture should take into account the interplay between caste ideologies, hierarchy and equality.

From the analysis of caste culture in six dimensions we have moved to the interpretative level in Part III to attain a clearer view (though analysis and interpretation cannot be separated in watertight compartment). In the caste cultural analysis we saw people struggling in the ambivalence and discontent with the caste system, which fills life with injustice and yet is viewed as the moral basis of the traditional society, and as part of the natural order. Those who are at the bottom of the caste system find it not just an objective social fact but a disturbing social fate, creating a problem of meaning and a problem for survival. The crisis has demanded a countercultural interpretation and movement marked by a change in the perspectives and understanding of self and society. The goal of liberation for the victims of the caste cultural conflict may be achieved through self-discipline and the mediation of a saviour figure, as seen in major liberation movements. In the sixth chapter we have explored some of the countercultural trends and prophetic voices and movements in the caste cultural scene.

The Buddhist revolt against Brahminic domination based on purity and pollution served an antidote to Hindu religious arrogance. Buddhist movement initiated an alternative culture that has elements of universal humanism based on Buddha's teachings. The ultimate goal of the *arahatta* consists in the absence of acquisitiveness, oppressiveness and hatred, and of freedom from illusory knowledge. The monastic community that embodies this ideal is also a symbol of religious communism: they are called to share all things in common, even the morsel of food falling into the begging bowl. The *Bhakti* movement too was a protest movement against the cultural domination by the higher castes. The Bhakti movement has links with Sufism within Islam and finds expression in Kabir, Guru Nanak, Tukaram, etc. Not all leaders of the *Bhakti* movement were, however, radical or could withstand the high caste strategy of subjugation by co-option.

Mahatma Phule, another countercultural prophet, preached the gospel that for India social democracy was more vital than the independence from foreign rule. His vision was to free the *Shudras* and the *Atishudras* by cleansing the minds of his fellowmen and women from the outdated belief system that denied equal status to all human beings. He reinterpreted culture and history and envisaged an action-oriented approach by establishing the institutions that would translate the new cultural script into practice. Periyar E. V. Ramaswamy, known as *Thandai Periyar*, was a fighter from Tamilnadu who led the anti-Brahmin movement. The self-respect movement he started helped the socio-political emergence of non-Brahmin castes. His approach has helped create more awareness among people about inequality and other social evils that are systematically promoted by the dominant castes.

Ambedkarism is even today a living force in India. It is a Dalit movement; in a broader sense it is an anti-caste movement. Around the idea of individual and his rights Ambedkar built his theory of social and political organisation. Ambedkar aims at the emergence of a new economic order of the common good and welfare of all, and insists on the need for the implementation of a mixed economy, a restructuring of classes, etc. He prefers Buddhism as it gives three principles in combination, which no other religion does: *prajna, karuna* and *samata,* through which man can lead a happy life. His Buddhism can be called Neo-Buddhism. Its essence is morality and its mission on earth is the establishment of the kingdom of righteousness.

Gandhi's perception of the problems surrounding the caste cultural conflict is very complex. He was totally against the untouchability and was committed to its abolition, but at the same time he wanted to keep the caste system. On the question of Dalits and caste cultural conflict there were differences in the approach and method between Gandhi and Ambedkar, though they had the common mission: emancipation of the human beings and the country. On the question of removing untouchability one was evolutionary and the other revolutionary in the approach and the line of action. While Ambedkar mainly stood for the oppressed classes Gandhi stood for whole nation.

The resurgence of the Dalits in independent India with a new political identity is a threat to the major political parties whose leadership is mainly from the dominant castes. To illustrate the change taking place in the Indian political scene in the milieu of caste culture carrying the sign of a counterculture, we have had a glimpse into the way the Bahujan Samaj Party under the leadership of Kanshi Ram and Mayawati, has emerged as a force in the North-West India. The BSP has entered into the politics of alliance, as its leaders believed in the primacy of capturing political power as a means for socio-cultural reforms. This is a crystallisation of the strategy of Kanshi Ram, which he developed out of the great vision of Ambedkar.

Chapter six in Part III, "Indian Untouchables' Critique of the Caste Culture", as the title shows, has focussed is on their own critique of the caste culture when they live in its milieu, with its socio-culturally determined and religiously sanctioned way of life thrust upon them. We saw how human values like justice, equality, fraternity, community, etc., are the focus of their critique in such conflicting situations when the dominant castes construct a "crushing objecthood" for the Untouchables by excluding, distancing, stigmatising, and subordinating them. To survive in today's political culture, it is necessary for the Untouchables to have an effective cultural critique and an ideology. The critique they make develops from the inside, from within self, from with in a culture, in intimate ways.

The Untouchables are not just passive in internalising the image others hold of them, but they are in deep dialogue with culture in re-defining themselves, reimagining culture and self. Taking the pieces of culture apart they reassemble them, amend and supplement culture in the process giving a 'spin' to symbols and meanings. As moral and political discourses such reading they make sometimes contradict each other as culture can be visualised both as contested and shared. In the caste system a person does not want to be lower than others, and at the same time he/she wants to be higher. People are both for emancipation and domination.

Asceticism is a significant cultural form shared by both the Untouchables and the Brahmins. In the critique the Untouchables make, they try to liberate the concept of asceticism from the distortion by the upper caste stressing the "culture of the deprived" aimed at subverting unjustified inequality and the launching of an alternative symbolisation of the social world. The cultural and symbolic world-view of the Untouchable Dalits is a meaning system that arises from the depth of their collective experience. They are agents who make symbols to sustain, nurture and direct their lives.

In the search for an alternative culture or counterculture and the perspectives for doing theology in the context of caste conflicts and the resultant discontents in India, we have pointed out in the eighth chapter, three options the theologian has to make that are dynamically interrelated: the option for the poor – liberation; the option for the culture – inculturation; and the option for dialogue – interpretation. The option for the poor as a perspective means the choice one takes to love all in and through a partisan love for the oppressed. This option is a practical, existential reality; a way of living that codetermines one's manner of perceiving and understanding. Christian theologians are called to interpret the meaning and exigencies of Christian faith viewing the socio-cultural reality through the optic of the poor, identifying themselves with their struggles. This gives theology a privileged interpretative perspective, which is always in dialogue with other perspectives.

The "option for culture – inculturation" has emerged as an important countercultural perspective indispensable for a theology that wants to be contextual in the background of India's present cultural situation in general and caste cultural situation in particular. The dialectics between theology and culture is of great importance in theologising in India. Faith is a response to the Spirit of God transforming the human spirit. Theology is the perception of the word of God transforming the human culture. Hermeneutics is the way of interpreting the symbols of faith in a contextualised theological pursuit. Faith and theological reflection are always in correlation with the culture of a people. To the question, how does the Gospel community enter into dialogue with different cultures, both dominant and subaltern, when the Gospel has a special option for the poor, the Gospel community has to respond by obeying the Gospel command to opt for the poor and the underprivileged.

Theology, faith-seeking understanding, should be consistent with the faith praxis which enters into every dimension of God's salvific action, including the cultural, social and historical. The dialogical inter-dependence of the literary-critical, the historical-critical and the social-scientific, is the ideal, each offering correctives to the other levels. The truth is attained in a self-correcting, mutually enriching process of theological conversation. Every dialogue has mystery as its horizon. The path of theology is not one which leads from faith to clarity of knowledge, but rather a movement from faith to its realisation in life through dialogue.

The cultural interpretation understood as a dialogue between partners can only be conceived holistically and it is a therapeutic experience. In the process of dialogue, there is a moment of vulnerability during which we gain a precious insight into the psychological roots of our discourse and consequently its distortedness. This contributes to mutual correction and enrichment. This dialogal approach helps to discover how our theology is partially rooted in and related to structures of oppression; the discovery leads to a new methodological self-awareness capable of creating counter-theologies and counter-ideologies. The dialogal approach aims at a conversion among partners so as to bring about transformation and change in society.

In his words and deeds Jesus strikes a countercultural note, which for Christians in India, who are also surrounded by the caste reality and its struggles, contains the elements for the Christian vision of a new society. Jesus, a countercultural prophet, with his discourses and interpretation was a challenge to the dehumanising and oppressive structures and principalities of his time. The counterculture that Jesus proposes is valid today in the Indian context of caste crisis in its different dimensions: economic, political, personal, social, cultural, and religious. With these cultural dimensions in mind I have pursued the final chapter "Jesus and counterculture".

Jesus associated with the outcastes to set them free by recognising their humanity and acknowledging their dignity and worth. By showing an example of selfless service, self-sacrifice and the spirit of sharing with others in community, Jesus showed the neglected and rejected ones the way to awaken their selfhood, to rebuild their pride and rely on their status as daughters, sons and citizens before God. Jesus inaugurated a new society with a culture that is capable of bringing transformation and change to the dominated outcastes and untouchables. The liberative education and the liberative praxis that Jesus taught freed enslaved minds and loosened their bound tongue to assert their identity, dignity and creativity. This new society is not built on hierarchy, inequality and competition but on co-operation, equality, fraternity and liberty for all sections of people. To fashion such a society and culture demands a new vision that is prophetic as well as mystic.

The Cultural *Hermeneusis*

Every culture is capable of mediating God's presence in the language of its people. The self-communication of God through the word is appropriated through interpretation. Hermeneutics is the way of understanding reality by interpreting the language, through which a perception of reality in a particular context is communicated in another context. The interpretation of culture and tradition, a critical and creative process, is very much part of this theological activity. As hermeneutics, theology seeks a critical understanding based on the socio-cultural analysis, and challenges any culture that is de-humanising to pave the way for a counter-culture which is life-affirming, liberating and communitarian.

Hermeneutical studies have made it clear that interpretation and understanding is accompanied by the pre-understanding and pre-options of the interpreter in a particular context, in a horizon of meaning, in a given historical and cultural situation. But it is not easy to give a clear-cut definition of the present socio-cultural situation in India. Kappen expresses the plural and complex nature of the Indian culture thus: "It is characterised by the interplay of diverse and conflicting factors: the superimposition of bourgeois culture over the traditional, the uneven development of capitalism and of the culture germane to it, the overlapping of caste and class, the rise of ritually inferior castes to economic and political dominance, the ambivalence of socialist ideologies."[1] A holistic approach is needed to enter into the Indian world-view, which insists on the interrelatedness of everything and a cosmic wholeness, avoiding any sort of dichotomy. This integral and dialogal approach is basic for doing theology and interpretation in India, if it wants to meet the test of relevancy.

Contradictions and complexities do exist in the cultural situation of India, but this does not mean that there is no possibility for a radical cultural revolution. There is a longing for a free, egalitarian and just society and there were socio-cultural movements of protest in the past which challenged the logic of dominant code in the cultural ground. After a socio-cultural and historical survey Kappen draws following conclusions:

> (i) Far from being a monolithic whole, from the beginning Indian culture has been an uneasy combination of two opposing strands: one, priestly, patriarchal and elitist; the other, popular, matriarchal, virtually egalitarian. The first is ascetical and, in relation to one's fellowmen, tends to become sadistic; the second is life affirming, creative and self-expanding. The former has served as an ideology legitimising the institutionalised inequality of caste; the latter has always been a source of destruction and creation. Neither of the two strands existed in purity; each contains an admixture of the other. But it is the second that has generated the movements of protest in the past. If these movements proved abortive, it is because they were either neutralised or smothered by the guardians of the priestly-elitist tradition. The lesson for the future is clear: the forces that can re-create Indian society can emerge only from the repressed culture of the lower castes, outcastes and the tribals. (ii) What Hindu orthodoxy did to the dissenting movements from the Buddha onwards,

capitalism is doing to all critical forces in Indian society today. These are being co-opted in the service of commodity production and formal bourgeois democracy. Not even Indian communism has been able to withstand capitalism's integrating power. (iii) The contemporary situation is characterised, on the one hand, by the objective need for a total – and therefore also cultural – revolution, and, on the other, by the absence of a collective agent capable of bringing it about. Hence the challenge to mobilise the forces for change latent in the consciousness and the subconscious of the masses with a view to creating a counter-cultural movement. [2]

The resurgence of the Dalits and the lower castes in India constitute a new political force that has started to assert and organising themselves politically and socio-culturally. It is threatening the dominant castes. "The consciousness of the marginalised and the dominated class-castes, subjected and subdued by the caste ideology for many generations, was roused out of their inferiority-complex and intellectual subjection, due to many socio-cultural changes that took place rapidly. The democratic revolution, the promises of political parties and governments, the exercise of power through the franchise, the constitutional guarantee of a casteless egalitarian socialist society, etc., led to the rising expectations of people." [3]

In India many subaltern socio-cultural movements emerged in the past because of the cultural crises brought about by the cultural imperialism of Indian and Western origin. [4] Such movements can be called countercultural movements as they emerge from the discontent or the subaltern experience in different dimensions: economic, political, psychological, social, cultural, religious, etc. Self-reflection and a critique in the process of enlightenment can change attitudes. This presupposes strategic action capable of dissolving distortions and manipulations. People look forward to an alternative culture by rediscovering their cultural roots and heritage, and seek a new value system that paves the way to an egalitarian society. About the subaltern *hermeneusis*, that serves the basis of any counterculture, Thumma writes:

> Manifold movements and action groups that responded to the oppression of the people did go through a deep reflection process resulting in their ideology, that contains also their theology regarding the meaning of life, beliefs, the significance of their struggle, future vision, ultimate goals, value system, motives for action, faith-content, understanding of justice, love, suffering etc. As against the traditional classical religious doctrines and ideological tenets, people began to articulate their own interpretation of life and events, subjecting the classical theologies and elitist ideologies to severe critique. [5]

Any quest for a cultural identity or counterculture "must take the form of a dialectical supersession involving two inter-related moments: abolition of what is dehumanising and preservation of what is valuable in the prevailing conditions." [6] In the caste conflict, looking from the victim's point of view, the Dalit reality and consciousness can be understood at once as a scandal (because of dehumanisation) and a noble yearning for equality and solidarity. A. M. A. Raja explains: "Both, the negative experience of humiliation and the positive one seeking to inaugurate a new order of equality, together create the Dalit consciousness with its dynamic restlessness." [7] In the face of dominating and dehumanising forces it is important to have a clear vision and a leadership with prophetic voices, which pave the way for a counter-culture. Such counter-ideologies, anti-hegemonic thoughts spun out of moral imaginations and critique, affect the historical development and change of culture, thus leading to social transformation. The counterculture brings about an all-round development and fulfilment of a human person and his/her needs in community, working against all that is oppressive and dehumanising. L. Jeyaseelan summarises Kappen's view of an alternative cultural paradigm thus:

> Culture should take the care of the social, economic and political requirements of all without any room for complaint, ill will or domination. Therefore, he [Kappen] proposes a cultural paradigm wherein the needs of the body, one's relation to nature, the production of the holistic needs, the social concerns and love for knowledge take a pride of place. He insists that these elements should form the composite and holistic process of a cultural growth designed specifically for the well being of a community. This is very vital for the realisation of the vision and for the creation of a new society.[8]

In this process of reinterpretation, besides the rediscovery of the socio-political history and religious and cultural resources and texts, the subalterns unearth rich theological mines such as the Dalit *Sahitya,* with its pathos and calls for praxis, folklore, myths, etc. The subaltern solidarity which is built upon the shared experience of powerlessness is the real milieu and power-centre for the creation of a counterculture similar to the one envisioned by Jesus, which is built not on hierarchy, inequality and competition but on cooperation, equality, fraternity and liberty of all sections of society. Questions should be raised about the credentials of any religion, culture or tradition, whether they respond positively and creatively to the challenges posed by the humanisation process, or the call to make this world a better place to live in freedom, justice and dignity. The Church community, taking inspiration from Jesus, the incarnate Word of God, has to appropriate and realise the core message of liberation through a process of incarnation and identification with the suffering humanity, sharing their cup of sorrow and hoping with them for the dawn of a new day of love, truth, freedom and justice. It demands an immersion of baptism in the dalitness of the oppressed in order to remove its victims and plant them in the realm of freedom, dignity and creative living.

The closeness of the subalterns to nature and their community sense will enable them to vibrate with the divine and respond to its call to fashion anew the world, society and culture, assuring better conditions for living in freedom, justice and love. Society will then be characterised by the tribal values of antigreed and antipride, which derive from the closeness to nature and the community, as Jesus also envisaged in his plan for an alternative society. Soares-Prabhu beautifully shows the implications when these values are incorporated in the life of a community:

> Antigreed and antipride are, therefore, not just individual virtues which Jesus demanded from those who wished to follow him. They are the structuring principles of the alternative community he sought to build. They are, therefore, meant to be community values. They are to be realised not just in individuals who strive to be 'poor' (Lk 6:20) and 'humble' (Mt 5:3; 11:28) in the sense that has been explained above, but in the lifestyle and functioning of the community as a whole...That is, it [the Church] must demonstrate its poverty and its humility (its serviceability), as well as its option for the humble and the poor, in its transactions within the community (bishop-priest; priest-laity; men-women; rich-poor; clean caste-dalit), as well as in its uncompromising prophetic stance towards the huge, immensely greedy, power-hungry, and status-conscious world outside. [9]

Such a community which embodies the *Abba* experience of Jesus will have the characteristics of radical freedom, radical universalism, radical sharing, radical service and radical equality. [10] This is because human beings are not perceived in isolation, but situated in the social milieu of their family and caste, and even humankind is understood to be part of the whole cosmos (the world as the body of God). Such an approach is holistic, inclusive and integral, and this is really the Indian way of thinking. As the holistic Indian mind has the passion for wholeness, it "thinks dialectically, is tolerant of ambiguity, and is able to hold together seemingly contradictory aspects of reality as complementary parts of a never fully to be apprehended whole."[11]

When we say we approach the caste cultural reality with the threefold options, the option for the poor/dalit, the option for the culture and the option for dialogue, we mean to approach it integrally and holistically, which respect the socio-cultural situation of the basic human community or pluri-religious group of people living in India by basic human (and therefore gospel) values and striving for transformation of Indian society. People who are in tune with this approach will enter into the different dimensions of cultural life, economic, political, psychological, social, cultural, religious, etc., and will go for an integral interpretation of the Bible or any other texts exploring both its prophetic and mystic dimensions.

Invitation to a New Spirituality

Transformation and change in society and culture take place when its components are changed and transformed. When we say that liberation is central to theology, we mean that theology has the function of facilitating a human and collective life lived under the sense of the Divine. It aims at living in justice and freedom in the economical, political, social, personal, cultural and religious realms. Every human being is then invited to create a new history. This involves a new spirituality. For Dalits, this spirituality for liberation which works for a new humanity on the foundation of human dignity, has its roots in the experience of pathos. The Dalits need to identify their spiritual energies and actualise them. About such spirituality Raja writes:

> To serve the Dalit struggle for liberation, the spiritual energies embedded in the inner layers of the Dalit consciousness have to be identified, unveiled and affirmed. This potential found within the wounded Dalit psyche to heal the wounded human history could be called the Dalit spirituality. This spirituality has declared a war against the demonic legions in the form of the Brahminic brand of purity, the casteist stratification and the *Hindutva* attempt to privilege the privileged. [12]

Such a vision of spiritual transformation enables humans to transcend themselves and reach towards the ultimate possibilities of their existence. It also takes the form of a prophetic critique of the socio-cultural domination and oppression. Spirituality draws from the deepest meaning of existence and leads to a commitment to realise the divine reign of righteousness in a new egalitarian and just society. It is important to understand and identify the spiritual strength springing from the consciousness of the need for the liberative struggles. Raja discusses in detail the anatomy of Dalit spirituality, which aims at finding out the various life-affirming aspects of culture and the function it has in the liberative struggle, and gives the various dynamics operative in it:

> Various dynamics simultaneously operative in Dalit spirituality can be pinpointed in the following transitions:
>
> From Wounded Past into a Realistic Present:
>   the spirit of restlessness and revolt;
>   the spirit of locating, naming and destroying the enemy;
>   the spirit of collective search.
> From a Realistic Present into a Promoting Future:
>   the spirit of 'here and now' in encountering the sacred;
>   the spirit of solidarity with the co-victims;
>   the spirit of 'letting go' celebration.
> From a Promising Future into a Liberative Harmony:
>   the spirit of inclusive integration;
>   the spirit of preserving hope;
>   the spirit of creative dreams.
> The interplay of all these movements in the individuals of the vulnerable Dalit communities gives birth to the inner power to put up a relentless struggle against the anti-Dalit forces. [13]

The transitions: in the first, the Dalits seek to rally around the collective memory of the dehumanising alienation, and so it is a rallying transition; in the second, they get a foretaste of self-empowerment to consolidate themselves, and it is called the consolidating transition; in the third, they transcend themselves and enter into the messianic roles of emancipating the oppressed in other walks of life, and so is called the all-embracing transition. Three transitions do not strictly function in a chronological sequence, but can be active simultaneously.

This spiritual empowerment with a new value system enables people to commit themselves to work for the establishment of a new society in the style of divine reign. In a society that is sharply divided between rich and poor, powerful and powerless, exploiters and exploited, dominant and subaltern, etc., Christian discipleship demands that we take the side of the poor. Thumma draws the characteristics of such a society for which the spiritually empowered people are working:

> They have a holistic vision of an ideal society, which is truly democratic, socialistic, secular, pluralistic and participatory. They aim at an integral ethical revolution at all levels and spheres. Economic self-reliance and self-sufficiency, social self-respect and self-dignity, political self-rule and self-governance are important goals of the envisioned new society. People's liberative praxis and theology consist in spreading this new vision, and struggle for the same. New egalitarian relationships between men and women and the people of different castes and classes are fostered in the new world order.[14]

Spirituality is essentially an undertaking springing from the deepest meaning of human existence in community and culture. Seen from the vantage point of the primal source of religion, the encounter with the divine here and now, a spirituality that is capable of effecting a counterculture will be "creative-subversive, telluric, erotic-*agapic*, aesthetic and communitarian."[15] Spirituality is our connectedness to God, to our human roots, to the rest of nature and to ourselves. It is a cry for life and for the power to resist oppression, death and the agents of death. It fulfils the quest for self-discovery, self-affirmation and self-inclusion, so that everybody can live as fully human and fully alive, as designed by God.

NOTES

1 S. Kappen, *Jesus and Culture*, 40.
2 *ibid*, 45.
3 A. Thumma, *Voices of the Victims*, 11.
4 Cf. J.N. Farquhar, *Modern Religious Movements in India*, New York: Macmillan, 1967; M.S.A. Rao (ed.), *Social Movements in India*, 2 Vols., Delhi: Manohar Publications, 1978,1979.
5 Thumma, *Voices from the Victims*, 18.
6 Kappen, *Jesus and Society*, 117.
7 A. M. A. Raja, "Harmony in the midst of Anarchy: Anatomy of the Spirit of Dalit Liberation", *Vidyajyoti*, 63(1999), 416.
8 L. Jeyaseelan, *Towards a Counter-culture....* ,76.
9 George Soares-Prabhu, "Antigreed and Antipride", in Isaac Padinjarekuttu (ed.), *Biblical Themes for a Contextual Theology*, Pune: JDV, 1999, 256.
10 *ibid*, 243-247.
11 George Soares-Prabhu, "Interpreting the Bible in India Today", in Francis X. D'Sa (ed.), *Theology of Liberation: An Indian Biblical Perspective*, Pune: JDV, 2001, 9.
12 A.M.A. Raja, "Harmony in the ..., 416.
13 *ibid*, 417.
14 A. Thumma, *Wisdom of the Weak*, 252.
15 S. Kappen, "Spirituality in the age of Recolonisation", Bangalore: *Visthar*, 1995, 8-9.

BIBLIOGRAPHY

A. BOOKS ON CASTE AND CULTURE

Aloka, P., *Mleechas in Early India*, Delhi: Munshiram Manoharlal, 1991.

Amaladoss, M., *A Call to Community*, Anand: Gujarat Sahitya Prakash, 1994.

Ambedkar, B. R., *Annihilation of Caste*, New Delhi: Arnold Publications, 1990.

Ambedkar, B. R., *The Buddha and His Dhamma*, Bombay: Siddhartha Publications, 1991 (1957).

Anand, C. C., *Equality, Justice and Reverse Discrimination*, New Delhi: Mittal Publications, 1987.

Anand, M. R., *Untouchable*, New Delhi: Arnold Publications, 1981.

Anand M. and Eleanor Z. (eds), *An Anthology of Dalit Literature*, New Delhi: Gyan Publications, 1992.

Antony, M. J., *Dalit Rights*, New Delhi: ISI, 1998.

Ashis, Nandy (ed.), *Science, Hegemony and violence*, New Delhi: Oxford University Press, 1992.

Atal, Yogesh, *Changing Patterns of Caste*, New Delhi: National, 1979.

Augustine, A. G., *Neethiku Vendiulla Porattam* (Mal.), Vaikom: Hobby Publishers, 1996.

Augustine, P. A., *Social Equality in Indian Society: The Elusive Goa*, New Delhi: Concept Publishing Co., 1991.

Ayrookuzhiel, A. M. A., *The Dalit Desiyata*, Delhi: ISPCK, 1990.

Ayrookuzhiel, A. M. A., *The Sacred in Popular Hinduism*, Madras: CLS, 1983.

Baker, Sophie, *Caste*, Calcutta: Rupa & Co., 1991.

Barid, Obert D. (ed.), *Religion in Modern India*, Delhi: Manohar Pub., 1981.

Basham, A. L., *The Wonder That Was India*, London: Fontana, 1971.

Basu, Tapan et al, *Khaki Shorts and Saffron Flags: A critique of the Hindu Right*, Hyderabad: Orient Longman, 1993.

Benjamin, J., *Scheduled Castes in Indian Politics and Society,* New Delhi: Ess Ess Publications, 1989.

Berwa, Laxmi N., *Asian Dalit Solidarity*, Delhi: ISPCK, 2000.

Beteille, Andre, *Caste, Class and Power*, Bombay: Oxford University Press, 1996.

Beteille, Andre (ed.), *Equality and Inequality: Theory and Practice*, Delhi: Oxford University Press, 1983.

Beteille, Andre, *The Idea of Natural Inequality and Other Essays*, Delhi: Oxford University Press, 1983.

Biswas, Swapan K. *Gods, False-Gods and the Untouchables*, Delhi: Orion Books, 1998.

Blau, Judith, *The Shape of Culture*, New York: Cambridge University Press, 1989.

Braganza, Karuna Mary and Peeradina Saleem, *Cultural Forces Shaping India*, Delhi: Macmillan India Ltd., 1989.

Breman, J., *Patronage and Exploitation*, Barley: University of California Press, 1974.

Caitanya, Krishna, *A Profile of Indian Culture*, New Delhi: Indian Book Co., 1975.

Caplan, Lionel, *Religion and Power: Essays on the Christian Community in Madras*, Madras: CLS, 1989.

Carman, J. B. & Marglin, F. A. (eds.), *Purity and Auspiciousness in Indian Society*, Leiden: E. J. Brill, 1985.

Charsley, Simon R. & Karanth, G. K. (eds.), *Challenging Untouchability*, New Delhi: Sage Publications, 1998.

Chatterji, S. K. & Manbry, H. P., *Culture Religion and Society*, Delhi: ISPCK, 1994.

Chaubisa, M. C., *Caste, Tribe and Exploitation*, Udaipur: Himanshu Publication, 1988.

Clifford, James, *The Predicament of Culture*, Cambridge: Harvard University Press, 1988.

Cornia, G. A., Jolly, R. & Stewart, F. (eds.), *Adjustment with the Human Force, Protecting the Valuable and Promoting Growth* (Vol. 1), Oxford: Clarendon Press, 1987.

D'Souza, V. S., *Inequality and its Perpetuation*, Delhi: Manohar, 1981.

Daily, *Givan Sakshi* (Hindi), Patna: Navjyoti Niketan, 1991.

Dangle, Arjun (ed.), *Homeless in my Land: Translations from Modern Marathi Dalit Short Stories*, Bombay: Orient Longman Ltd., 1994.

Das, D. P., *The Untouchable Story*, New Delhi: Allied Publications, 1985.

Das, Soman (ed.), *Christian Faith and Multi-form Culture in India*, Bangalore: UTC, 1987.

Das, Veena, *Structure and Cognition: Aspects of Hindu Caste and Rituals* (second edition), Delhi: Oxford university Press, 1982.

Dasan A. S. & Shenoy B. V. (eds.), *India: a People Betrayed*, Mysore: Good Will Fellowship Academy, 1993.

Desai, A. R. (ed.), *Caste and Communal Violence in Independent India*, Bombay: C. G. Shah Memmorial Trust, 1985.

Deshpande, Vasant, *Towards Social Integration*, Pune: Nehru Institute of Social Studies,1978.

Desrochers, J., *Towards a New India*, Bangalore: CSA,1995.

Devasahayam, V. (ed.), *Dalits and women*, Madras: Gurukul Summar Institute, 1992.

Dietrich, G., *Culture Religion and Development*, Bangalore: CSA, 1978.

Doglas, Mary, *Purity and Danger*, London: Routledge and Kegon Paul, 1982.

Dogra, Bharat, *20th Century Failures and the Challenges of the last decade*, New Delhi: Authors Publications, 1992.

Dogra, Bharat, *India , Despair and Hope*, New Delhi: Authors Publications, 1992.

Dongle, Arjun (ed.), *Poisoned Bread: Translations from Modern Marathi Dalit Literature*, Bombay: Orient Longman, 1992.

Dumont, Louis, *Homo Hierarchicus: The Caste System and its Implications*, Delhi: Oxford University Press, 1988.

Embree, Ainslee T., *Utopias in Conflict, Religion and Nationalism in Modern India*, Delhi: Oxford University Press, 1992.

Famon, F., *The Wretched of the earth*, London: Penguin, 1967.

Fernandez, Walter, *Inequality its Bases and searches for Solutions*, Delhi: ISI, 1986.

Fernandez, Walter, *The Indigenous question: Search for an Identity*, Delhi: ISI, 1993.

Forrester, Duncan B., *Caste and Christianity*, London: Curzon Press Ltd., 1980.

Freeman, James M., *Untouchable. An Indian Life History*, Stanford: Stanford University Press, 1979.

Freire, Paulo & Shor, Ira, *A Pedagogy for Liberation*, Beigin & Garvey, 1987.

Freire, Paulo, *Cultural Action for Freedom*, London: Penguin Books, 1972.

Fuller, C. J. (ed.), *Caste Today*, Delhi: Oxford University Press, 1996.

Geertz, C. (ed.), *Interpretation of Cultures*, New York: Basic Books, 1973.

Ghurye, G. S., *Caste and Class in India*, Bombay: Popular Prakashan, 1950.

Gokhle, Jayshree, *From Concessions to Confrontation: The Policies of an Indian Untouchable Community*, Bombay: Popular Prakashan, 1993.

Gould, Harld A., *Caste Adaptation in Modernising Indian Society. The Hindu Caste System*, Vol. 2, Delhi: Chanakya Publication, 1988.

Gould, Harld A., *The Sacralisation of a Social Order. The Hindu Caste system* (Vol. 1), Delhi: Chanakya Publications, 1987.

Grossberg, L., Carynelson & Paula Trickler (eds.), *Cultural Studies*, New York: Routeldge, 1992.

Guha, Ranjit, *Subaltern Studies* (Vol. 1,VI), Delhi: Oxford University Press, 1982, 1985.

Gupta, A. R., *Caste Hierarchy and Social Change,* New Delhi: Jyotsana Prakasan, 1984.

Gupta, Dipankar (ed.), *Social Stratification,* Delhi: Oxford University Press, 1992.

Hall, J. R. & M. J, Netz, *Culture,* Prentice Hall, 1993.

Heesterman, J. C., *The Inner Conflict of Tradition. Essays in Indian Ritual, Kingship and Society,* Delhi: Oxford University Press, 1985.

Hutton, J. H., *Caste in India,* Bombay: Oxford University Press, 1980.

Ilaiah, Kancha, *God as Political Philosopher: Buddha's Challenge to Brahminism,* Kolktta: Samy, 2001.

Ilaiah, Kancha, *Why I am not a Hindu,* Calcutta: Mandira Sen, 1996.

Inder, Donald, *Imaging India,* Oxford: Basil Blackwell, 1990.

Iyer, V. R. K., Dr. *Ambedkar and Dalit Future,* Delhi: B. R. Publishing Corporation, 1990.

Jayaraman, R., *Caste and Class: Dynamics of Inequality in Indian society,* Delhi: Hindusthan Publishing Corporation, 1981.

Joshi, P. C., *Culture, Communication and Social Change,* Delhi: Vikas Publishing House, 1989.

Kadam, K. N. (ed.), *Social Inequality,* Hammondsworth: Penguin Books, 1969.

Kadam, K. N., *Backward Classes in Contemporary India,* Delhi: Oxford University Press, 1992.

Kadam, K. N., Dr. *Baba Saheb Ambedkar and the Significance of His Movement,* Bombay: Popular Prakashan, 1991.

Kadam, K. N., *Society and Politics in India. Essays in a Comparative Perspective,* Delhi: Oxford University press, 1992.

Kample, J. P., *Pursuit of Equality in Indian History,* Delhi: National, 1985.

Kample, J. R., *Rise and Awakening of the Depressed classes in India,* New Delhi: National Publishing House, 1979.

Kample, J. R., *The Depressed Classes in India*, New Delhi: ICSSR, 1979.

Kample, N. D., *Atrocities on Scheduled Caste in Post Independent India*, Delhi: Select Book Service Syndicate, 1986.

Kananaikil, Jose, *Scheduled Castes in Search of Justice*(I&II), New Delhi: ISI, 1986.

Kannanaikal, J. (ed.), *Schedule Caste and the Struggle against Inequality*, Delhi: ISI, 1983.

Kappen, S., *Cultural Revolution*, Bombay: BILD, 1983.

Karwe, Iravati, *Hindu Society: An Interpretation* (2nd edition), Pune: Deshmukh Prakashan, 1968.

Khare, R. S., *Cultural Diversity and Social Discontent*, New Delhi: Sage Publications,1998.

Khare, R. S., *The Untouchable as Himself: Ideology, Identity, and Pragmatism among the Lucknow Chamars,* New York:Cambridge University Press, 1984.

Kly, Y. N., *International Law and Dalits in India*, Geneeva: Dalit Liberation Trust, 1989.

Kolenda, P., *Caste, Cult and Hierarchy*, Meerut: Ved Prakash Vatuk, 1983.

Kolenda, Pauline M., *Caste in Contemporary India, Beyond Organic Solidarity*, Mento Park: The Benjamin Cunnings Publishing Co., 1972.

Kolpe, S. B., *Upsurge of Sudras and Atisudras*, Bombay: Clarity Publications, 1994.

Kosambi, D. D., *Myth and Reality*, Bombay: Popular Prakasan, 1962.

Kosambi, D. D., *The Culture and Civilisation of Ancient India*, New Delhi: Vikas Publications, 1977.

Kotani, H (ed.), *Caste System, Untouchability and Depressed*, Delhi: Manohar, 1999.

Kraft, C. H., *Christianity in Culture*, New York: Orbis Books, 1994.

Kroeber, A. L., and Klyde Kluckhohn, *Culture: A critical Review of Concepts and Definitions,* Cambridge: Harvard University, 1952.

Kumarappa, Bharathan (ed.), *The Removal of the Untouchability*, Ahmedabad: Navasivam Press, 1954.

Lourdusamy, Stan, *Religion as a Social Protest*, Calcutta: Multi Book Agency, 1993.

Lynch, O. M., *Politics of Untouchability*, Delhi: National Publishing House, 1974.

Lynch, Owen and Others (eds.), *Structure and Change in Indian society*, Chicago: Aldme Publishing Co., 1963.

Madan, T. N., *Culture and Development*, Delhi: Oxford University Press, 1983.

Madhu, Limaye, *Manu, Gandhi and Ambedkar*, Delhi: Cryas Publishing House, 1995.

Mahar, J. M. (ed.), *The Untouchable in Contemporary India*, Arizona: University of Arizona Press, 1972.

Maliekal, John, *Caste in India Today*, Bangalore: CSA Publications, 1980.

Malik, S. C. *Determinants of Social Status in India*, Simla: Indian Institute of Advanced Study, 1986.

Marriot, Mckim (ed.), *India Through Indian Categories*, New Delhi: Sage Publications, 1990.

Massey, J. & Das, Somen (eds), *Dalit Solidarity*, Delhi: ISPCK, 1995.

Massey, J. (ed.), *Indegenous People, Dalits: Dalit Issues in Today's Theological Debate*, Delhi: ISPCK, 1994.

Massey, J., Roots: *A Concise History of Dalits,* Delhi: ISPCK, 1991.

Massey, James, *Dalits in India*, New Delhi: Manohar, 1995.

Mathew, George (ed.), *Dignity for All: Essays in Socialism and Democracy*, Delhi: Ajanta Publications, 1991.

Mathew, P. & A., Murickan (eds.), *Religion, Ideology and Counter-culture*, Bangalore: Horizon Books, 1987.

McGilvray, Dennis B. (ed.), *Caste Ideology and Interaction,* New York: Cambridge University Press, 1982.

Menamparampil, T., *The Challenge of Cultures*, Bombay: St. Pauls, 1996.

Michael, S. M. (ed.), *Dalits in Modern India*, New Delhi: Visthar Publications, 1999.

Milner, A., *Contemporary Cultural Theory*, UCL Press, 1994.

Mishra, R. B., *Caste and Caste Conflict in Rural Society*, New Delhi: Commonwealth Publishers, 1989.

Mitra, S., *Indian Vision and Fulfilment*, D. B. Taraporevala Sons & Co., 1972.

Moore, Barrington Jr., *Authority and Inequality under Capitalism and Socialism*, Oxford: Clarendon Press, 1987.

Mukherjee, P., *Beyond four Varnas: The Untouchables in India*, Delhi: Motilal Banarasidas, 1988.

Murali, Kaviyoor, *Dalitarkeruthia, Sivishesham* (Mal.), Kottayam: Current Books, 1997.

Murthy, H. V., Srinivasa *et al*, *Essays on Indian History and Culture*, New Delhi: Mittal Publications, 1990.

Nadkarni, M. V, Seetharmu, A. S. & Aziz, Abdul, *India: The Emerging Challenges. Essays in Honour of VKRV Rao,* New Delhi: Sage Publications, 1991.

Nandy, Ashis (ed.), *Science, Hegemony and Violence, A Requiem for Modernity,* Delhi: OUP, 1990.

Narain, A. K. & Ahir, D. C. (eds.), *Dr. Ambedkar, Buddhism and Social Change*, Delhi: B. R. Publishing Corporation, 1994.

Nath, Trilok, *Politics of the Depressed Classes*, Delhi: Deputy Publications, 1987.

Nida, E. A. &Reyburn, W. D., *Meaning Across Cultures*, New York: Orbis Books, 1981.

Niebuhr, H. Richard, *Christ and Culture,* New York: Harper & Row, 1951.

O'Hanlon, Rosalind, *Caste, Conflict and Ideology:Mahatma Jyotirao Phule and Low Caste Protest in Nineteenth Century Western India*, New York: Cambridge University Press, 1985.

Omvedt, Gail, *Dalit Visions: The Anti-caste Movement and the Construction of an Indian Identity*, Delhi: Orient Longman, 1995.

Omvedt, Gail, *Dalits and the Democratic Revolution*, New Delhi: Sage Publications, 1994.

Omvedt, Gail (ed.), *Land, Caste and Politics in Indian States*, Delhi: Authors' guild Publication, 1982.

Oommen, George & J. C. B., Webster (ed.), *Local Dalit Christian History*, Delhi: ISPCK, 2002.

Ottanla, Rosalind, *Caste, Conflict and Ideology*, New York: Cambridge University Press, 1985.

Pandey, Shashi Ranjan, *Community Action for Social Justice*, New Delhi: Sage Publications, 1991.

Pandian, J, *Caste Nationalism and Ethnicity*, London: Sangam Books, 1987.

Panickar, R. (ed.), *History, Politics and Culture*, New Delhi: Manohar, 1991.

Panikar, K. N., *Culture, Ideology, Hegemony*, New Delhi: Tulika, 1995.

Parvathamma, C., *Scheduled Castes at the Cross-roads*, New Delhi: Ashish Publishing House, 1989.

Parish, S. M., *Hierarchy and its Discontents: Culture and the Politics of Consciousness in Caste Society*, Delhi: Oxford University Press, 1997.

Pendse, Sandeep (ed.), *At The Cross-Roads: Dalit Movement Today*, Bombay: Vikas Adhyayan Kendra, 1994.

Peter, Berger, *The Hierarchical Imperative*, Anchor Doubleday, 1980.

Pillai, S. Devadas (ed.), *Aspects of Changing India. Studies in Honour of Pro. G. S. Ghurye,* Bombay: Popular Prakasan, 1976.

Pinto, Ambrose, *Dalit Christians: A Socio Economic Survey*, Bangalore: Ashirvad, 1992.

Pinto, Ambrose, *Dalits: Assertion for Identity*, New Delhi: ISI, 1999.

Pobee, John S. (ed.), *Culture, Women and Theology*, Delhi: ISPCK, 1994.

Prabhakar, M. E., *Liberty to the Captives*, Deenapur, 1987.

Prasad, D. M. C., *Dalit Christian Consciousness*, Bangalore: Rachana Publications, 1994.

Prasad, R. C., *Ambedkarism*, Delhi: Motilal Banarasidas, 1993.

Pulus, K. &Indira, J. Paridh, *Crossroads of Culture*, New Delhi: Saya Publications, 1995.

Quigley, Declan, *The Interpretation of Caste*, Oxford: Clarendan Press, 1995.

Radhakrishnan, S., *Our Heritage*, New Delhi: Orient Paperbacks, 1973.

Raj, M. C., *From the Periphery to Centre*, Tumkur: REDS, 1998.

Raj, Sebasti L. & Xavier G. F., Raj (eds.), *Caste Culture in Indian Church*, New Delhi: ISI, 1993.

Rajashekar, V. T. & Gopinath, M., *Textbook on Dalit Movement in India*, 1994.

Rajashekar, V. T., *Brahminism: The Curse of India*, Bangalore: Dalit Sahitya Academy, 1981.

Rajashekar, V. T., *The Dilemma of the Class & Caste*, Bangalore: Dalit Sahitya Akademy, 1984.

Rajashekhriah, A. M., *B. R. Ambedkar: The Quest for Social Justice*, New Delhi: Uppal Publishing House, 1989.

Ram, Nandu, *Beyond Ambedkar*, New Delhi: Har-anand Publications, 1995.

Ram, Nandu, *The Mobile Scheduled Castes: Rise of a new Middle Class*, Delhi: Hindusthan Publishing Corporation, 1988.

Rao, K. P., *Caste and Alternative Culture*, Madras: Gurukul, Lutheran Theological College, 1995.

Rao, M. S. A., *Social Movements and Social Transformation: A Study of two Backward Classes Movement in India*, Delhi, 1979.

Reddy, P. Ranjani (Dr.), *The Role of Dominant Castes in Indian Politics*, New Delhi: Uppal Publishing House, 1987.

Richard, Taylor (ed.), *Society and Religion*, Madras: CLS, 1976.

Robb, Peter, *Dalit Movements and the Meaning of Labour in India*, Delhi: Oxford University Press, 1993.

Russel, Burman, *Modern Culture and Critical Theory*, Madison: University of Wisconsin Press, 1989.

Sathyamurthy, T. V., *Region, Religion, Caste, Gender and Culture in Contemporary India*, Delhi: Oxford University Press, 1998.

Schluchter, Wolfgang, *Rationalism, Religion and Domination*, Berkeley: University of California Press, 1989.

Sebastian, M., *Liberating the Caged Dalit Panther*, Madras: Emerald Publishers, 1994.

Shah, A. B., *Religion and Society in India*, Bombay: Soaiya Publications, 1981.

Shah, Ghanshyam, *Social Movements in India*, New Delhi: Sage Publications, 1990.

Sharad, Patel, *Dasa-Sudra Slavery*, New Delhi: Allied Publishers, 1982.

Sharma, K. L. (ed.), *Caste and Class in India*, New Delhi: Rawat Publications,1994.

Sharma, Ram Avthar, *Justice and Social Order in India*, Delhi: Intellectual Publishing House, 1984.

Shashi,S.S. (ed.), *Ambedkar and Social Justice*, New Delhi: Government of India, 1992.

Singh, Harijinder, *Caste Among Non Hindus in India*, New Delhi, National, 1977.

Singh, K. K., *Patterns of Caste Tensions*, New Delhi: Ashish Publishing House, 1967.

Singh, V. P. (ed.), *Class Structure and Cultural Dynamics*, New Delhi: Commonwealth Publishers, 1992.

Singh, V. P. (ed.), *Community and Caste in Tradition*, New Delhi: Commonwealth Publishers,1992.

Singh, Yogendra, *Social Stratification and Social Change in India*, Delhi: Manohar,1977.

Singh, Virendra Prakash (ed.), *Caste System and Social Change*, New Delhi: Common Wealth Publications, 1992.

Sivaramamurthy, C., *Some Aspects of Indian Culture*, New Delhi, Publications Division, 1994.

Srinivas, M. N. & Others (eds.), *Dimensions of Social Change in India*, New Delhi: Allied Publishers, 1978.

Srinivas, M. N., *The Dominant Caste and other Essays*, Delhi: Oxford University Press, 1987.

Starke, Linda, *Signs of Hope, Working Towards Our Common Future*, Oxford: Oxford University Press, 1990.

Subhaya, Dasgupta, *Hindu Ethos and Challenge of Change*, New Delhi: Arnold Hermemann, 1977.

Sukumaran, Kallada, *Dalit Bandhuvinte Dalith Darsana Granthangal* (Mal.), Peermade: Dr. Ambedkar Bhavan, 1993.

Sunder, B. Shyam, They Burn the 160,000,000 Untouchables of India, Bangalore: Dalit Sahitya Academy, 1987.

Tanner, Kathryn, *Theories of Culture: A New Agenda for Theology*, Augsburg: Fortress Press, 1997.

Thaper, Romesh (ed.), *Tribe, Caste and Religion in India*, Delhi: Macmillan, 1977.

Wilson, K., *Between Mythology and Technology*, Madras: The Centre for Research on New International Economic Order, 1982.

Wilson, K., *Dialectics of Consciousness: Problems of Development*, Madras: Oneworld Educational Trust, 1993.

Wilson, K., *The Twice Alienated*, Hyderabad: Booklinks Corporation, 1982.

Zelliot, Eleanor, From Untouchable to Dalit,. Essays on Ambedkar Movement, New Delhi: Manohar, 1992.

B. BOOKS ON THEOLOGY AND HERMENEUTICS

Abraham, K. C., *Liberative Solidarity*, Thiruvalla, Christava Sahitya Samithi, 1996.

Abraham, K. C., *Third World Theologies*, New York: Orbis Books, 1990.

Bibliography 291

Abraham, K. C., *Two Essays*, Bangalore: BTESSC, (n.d.).

Alangaram, A., *Christ of the Asian Peoples*, Bangalore: ATC, 2001.

Amaladoss, M. (ed.), *Globalisation and its Victims*, Delhi: ISPCK, 1999.

Amaladoss, M., *Beyond Inculturation*, Delhi: ISPCK, 1998.

Amaladoss, M., *Life in Freedom: Liberation Theologies from Asia*, Anand: GSP, 1997.

Amaladoss, M., T. K. John and G. Gispert-Sauch (eds.), *Theologising in India*, Bangalore: Theological Publication in India, 1981.

Amaladoss, M., *Towards Fullness: Searching for an Integral Spirituality*, Bangalore: NBCLC, 1994.

Amalorpavadass, D. S. (ed.), *The Indian Church in the struggle for a new society*, Bangalore: NBCLC, 1981.

Amirtham, S. and J. S. Pobee (eds.), *Theology by People: Reflection in Doing Theology in Community*, Geneeva: WCC, 1986.

Anderson, G. S. and T. F. Stransky (eds.), *Third World Theologies*, New York: Grand Rapids, 1979 (1976).

Anthony, Francis-Vincent, *Ecclesial Praxis on Inculturation*, Rome: LAS, 1997.

Appavoo, T., *Folklore in Social Change*, Madurai: TTS, 1986.

Arbuckle, G., *Earthing the Gospel*, New York: Orbis Books, 1990.

Arokiasamy, S. and G. Gispert-Sauch (eds.), *Liberation in Asia – Theological Perspectives,* Anand: GSP, 1991.

Arulraja, M. R., *Jesus The Dalit*, Hyderabad: Volunteer Centre, 1996.

Balasundaram, Franklin J., *Contemporary Asian Christian Theology*, Delhi: ISPCK, 1995.

Balasuriya, Tissa, *Globalisation and Human Solidarity*, Thiruvalla: Christhava Sahithya Samiti, 2000.

Balasurya, Tissa, *Jesus Christ and Human Liberation*, Colombo: CSR, 1981.

Balasurya, Tissa, *Planetary Theology*, London: SCM, 1984.

Battummalai, S., *An introduction to Asian Theology*, Delhi: ISPCK, 1991.

Berger, Bennet, *The Survival of a Counter-culture: Ideological Works and Everyday Life among Rural Communards*, Berkley: University of California Press, 1981.

Bevans, S. B., *Models of Contextual Theology*, New York: Orbis Books, 1992.

Brown, Robert McAfee, *Theology in a New Key, Responding to Liberation Themes*, Delhi: Lithose Publications, 1983.

Chilton, Bruce & Jim Mc Donald, *Jesus and the Ethics of the Kingdom*, London: SPCK. 1987.

Clarke, Sathyanathan, *Dalits and Christianity: Subaltern Religion and Liberation Theology in India*, New Delhi: Oxford University Press, 1999.

Coggins, R. J. & J. L., Houlden (eds.), *A Dictionary of Biblical Interpretation*, London: SCM, 1990.

Colaco, J. (ed.), *Jesus Christ in Asian Suffering and Hope*, Chennai: CLS, 1977.

Collins, R., *Models of Theological Reflection*, Lanham: University Press of America, 1984.

Cone, James, *God of the Oppressed*, New York: Seabury Press, 1972.

Croatto, Severino, *Biblical Hermeneutics*, New York: Orbis Books, 1987.

Crollius, A. A. R. (ed.), *Inculturation: Working Papers on Living Faith and Cultures*, Rome: Pontifical Gregorian University, 1984.

D'Lima, Errol & Max, Gonsalves (eds.), *What does Jesus Christ Mean?*, Bangalore: Dharmaram Publications, 2001.

Das, Somen, *Christian Spirituality and Indian Reality*, Bombay: BUILD, 1987.

De mesa, Jose M. & Lode L., Wostyn, *Doing Theology*, Philippines: Claretian Publications, 1990.

Devasahayam, V. (ed.), *Frontiers of Dalit Theology*, Madras: Gurukul Lutheran Theological College & Research Institute, 1997.

Devasahayam, V., *Outside the Camp, Biblical Studies in Dalit Perspective*, Chennai: Gurukul, 1992.

Dietrich, Gabriele, *Culture Religion and Development*, Bangalore: CSA, 1991.

Engineer, Asghar Ali (ed.), *Religion and Liberation*, Mumbai: Institute of Islamic Studies, 1990.

Fabella, Virginia &Sugirtharaja, R. S. (eds.), *Dictionary of the Third World Theologies*, New York: Orbis Books, 2000.

Fabella, Virginia (ed.), *Asia's Struggles for Full Humanity: Towards a Relevant Theology*, New York: Orbis Books, 1980.

Ferm, D. W., *Third World Liberation Theologies*, New York: Orbis Books, 1986.

Fernandes, Erasto & Joji, Kunduru (eds.), *Renewed Efforts at Inculturation for an Indian Church*, Bangalore: Dharmaram Publications, 2002.

Geffre, Claude, *The Risk of Interpretation*, New Jersey: Paulist Press, 1987.

Gottwald, Norman K. (ed.), *The Bible and Liberation*, New York: Orbis Books, 1989.

Grady, J. F. O., *Models of Jesus*, New York: Doubleday, 1981.

Haight, Roger, *Dynamics of Theology*, New York: Paulist Press, 1990.

Irudayaraj, X. (ed.), *Liberation and Dialogue*, Bangalore: Claretian Publications, 1989.

Irudayaraj, X., *Emerging Dalit Theology*, Madras: Madras Theological Forrum, 1987.

Jayakumar, Samuel, *Dalit Consciousness and Christian Conversion*, Delhi: ISPCK,1999.

Jeanrond, Werner G., *Theological Hermeneutics, Development and Significance*, New York: Crossroad, 1991.

Jeyaseelan, L., *Towards a Counter-Culture: Sebastian Kappen's Contribution*, Delhi: ISPCK, 1999.

John T. K. (ed.), *Bread and Breath*, Anand: GSP, 1991.

Joshi, Barbara (ed.), *Untouchables: Voices of the Dalit Liberation Movement*, New Delhi: Select Book, 1986.

Kappen, S, *Jesus and Culture*, Delhi: ISPCK, 2002.

Kappen, S., *Jesus and Society*, Delhi: ISPCK,2002.
Kappen, S., *Tradition Modernity Counterculture*, Bangalore: Visthar,1994.
Kavungal, Jacob & F., Hrangkhuma (eds.), *Christ and Cultures*, Bombay: St. Pauls, 1994.
Khan, Benjamin (ed.), *Dalit Christian Movement and Christian Theology*, Indore: New Christian Perspective Association, 1995.
Kochuthara, Thomas, *Theology of Liberation and Ideology Critique*, New Delhi: Intercultural Publications, 1993.
Kung, Hans and David Tracy (eds.), *Paradigm Change in Theology: A Symposium for Future,* Edinburgh: T & T Clark, 1989.
Kurien, C. T., *Growth and Justice, Aspects of Indian Development Experience*, Madras: Oxford University Press, 1972.
Lohfink, Norber F., *Option for the Poor*, California: BIBAL Press, 1987.
Massey, J., *Towards a Dalit Hermeneutics*, Delhi: ISPCK, 1991.
Mattam, J. & P., Arokiadoss (eds.), *Hindutva: An Indian Christian Response*, Bangalore: Dhamaram Publications, 2002.
McGovern, Arthur F., *Liberation Theology and its Critics*, New York: Orbis Books, 1989.
McKim, Donald K., *A Guide to Contemporary Hermeneutics*, Michigan: W.B. Eerdmans Publishing Company, 1986.
Niles, D. Preman (ed.), *Minjung Theology: People as Subject of History*, Singapore: Christian Conference of Asia, 1981.
Nirmal, A. P. (ed.), *Towards a Common Dalit Ideology*, Madras: Gurukul, 1989.
Nirmal, A. P., *A Reader in Dalit Theology*, Madras: Gurukul, 1991.
Nirmal, A. P., *Heuristic Explorations*, Madras: CLS, 1990.
Nolan, *Albert*, *Jesus Before Christianity*, Philippines: Claretian Publications, 1988.
O'Brien, J., *Theology and the Option for the Poor*, Minnesota; Liturgical Press, 1992.
Oommen, T. K., *Protest and Change, Studies in Social Movements*, Delhi: Sage, 1990.

Panikkar, Raimundo, *Myth, Faith and Hermeneutics, Cross Cultural studies,* Bangalore: ATC, 1983.

Parappally, Jacob (ed.), *Theologising in the Context: Statements of the Indian Theological Association,* Bangalore, Dharmaram Publications, 2002.

Pathil, Kuncheria (ed.), *Socio-Cultural Analysis in Theologising,* Bangalore: ITA, 1987.

Patmury, Joseph (ed.), *Doing Theology with the Poetic Traditions of India,* Bangalore: SATHRI, 1996.

Pieris, A., *An Asian Theology of Liberation,* Edinburgh: T & T Clark,1988.

Pieris, A., *Love Meets Wisdom,* New York: Orbis Books, 1988.

Prabhakar, M. E. (ed.), *Towards a Dalit Theology,* Bangalore: CISRS & CDLM, 1988.

Puthanagady, Paul (ed.), *Towards an Indian Theology of Liberation,* Bangalore: NBCLC, 1986.

Raj, Antony, *Betraying the Hope of the Poor,* Madurai: IDEAS, 1990.

Rajashekar, V. T., *Christians and Dalit Liberation,* Bangalore: Dalit Sahitya Academy, 1987.

Robinson, G. (ed.), *Religions of the Marginalised,* Delhi: ISPCK, 1998.

Rowland,C and M. Corner, *Liberating Exegesis: The Challenge of Liberation Theology to Biblical Studies,* Westminster: John Knox, 1989.

Sahay, K. N., *Christianity and Cultural Changes in India,* New Delhi: Inter-India Publications, 1986.

Sahi, Jyoti, *Stepping Stones: Reflections on Theology of Indian Christian Culture,* Bangalore: ATC, 1986.

Said, Edward, *Culture and Imperialism,* London: Vintage, 1993.

Samartha, S. J., *The Search for a New Hermeneutic in Asian Christian Theology,* Bangalore: BTESSC,1987.

Segundo, J, L., Liberation of Theology, New York: Orbis Books, 1976.

Segundo, J. L., *Faith and Ideologies*, New York: Orbis Books, 1982.

Soares-Prabhu, G. M., *Collected Writings of George M. Soares-Prabhu, S. J., Vol. 4*, D'Sa, Francis X. (ed.), *Theology of Liberation: An Indian Biblical Perspective*, Pune: Jnana-Deepa Vidyapeeth Theology Series, 2001.

Soares-Prabhu, G. M., *Collected Writings of George M. Soares-Prabhu, S. J., Vol. 2*, Kuthirakkattel, S. (ed.), *A Biblical Theology for India*, Pune: Jnana Deepa Vidyapeeth Theology Series, 1999.

Soares-Prabhu, G. M., *Collected Writings of George M. Soares-Prabhu, S. J., Vol. 1*, Padinjarekuttu, I. (ed.), *Biblical Themes for a Contextual Theology Today*, Pune: Jnana Deepa Vidyapeeth Theology Series, 1999.

Students Council (ed.), *Human Liberation in the Indian Context*, Pune: JDV, 1983.

Sugirtharaja, R. S. (ed.), *Voices from the Margin*, New York: Orbis Books, 1991.

Sugirtharaja, R. S., *Bible and the Third World*, Cambridge: Camebridge University Press, 2001.

Sumitra, Sunand, *Theology from an Indian Perspective*, Bangalore: Theological Book Trust, 1990.

Takenaka, Masao, *God is Rice: Asian Culture and Christian Faith*, Geneva: WCC, 1986.

Thomas, M. M., *Religion and the Revolt of the Oppressed*, Delhi: ISPCK, 1981.

Thomas, M. M., *Secular Ideologies of India and the Secular meaning of Christ*, Madras: CLS, 1980.

Thumma, Anthoniraj, *Breaking Barriers: Liberation of Dialogue and Dialogue of Liberation*, Delhi: ISPCK, 2000.

Thumma, Anthoniraj, *Dalit Liberation Theology*, Delhi: ISPCK, 2000.

Thumma, Anthoniraj, *Springs from the Subalterns*, Delhi: ISPCK, 1999.

Thumma, Anthoniraj, *Voices of the Victims*, Delhi: ISPCK, 1999.

Thumma, Anthoniraj, *Wisdom of the Weak: Foundations of People's Theology*, Delhi: ISPCK, 2000.

Torres, Sergio and Virginia Fabella (eds.), *Doing Theology in a Divided World*, New York: Orbis Books, 1985.

Tracy, David, *Analogical imagination: Christian Theology and the Culture of pluralism*, New York: Crossroad, 1981.

Vattamattam, J and Others (eds.), *Liberative Struggles in a Violent Society*, Hyderabad: A Forum Publication, 1990.

Webster, John C. B., *Pastor to Dalits*, Delhi: ISPCK, 1995.

Webster, John C. B., *Religion and Dalit Liberation*, New Delhi: Manohar, 1999.

Webster, John C. B., *Towards Dalit Liberation: From Indian Church to Indian Theology, An Attempt at theological Reconstruction*, Chennai: Dalit Liberation Education Trust, 1991.

Wilfred, Felix (ed.), *Leave the Temple: Indian Path to Human Liberation*, New York, Orbis Books, 1992.

Wilfred, Felix, *Asian Dreams and Christian Hope*, Delhi: ISPCK, 2000.

Wilfred, Felix, *On the Banks of Ganges*, Delhi: ISPCK, 2002.

Wilfred, Felix, *From the Dusty Soil: Contextual Interpretation of Christianity*, Madras: University of Madras, 1995.

Wilfred, Felix, *Sunset in the East?*, Madras: University of Madras, 1991.

Williams, Raymond, *Resource of Hope, Culture, Democracy, Socialism*, London: Verso, 1989.

Wilson, K., *Invocation to the Human*, Hyderabad: Scientific Services, 1987.

C. ARTICLES

Abraham, K. C., "Globalisation: A Gospel and Culture Perspective", *International Review of Mission*", 135, 336 (1996), pp. 85-92.

Abraham, K. C., "Paradigm Shift in Contemporary Theological Thinking", *Theology of Times,* 1988, pp. 18-26.

Agera, C. R, "Vital Hermeneutics: The Problem of Meaning in Life and its Relation to Religion", *Journal Of Dharma,* 11, 4(1986), pp. 379-396.

Aggins, B. and Rajiv Lochan, "Religion and Social Change: The Case of Jyotiba Phule", *Social Action,* 39 (1989), pp.142-150.

Amaladoss, M., " Hermeneutic of Tradition and Social Change", *Indian Theological studies,* 27, 2(1990), pp. 113-132.

Amaladoss, M., "A Christian Vision of a new Society", *Jnanadeepa,* 2, 1(1999), pp. 111-122.

Amaladoss, M., "Building Community", *Jeevadhara,* 24, 141(1994), pp. 165-175.

Amaladoss, M., "Culture and Dialogue", *Vidyajyoti,* 49(1985), pp. 6-15.

Amaladoss, M., "Difficult Dialogue", *Vidyajyoti,* 62(1998), pp. 567-577.

Amaladoss, M., "Faith and Symbols, the Flute and the *Chakra,* the Cross and the Crescent", *Jeevadhara,* 20, 117(1990), pp. 209-220.

Amaladoss, M., "Folk Culture as Counter-culture the Dalit Experience", *Jeevadhara,* 139(1994), pp. 31-42.

Amaladoss, M., "From Experience to Theology", *Vidyajyoti,* 61(1997), pp. 372-385.

Amaladoss, M., "Inculturation and Internationality", *EAPR,* 29(1992), pp. 238-252.

Amaladoss, M., "Liberation an Inter-religious Project", *EAPR,* 28(1991), pp. 4-33.

Amaladoss, M., "Mission in a Post-Modern World: A call to be Counter-cultural", *Vidyajyoti,* 60, 9(1996), pp. 569-581.

Amaladoss, M., "Periyar and Liberation in Tamilnadu", in *Towards an Indian Theology of Liberation,* Puthanangady, P. (ed), Bangalore:ITA *&NBCLC,* 1986, pp. 184- 198.

Amaladoss, M., "Changing Culture and Religion", *Jeevadhara*, 22, 127(1992), pp. 7-18.

Amaladoss, M., "Towards a Culture of Wholeness", *Vidyajyoti*, 47(1983), pp. 67-76.

Ambrose, Y., "Culture Liberating or Alienating?", *Jeevadhara*, 22, 127(1992), pp. 26- 32.

Ana, J. De Santa, "Cultures in Tension and Dialogue", *International Review of Mission*, 135, 336(1996), pp. 93-102.

Ananth, V. Krishna, "The Dalit Factor They Cannot Do Without", *The Hindu*, Sept. 26, 1999, p. 13.

Aram, I. A., "Craze for Power, Communal Politics and Subaltern Politics", *Integral Liberation*, 6, 2(2002), pp. 97-105.

Ariaraja, Wesley S., The rise of Dalit Consciousness and Hindu Christian Dialogue", *Studies in Interreligious Dialogue*, 2(1992), pp. 101-110.

Arulraja, A. M., "Towards a Dalit Reading of the Bible: Some Hermeneutical Reflections", *Jeevadhara*, 26, 151(1996), pp. 29-34.

Ayrookuzhiel A. M. A., "Dalit Liberation- Some Reflections on their Ideological Predicament", *Religion and Society*, 35, 2(1989), pp. 47-52.

Ayrookuzhiel A. M. A., "Religion a Way of Salvation or an Ideology of oppression of the Poor Dimension of the Hindu Village Religion", *Religion and Society*, 32, 1(1985), pp. 3-23.

Ayrookuzhiel A. M. A., "The Role of Religion in the Dalit Liberation: Some Reflections", *Kerala Sociological Society*, 12, 1(1989), pp. 46-63.

Ayrookuzhiel A. M. A., Ideological Nature of the Emerging Dalit Consciousness", *Journal of Dharma*, 37, 3(1990), pp. 14-23.

Ayrookuzhiel, A. M. A., "Christian Dalits in Revolt", *Jeevadhara*, 23, 136(1993), pp. 269-273.

Ayrookuzhiel, A. M. A., "Religio-Cultural Factors and the Struggle of the Dalits for Social Equality", *Samata*, 2(1985), pp. 1626.

Ayrookuzhiel, A. M. A., The Dalits, Religions and Inter-faith Dialogue", *Hindu Christian Studies Bulletin*, 7(1994), pp. 13-19.

Azariah, M., "Doing Theology in India Today", *NCCR*, 108, 2(1988), pp. 93-101.

Balasundaram, Franklyn J., "Dalit Theological Perspectives- Arvind P. Nirmal, A Case, *Voices from the Third World*, 15, 2(1992), pp. 74-103.

Balasuriya, Tissa, "Emerging Theologies of Asian Liberation", *Cocillium*, 1988, pp. 35- 45.

Banana, Canaan, "The Biblical Basis for Liberation Struggles", *International Review of Mission*, 68, 272(1979), pp. 417-423.

Baxi, Upendra, "Relevance of Ambedkar Today", *NCCR,* 111, 11(1991), pp. 1416-1429.

Berreman, Gerald, D., " The Brahminical View of Caste", *Contributions to Indian Sociology*, 5(1970), pp. 16-23.

Bruck, M. Von, "Holistic Vision in Eastern Religions. Reality as Consciousness", *Indian Theological Studies*, 22, 1(1985), pp. 28-61.

Casti, J., "Inculturation in Asia: Religious and Cultural Aspects", *Indian Missiological Review*, 7, 3(1985), pp. 217-245.

CCBI Consultation on "A Dialogue of Cultures-Cultural Issues in Mission (March 7-9, 2000)", *Indian Theological Studies*, 37, 2(2000), pp. 193-202.

Chandhoke, Neera, "Rethinking Reservation", *The Hindu*, Nov. 4, 1999, p. 9.

Chatterji, S. K., "Social Aspects of Dalit Ideology", *Journal of Dharma*, 37, 3(1990), pp. 3-13.

Chinnappa, P., "A Pastoral Approach to Inter-caste Problems", *Third Millennium*, 3, 3(2000), pp. 92-101.

Clarke, Satyanathan, "Subaltern Culture as Resource for People's Liberation: A Critical Inquiry into Dalit Culture Theory", *Religion and Society*, 44, 4(1997), pp. 84-105.

D'sa, Francis X., "A Hermeneutic of Theological Language: The Relationship between Reality, Language, History and Faith", *Third Millennium*, 3, 4(2000), pp. 6-23.

Daniel, Ayub, "Dalit Theology: Punjab Perspective", *Religion and Society*, 38, 2(1991), pp. 58-64.

Deenabandhu, M., "New Prospects for Dalit Theology", *NCCR*, 108, 2(1988), pp. 67- 69.

Desbruslais, Cyril, "A Liberative Vision for a Pluralistic Society", *Vidyajyoti*, 95(1995), pp. 711-717.

Dupuis, Jacques, "Jesus with an Asian Face", *Third Millennium*, 2, 1(1999), pp.6-17.

Engineer, A. A., "On Inter-cultural Dialogue", *The Hindu*, Nov. 4, 1999, p.9.

Gispert-Sauch, G., " Jesus the Good Dalit", *Vidyajyoti*, 65, 7(2001), pp. 519-520.

Gispert-Sauch, G., "Notes for an Indian Christology", *Vidyajyoti*, 61(1977), pp. 757- 765.

Gispert-Sauch, G., "Theological Method in Hinduism", Vidyajyoti, 61(1999), 667-679.

Gladstone, J. W., "Caste, Religion and People's Movements in Kerala", *Religion and Society*, 32, 1(1985), pp. 24-35.

Heredia, Rudolf C., "Gandhi's *Hind Swaraj*: Need for a New Hermeneutic (II)", *Vidyajyoti*, 63(1999), pp. 733-748.

Heredia, Rudolf C., "Gandhi's *Hind Swaraj*: Need for a New Hermeneutic (I)", *Vidyajyoti*, 63(1999), pp. 638-650.

Heredia, Rudolf, "Subaltern Interrogations of Hindu Nationalism. Need for a New Hermeneutic (I)", *Vidyajyoti,* 66, 10(2002), pp. 822-835.

Heredia, Rudolf, "Subaltern Interrogations on Hindu Nationalism. Need for a New Hermeneutic (II)", *Vidyajyoti*, 66, 11(2002), pp. 914-922.

Ilaiah, Kancha, "Caste and the U.N. meet", *The Hindu*, Aug. 21, 2001, P. 10.

Ilaiah, Kancha, Countering the Counter-revolution", *The Hindu*, March 20, 2000, p. 10.

Ilaiah, Kancha, "Globalisation and Hindutva', in *Globalisation*, R. Visvanath (ed), 1998, 35.

Jebraj, D., "Paradigms in Dalit Theology", *AETEI*,6, 2(1993), pp. 11-17.

Kadam, K. N., "Race, Caste and Gender", *Man*, 5, 25(1990), pp. 489-504.

Kananaikil, J., "Emerging Dalit Theology in India", *Social Action*, 43, 5(1993), pp. 401- 412.

Kannanaikil, J., "Religion, Culture and Power: The Case of the Scheduled Castes in India", *Religion and Society*, 33, 2(1986), pp. 27-32.

Kappen, S., "Dialectic of Faith and Unfaith", *Jeevadhara*, 20, 117(1990), pp. 165-168.

Karotempel, S., " Christian Mission and Cultural Formation amidst Conflict of Cultures", *Indian Missiological Review*, 17, 3(1985), pp. 267-278.

Koonthanam, G., " Yahweh the Defender of Dalits: A Reflection on Isaiah 3:12-15", *Jeevadhara*, 22, 128(1992), pp. 112-123.

Lobo, Lancy, "Regional Cultures and Religion", *Vidyajyoti,* 57, 4(1993), pp. 231-242.

Madtha, W.,"Dalit Theology: Voice of the Oppressed", *Journal of Dharma,* 16, 1(1991), pp. 74-92.

Manuswamy, U., "Dalit Christians: Their Plight with in the Church in India", *Christujyot*i, 7, 1(1991), pp. 92-116.

Mariaselvam, A., "The Cry of the Dalits", *Jeevadhara*, 22, 128(1992), pp. 124-139.

Marriott, McKim, "Caste Systems", in *Encyclopedia Britanica*, 3(1973), pp. 982-991.

Martin, M. S., "Towards an Indian Theology of Liberation, ITA Statement (1985)", *Indian Theological studies*, 23, 1(1986), pp. 61-64.

Bibliography

Massey, J., " Christian Dalits in India: An Analysis", *Journal of Dharma*, 37, 3(1990), pp. 40-53.

Massey, J., "Christian Dalits: A Historical Perspective", *Journal of Dharma*, 16, 1(1991), pp. 44-60.

Michael, S. M., "The Cultural Context of the Rise of Hindutva and Dalit Forces", *Vidyajyoti,* 60(1996), pp. 294-310.

Nalunnakkal, G. M., "The Dalit Question", *Third Millennium*, 1, 1(1998), pp. 74-82.

Naravane, Vaiju, "Hindutva is not Indian", *The Hindu*, April 18, 2000, p. 10.

Natarajan, R., "Casting the Vote or Voting the Caste", *The Hindu*, Aug. 15, 1999, p. A.

Neuner, J., "Jesus the Prophet", *Vidyajyoti,* 47, 11(1983), pp.526-540.

Nirmal, A. P., "What is Dalit Theology", *NCCR*, 108, 2(1988), pp. 70-87.

Omvedt, Gail, "Dalits and Elections (II)", *The Hindu*, Nov. 6, 1999, p. 10.

Painadath, S., "Hermeneutics in Indian Theology", *Vidyajyoti*, 62, 5(1998), pp. 303-314.

Painadath, S., "Spiritual Dynamics of Dialogue", *Vidyajyoti*,60, 12(1996), pp. 813-824.

Painadath, S., "Theologising As Doing Mission: Inter-religious Hermeneutics in Theology", *Third Millennium*, 4, 4(2001), pp. 6-21.

Painadath, S., "Towards an Inter-religious Hermeneutics", *Word and Worship*, 20, 3(1987), pp. 83-90.

Painadath, S., " Spirituality, Christian and Secular", *Christu Jyoti*, 7, 4(1991), pp. 10-20.

Pattery, G., "Inculturation and Liberation", *EAPR*, 30(1993), pp. 317-345.

Phan, Peter C., "Jesus The Christ with an Asian Face", *Theological Studies*, 57(1996), pp. 399-430.

Pieris, Aloysius, "Non Christian Religions and Cultures in Third World Theology", *Vidyajyoti*, 1982, pp. 158-170.

Pillai, M., "Cultural Hegemony: Its Traditional Roots and the Present Manifestation", *Jeevadhara*, 22, 127(1992), pp. 33-48.

Pinto, Ambrose, "The Concept of Reservation: Culture versus Religion", *Vidyajyoti*, 62(1998), pp. 487-497.

Prabhakar, M. E., " Christian Dalits", *Religion and Society*, 34, 3(1988), pp. 23-34.

Prabhakar, M. E., " Reservation for Equality and Justice", *Religion and Society*, 37, 4(1990), pp. 3-29.

Prabhakar, M. E., "Developing a Common Ideology of Dalits of Christian Origin and Other Faiths", *Journal of Dharma*, 37, 3(1990), pp. 24-39.

Prasad, C. B., &Bechain, S. S., "Where the non-Dalit Commentators Err", *The Hindu*, Jan. 4, 2000, p. 21.

Puthenangady, P., "Which Culture for Inculturation: the Dominant or the Popular", *EAPR,* 30(1993), pp. 295-310.

Raj, M. C., "A Dalit Perspective on Pluralism", *Integral Liberation*, 6, 3(2002), pp. 191- 199.

Raj, M. C., "Brahminism Denies Religious, Cultural & Educational Rights of Dalits", *People's Reporter*, May 25-June10, 2001, p. 4.

Raja, A. M. A., "Harmony in the midst of Anarchy: The Anatomy of the Spirit of Dalit Liberation", *Vidyajyoti,* 63(1999), pp. 416-428.

Raja, A. M. A., "Living through the Conflicts: The Spirit of Subaltern Resurgence", *Vidyajyoti*, 65, 6(2001), pp. 465-476.

Raja, A. M. A., "Reading the Bible from a Dalit Location: Some Points for Interpretation", *Indian Theological Studies*, 36, 1(1999), pp. 73-87.

Raja, A. M. A., "The Authority of Jesus: A Dalit Reading of Mk 11:27-33", *Jeevadhara,*25, 146(1995), pp.123-139.

.**Raja, A. M. A.**, "Exorcism and Dalit Self-Affirmation", *Vidyajyoti,* 60, 12(1996), pp. 843-851.

Raja, Hilda, "Caste Discrimination is Racism?",*The Hindu*, Aug. 21, 2001,OB.1 **Rasquinha, Dionysius**, "A Brief Historical Analysis of the Emergence of Dalit Christian Theology", *Vidyajyoti,* 66, 5(2002), pp. 353-370.

Rayan Samuel, "Outside the Gate, Sharing the Insult", *Jeevadhara,* 11, 63(1981) pp. 203-231.

Rayan, S., "Indian Realities and the Wholeness of Christ", *IRM,* 4, 3(1982), pp. 255-275.

Rayan, Samuel, "Flesh of India's Flesh", *Jeevadhara,* 33(1976), pp. 259-267.

Rayan, Samuel, "Jesus and the Struggles of the Masses in India", *Third Millennium,* 2, 1(1999), pp. 18-31.

Rayan, Samuel, "People's Theology", *Jeevadhara,* 22, 129(1992), pp. 175-202.

Ryerson, C. A., "Religion, Culture and Power: Hinduism and Justice", *Religion and Society,* 33, 2(1986), pp. 5-26.

Samartha, S., "Religion, Culture and Power – Three Bible Studies", *Religion and Society,* 34, 1(1987), pp. 66-79.

Sebastian, Simon, "Inculturation as a Dialogue with the Poor", *Vidyajyoti,* 65, 6(2001), pp. 416-429.

Sheth, D. L., "Politics of Caste Conflict", *Seminar,* 233(1979), pp. 29-36.

Soares-Prabhu, G., "The Bible as the Magna Carta of Movements for Liberation and Human Rights", *Concillium,* 1(1995), pp. 85-96.

Staff Reporter, "Culture has Power to Transform People", *The Hindu,* Dec. 16, 1999, p. 3.

Stanislaus, L., "Liberative Mission among the Dalits: Challenges to the Church", *Third Millennium,* 2, 1(1999), pp. 60-71.

Starkloff, C. F., "Inculturation and Cultural Systems (Part I)", *Theological Studies,* 55, 1(1994), pp. 66-81.

Starkloff, C. F., "Inculturation and Cultural Systems (Part II)", *Theological Studies,* 55, 2(1994), pp. 274-294.

Statement of an EATWOT Consultation (at New Delhi on 1st to 5th Dec., 1987), "Religion and Liberation", *Basic community Service,* pp. 1-7.

Sudhakaran, Jacob, "Anti-Dalit Theology of Indian Renaissance", *NCCR,* 117, 9(1997), pp. 602-615.

Velankunnel, Joseph, "Hindutva and the Search for a *Svadeshi* Theocracy", *Vidyajyoti,* 65, 6(2001), pp. 450-464.

Vellaringatt, J., "The Secular Face of Hinduism", *Vidyajyoti*, 65, 9(2001), pp. 645-652.

Waldenfels, Hans, "On the Hermeneutics of Intercultural Encounter", *Studies in Interreligious Dialogue*, 2, 1(1992), pp. 31-50.

Wilfred, Felix, "Church's commitment to the Poor in the Age of Globalisation", *Vidyajyoti*, 62(1998), pp. 79-95.

Wilfred, Felix, "Inculturation as a Hermeneutical Question", *Vidyajyoti*, 42, 9(1988), pp. 422-436.

Wilfred, Felix, "On the Threshold of the 1990's: Emerging Trends and Socio-cultural Processes at the Turn of the Century", *Jeevadhara*,20, 115(1990), pp. 57-71.

Wilfred, Felix, "Towards a Better Understanding of Asian Theology", *Vidyajyoti*, 62(1998), pp. 890-915.

Wilfred, Felix, "Inculturation as a Hermeneutical question", *Vidyajyoti,* 52, 9(1988), pp. 422-436.

Wilson, K., "Political Perspectives of Dalits in Contemporary India", *NCCR*, 111, 11(1991), pp. 1438-1446.

INDEX

A

Actors, caste xxii, 72, 74, 78, 83, 85, 119, 120, 167, 172, 178, 261, 262
Adivasis 26, 27
Amaladoss, M. xxiii, 36, 49, 51, 53, 88, 90, 110, 122, 127, 129, 227, 261
Ambedkar xix, 12, 94, 148, 150, 151, 152, 155, 156, 157, 158, 163, 199, 265
Ambedkarism 264
Analysis xxii, 19, 48, 72, 79, 130, 175, 197, 258, 261, 263, 269
Analysis, Marxian, xxii
Ascetic and Householder 125
Apartheid 25
Approach, holistic 197, 270
Aryans 4, 7, 8, 11, 52
Ascetics 174, 180, 182, 183, 185
Authoritarianism 100
Authoritarianism, Patriarchal 99, 100

B

Basavanna 18
Beteille, Andre xxiii, 2, 37, 38, 39, 42, 105

Buddha xix, 7, 15, 138, 139, 150, 151, 163, 270
Buddhism 9, 15, 140, 150, 151, 152, 153, 265

C

Caste and class 6, 43, 44, 55, 270
Casteism 17, 99
Castes, intermediate 4
Centrality of culture 202
Christianity 9, 18, 33, 152, 261
Clarke, Sathianathan 174, 188, 192, 196
Commitment xx, 54, 58, 98, 152, 232, 244, 276
Communication, distorted 173
Confrontations 120, 121, 225
Counter-ideologies 61, 174, 175, 178, 190, 212, 268, 272
Counterculture xix, 33, 192, 214, 244, 259, 266, 272, 273, 277
Countercultural, alternative xix
Countercultural perspectives xxii, 191, 192, 260, 261
Crisis, cultural xix, 214, 215
Critique, Untouchables' 166, 167, 265
Cultural, caste analysis 72, 110, 129, 137, 263
Cultural, explorative xxii

D

Dalits and Christianity 33
Dalit culture 2, 48, 53, 174, 188, 260
Democracy 2, 22, 37, 39, 88, 96, 97, 101, 149, 168, 264, 271
Dialogue xxii, 170, 183, 191, 194, 195, 201, 208, 209, 211, 267, 268, 275
Discontent xvii, 14, 23, 55, 56, 71, 137, 262, 271
Discriminations, social 25, 148
Dissent 56, 119, 138, 230, 262
Dissimulation 173, 175, 176, 189
Dominant and Subaltern Cultures 52
Domination, cultural xviii, 92, 117, 147, 276
Dumont, Louis 54
Dynamics, cultural xxiv, 10, 22, 48, 53, 87, 119, 261

E

E., Periyar V. Ramaswamy 147, 148, 163, 264
Emancipation of the Dalits 192, 196
Equality 17, 18, 36, 42, 49, 88, 94, 107, 108, 109, 113, 114, 115, 118, 120, 121, 126, 128, 129, 141, 149, 152, 155, 158, 181, 199, 200, 230, 244, 259, 263, 269, 272, 274
Ethnicisation 42, 43
Exclusion 9, 76, 82, 118, 183
Experience xxii, 2, 187, 194, 195, 196, 198, 208, 209, 211, 216, 217, 218, 221, 233, 234, 258, 260, 261, 272

F

Fellowship, Table 237, 238, 240, 242
Freeman, James 32

G

Gandhi, Mahatma xix, 13, 154, 155
Globalisation 92, 93
Globalisation and Brahminism 92
Gould, Harold 6
Groups, cultural 10, 104

H

Hermeneusis, Cultural xxi, 261, 269
Hermeneutics, cultural 258, 260
Hermeneutics, subaltern 199
Hierarchical xvii, 241, 258
Hierarchicus, Homo 54, 261
Hindutva 43, 95, 102, 112, 275
Historical perspective 2, 3, 72

I

Ilaiah, Kancha xxiii
Impact of Modernity 36
Inculturation xxi, 192, 200, 203, 206, 267
Indigenisation xxi
Ideological structure 51, 261
Inculturation 200
Inferiority-complex 33, 271
Institutions, Political 100
Integration, cultural 10
Interplay of Hierarchy and Equality 117
Interpretation xxi, 130, 137, 148, 153, 192, 205, 208, 210, 212, 213, 225, 258, 261, 267, 275

Interpretation, Counter-cultural 137, 214, 239
Islam 9, 17, 36, 141, 152, 264

J

J., C. Fuller, xxiii, 7, 105, 186
Jati 4, 5, 21, 22, 155
Jesus and counter-culture 213

K

Kabir 16, 140, 141, 143, 264
Kappen, S. xxiii, 50, 144, 204, 215, 217, 222, 224, 228, 231, 232, 238, 240, 241, 242, 243, 245, 269, 270, 273
Karma and Hierarchy 127
Karuna 15, 140, 152, 265
Kingdom of God 219, 220, 221, 224, 234, 227, 232, 236, 244
Kumar, Suniti Chatterji 11

M

M., S. Parish xxiii, 51, 54, 55, 56, 73, 115, 121, 129, 173, 184, 189
Maitri 15, 140
Manusmrti 5, 12, 13, 148, 152
Marginalisation 9, 174, 211
Max Muller 2
Mobility 9, 11, 19, 22, 37, 40, 45, 91, 260
Modernisation 2, 22, 46, 178
Movement, Bhakti 15, 16, 140, 141, 142, 143, 144, 145, 264
Movement, BSP 156, 157, 163
Movement, Counter-cultural xix, 214, 244, 271
Muslims 17, 42, 143, 161

N

Narayana, Sri Guru xix
Nirvana 15

O

Oppressions, Caste 28
Option for Dialogue 192, 207, 267, 275
Option for the Culture 192, 267, 275, 200
Option for the Poor 192, 193, 194, 195, 221, 267, 275
Outcastes 5, 11, 14, 145, 217, 226, 236, 237, 244, 268, 270

P

Panikkar, Raymond 205
Phenomenological 3
Phule, Jotibha xix
Phule, Mahatma 145, 147, 264
Politics of Asceticism 181
Politics of consciousness 58, 59, 129, 263
Politics of culture 59, 168
Poverty xxi, 93, 109, 191, 201, 223, 258, 274
Praxis, subaltern 199
Production and distribution 90, 94, 262
Pulling, Chariot 72, 73, 80, 88
Purity, ritual 4, 6, 15, 20, 141, 238, 240, 242
Purity and pollution 17, 103, 122, 138, 262, 264

R

Religiosity, pluriform xxi, 258
Religious ethos 2

Response, Christian 214
Revolt, Buddhist 138, 264
Revolution, Cultural 33, 237, 244, 270

S

S., R. Khare 180
Sangha 15
Sankara-jati 4
Sanskritisation 9, 20, 21, 40
Secularisation 37
Sikhism 9, 17, 144
Singh, Yogedra 46
Soares-Prabhu, George, xxiii, 191
Solidarity, Subaltern 188, 273
Specialisation, occupational 3
Spirituality, New 275
Structures, ideological 89
Struggle of the oppressed xix, 259
Subalterns 33, 166, 174, 187, 199, 273
Substantialisation 41, 43
Sufism 141, 142, 264
Suspicioin, hermeneutical xxiv
Symbolic or meaning structures 89
system, Jajmani 90

T

Thapar, Romila 11
Theologians xx, 35, 195, 267
Theological perspectives xix, 259
Theology, Contextual xx, 191
Transformation, Modern of Caste 40

U

Untouchables 5, 8, 18, 22, 24, 33, 43, 76, 77, 82, 104, 122, 149, 156, 167, 170, 171, 176, 178, 179, 180, 182, 187, 189, 266

V

Varna 4, 5, 11, 140, 153, 164
Victims xxii, 25, 27, 33, 56, 92, 110, 115, 188, 226, 235, 260, 273
View, subaltern xxi
Violence, Caste 24

W

Wilfred, Felix xxiii, 197, 201, 202, 207, 225
Writings, Dalit 28

www.ingramcontent.com/pod-product-compliance
Lightning Source LLC
Chambersburg PA
CBHW060108170426
43198CB00010B/819